Personality as Art

~

Artistic approaches in psychology

Peter K. Chadwick

With contributions by
Colette Meury and
Jonathan Smith

PCCS BOOKS
Ross-on-Wye

PCCS BOOKS
Llangarron
Ross-on-Wye
Herefordshire
HR9 6PT
UK
Tel +44 (0)1989 77 07 07
www.pccs-books.co.uk

Personality as Art:
Artistic approaches in psychology

ISBN 1 898059 35 7

Cover design by Denis Postle.
Printed by Bookcraft, Midsomer Norton, Somerset, UK

Dedication

For my students past and present

'Being natural is such a very difficult pose to keep up.'
Oscar Wilde.

'Truth is independent of facts always.'
Oscar Wilde

'The highest aim of art is expression; the true function of the artist is to express yourself. '
Gustav Moreau

'Expression is one and the same thing as decoration. '
Matisse.

Acknowledgements

Large tracts of Chapter 12 here: 'Oscar Wilde: the differentiated personality' were taken from Chadwick, P.K. (1997) 'Oscar Wilde: Psychologist' which was first published in *Changes*, v15, No 3, August, pp.163–74. © John Wiley and Sons Limited. Reproduced with permission.

The section in Chapter 15 dealing with therapeutic approaches to paranoia drew heavily on a pamphlet: Chadwick, P.K. (1999) *Understanding Paranoia* Mind Publications © Mind 1999 (National Association for Mental Health). Reprinted with permission.

I also am grateful to Desmond Marshall; Ivo Wiesner; Jill Chadwick and Trevor Pastaro for permission to publish the photographs of them that appear in Chapters 6, 7, 8 and 10 respectively.

PCCS Books — publishers of counselling, psychotherapy and critical psychology texts

CRITICAL PSYCHOLOGY DIVISION

Commissioning Editors: Craig Newnes and Guy Holmes

This is Madness:
A Critical Look at Psychiatry and the Future of Mental Health
Services
Edited by **Craig Newnes, Guy Holmes** and **Cailzie Dunn**
ISBN 1 898059 25 X   1999

This is Madness Too:
Critical Perspectives on Mental Health Services
Edited by **Craig Newnes, Guy Holmes** and **Cailzie Dunn**
ISBN 1 898059 37 3   2001

Personality as Art:
Artistic approaches in psychology
Peter Chadwick
ISBN 1898059 35 7   2001

Spirituality and Psychotherapy
Edited by **Simon King-Spooner** and **Craig Newnes**
ISBN 1898059 39 X   2001

Contents

Figures

Tables

Preface

There is an enormous amount of latent energy in the student population for artistic approaches in psychology that is being ruthlessly and fiercely held at bay by the way we currently practise the subject. It is high time this energy was released. This book therefore is written mainly for students of psychology, particularly undergraduates and postgraduates and for clinical psychologists, clinical psychology trainees and personality researchers. However, psychiatrists, mental health and community psychiatric nurses, psychiatric social workers and mental health help-line workers may also find much material here of interest. Parents and partners of people with major mental health problems are also addressed, particularly in Chapter 15. The core topic is the description, understanding and 'capturing' of the individual personality but using *artistic* as well as scientific methods to achieve this. The five biographical sketches that I present in Part III of the book (Chapters 6–11) are mostly of people who have struggled, as millions do, with problems that would lead them to be regarded as abnormal to some degree by clinicians. But despite this there is an essential beauty to them, as there is in all people, that needs to be appreciated and studied as in many ways the very foundation or armature of who and what they are. This issue of the beauty of the personality has been relatively neglected by personality researchers and psychiatrists in the twentieth century in comparison to the wealth of research devoted to the quantification of constructs and traits. Here it forms part of the backbone of this text.

I say that I am using artistic methods here as well as the methods of science to study personality. This means that I consider it worthwhile for example to consult the views of great writers on personality — which we see in Part IV. There are presented Wilde; Dostoyevsky; Blake; Larkin and others on the ways to regard and capture mind and personality. Other artistic methods I use here are the autobiographical sketch (Chapters 3–5), stream-of-consciousness writing (Chapter 9); dialogue (Chapter 6); music (Chapter 7); photography (Chapters 4, 6, 7, 8, 9 and 10); journal writing (Chapters 6 and 9) and poetry and prose-poetry (Chapters 6, 7 and 14).

The book begins with an introduction to the idea of artistic psychology (Chapter 1) and of what it really means and then presents in Chapter 2 the theorising of other psychologists in the fields of personality and abnormal psychology which could be seen as precursors of the present approach. My own autobiographical narrative follows in order to point out the limitations of standardised methods and to chart the personal and intellectual background to the present book — where the artist-experimenter and artist-practitioner identities are really put to work and the subjective and the objective find a blend. Particularly in Chapter 5 I raise the issue of the critical importance of the single case study. Contrary to nomothetic science it is only in the context of the individual that one can see the dynamic interplay of all factors from the biochemical to the spiritual in shaping how they are and what they are becoming. Should we want a paradigmatic psychology it is something we will only achieve if more studies of the single case reach the printed page. This approach, in which the intuitive and the empirical are dovetailed together, is then exemplified in Chapters 6 to 10.

Chapters 6–14 are, as I implied above, the vertebral column of the text (Parts III and IV) before we embark on discussing in Part V the practical implications of the present approach firstly to therapy (Chapter 15) and then to education (Chapter 16). The concluding chapter makes a strong plea for a more democratic psychology in which both scientific and artistic methods can find a place.

Two chapters here, Chapters 4 and 10, break — what for a lot of people is — the conspiracy of silence over transvestism. This is indeed regarded in the human sciences as a clinical condition but perhaps some would regard two chapters as excessive. I don't think so. Transvestism may well be in the region of ten times more common than homosexuality (see Chapter 10) but while discourse on the latter fills thousands of pages of texts, learned journals and serious magazines and newspapers, transvestism and the transvestite sensibility has so far been represented by relatively little narrative. As transvestites and transsexuals (collectively known as transgenderals) are now at last beginning to fight for their rights and for freedom from discrimination it is high time that charitable and insightful treatments of these ways of being appeared in learned works. It is sad and regrettable that such people should be ostracised from their children and sacked from their jobs (as often happens) for what they are — and it has to be said that much psychological and psychoanalytic writing by outsiders has done nothing at all to foster the dignity of these individuals (indeed some writers if anything have demeaned and scorned them at almost every opportunity). In these pages we see the activity of cross-dressing in men — and hence the self-construction of a 'female' personality — treated in a beneficent way from someone, myself, who has 'been there' and hence knows of the activity from both the inside and the outside. This enables both subjective and objective perspectives on this issue to be studied in detail (see for example Chapter 10 for objective profiles of the male and female personalities of two transvestites and one transsexual and Chapter 4 for the experience of 'being a woman though male').

Richard Hurd said, in 1782, 'when an architect examines a Gothic structure by Grecian rules he finds nothing but deformity'. This is a common problem in life and of course in the human sciences. Poetic clients facing scientific clinicians, theistic patients being dealt with by atheistic psychiatrists, and, inevitably, students who want to explore and discuss their intuitions and experiences being faced by lecturers who want to talk about neural networks, cognitive schemata and experimental design and statistics. This is certainly a more 'Gothic' and romantic work on personality than any previous tome on this topic. Doubtless many academics will 'find nothing but deformity' here but British clinical psychologists are a subversive lot, far less conforming to the *zeitgeist* in psychiatry than are our American counterparts. This is a text that I believe is deeply needed to put colour, warmth and music into the study of personality in a clinical context and one that the vast bulk of undergraduates, desperate to use all of their experience to enrich their competence as psychologists, will welcome and from which they will benefit.

The book is written in as accessible a style as I can manage. Opaqueness and obscurity are often used to deceive the reader into thinking that the text is more profound than really it is — that is not a strategy I have any interest in mimicking. In Part III my aim is to bring the experiences and personalities of the individuals alive, to marry form and content and to capture how they are to others. This requires both objective and subjective study. Chapter 9 also features an interesting exercise in stream-of-consciousness writing in which academic formalities are by-passed in the interests of realness.

I would like to close this preface, however, on a slightly more lyrical note to finally prepare the reader for what they will be confronted with here. In this book is love and hate; vanity and self-denigration; passion and despair. This is not a staid or self-concealing text. *Personality as Art* stands in relation to scientific psychology as does modern dance to classical ballet. Really it is a radical move: photographs of transvestites and posing men; musical scores to describe a person's personality; photographic collages; poems; narratives on dance, deviance, satin and sin; Oscar Wilde presented as a psychologist; alternative sexuality as a pathway to art; science as an inadequate education; this is all surely outrageous and cannot be permitted in a subject devoted to reaching 'Ballet Heaven' the zenith of classical ballet perfection. But such an attitude would betray ignorance of many converging trends in psychology over the past 10 to 15 years particularly in Britain. Although academic psychology has committed itself since the 1870s and certainly since 1913, with J.B. Watson's behaviourist revolt, to an essentially scientific identity it is timely to ask now, in these days of family-historical research (Eustace, 1993); theatre and psychiatry (Davis, 1995); rhetorical methods (Billig et al., 1988); qualitative research (Henwood and Nicolson, 1995; Banister et al., 1994); social constructionism (Gergen, 1985; Burr, 1995) and discourse analysis (Edwards and Potter, 1992), whether a conception of psychology as having a spectral harmony passing from science to art might not be permissible and more appropriate? In the end I leave the reader to judge.

This text, as I say, is aimed chiefly at students — who generally are more open-minded than specialist staff. In both its form and content I therefore have striven to maintain and enhance motivation which is so easily dulled by the grave and solemn approach of prototype academics. I leave this then as a generic paragraph for what this work really tries to reach and achieve: the most important thing in the teaching of psychology is to bring the subject alive — not to kill it stone dead with criticism and formalities. Relating psychology to life, including one's own, in an enthusiastic way, is probably the best way of doing this. This work is more of a personal offering and a way of doing psychology, and a set of suggestions and arguments about this, than a staid scholarly tome. Over the years I have come to feel that there is nothing worse for a university teacher than to see the dead eyes of a group of students taught for a year by a hard-line positivist. Their life experience seen as irrelevant; their intuitions valueless; their ideas bubbles to be popped by a fact; their enthusiasm sapped . . . 'insufficient evidence' . . . '*prove* it!' . . . 'how do you know you're right?!' . . . 'there must be nothing of *you* in the essay' . . . 'too much theory, not enough fact' . . . the soul-dead building abstract mountains of empirical rubble of no meaning and no vision in the service of a nineteenth-century philosophy that totally forgot that vitality must precede knowledge and that teachers are taught by their students. It is of no use talking to a positivist about what I am going to say but it may strike a chord in the receptive mind. A number of people, reported in Rogo (1990), have experienced — usually in altered states of consciousness — what has been described as 'celestial music'. It is sometimes spoken of as the music of the Heavens and against it even the finest works of Beethoven and Mozart are like strummings on a guitar. Although it is a mystical position to hold — and hence of rather limited interest to empirical psychologists[1] — it is my belief that this celestial music reflects something very profound about ourselves, the world and of our place in it. To see a Stradivarius being played by a fiddler is a terrible sight and, like the students with dead eyes, it damages the violin if continued. To reach to the depths and heights of the celestial music in the work that one does is something only a very few people such as Wagner, Newton, Milton and Einstein have ever even approached. For the rest of us it is simply not possible. In a way perhaps we are all Stradivariuses being played by a fiddler. But at least we can make the effort, see people as perhaps living instantiations of this 'deep music' and though reaching for the stars, maybe at least grasp the Moon.

This work has grown out of voluminous discussions particularly with students at Birkbeck College, University of London; the Open University; the Universities of Liverpool and Strathclyde; the City Literary Institute and Norwich City College — part of Anglia Polytechnic University. I thank them all. I would also like to thank the other members of the Borderliners group, formed by myself and Desmond Marshall in March 1992: Simon Blair; Geoff Garfield; Jane Howe; Jonathan Smith and Ivo Wiesner. The issue of artistic approaches in theory and therapy in psychology has risen innumerable times in the meetings of this group and the results of discussion have enriched me immensely.

Finally I would like to acknowledge the support of other academics who have been receptive to the general concepts expressed here over the last ten years. In particular I would like to thank Halla Beloff; David Harper; Rom Harré; Liam Hudson; Miller Mair; Richard Stevens; David Smail; Anthony Storr; Martina Thomson and Jane Ussher. Their open-mindedness on the conceptual and methodological issues discussed here has been a considerable source of encouragement.

Colette Meury, a singer-songwriter, arranger and vocal coach, and Jonathan Smith, a staff lecturer in psychology at Birkbeck College, I would like to thank for their efforts in Chapters 7 and 14 respectively and Merlin Holland, grandson of Oscar Wilde, also for reading an earlier draft of Chapter 12 and for his constructive comments and encouragement. Chapter 2 was facilitated by a helpful discussion with Chris Brewin and Chapter 10 nourished by discussion with Glenn Wilson. Craig Newnes and Guy Holmes both read the entire manuscript and made innumerable helpful comments.

The manuscript was typed by my friend and confidante Sylvia Greenwood whose near flawless rendering of my handwriting is a testament to her extraordinary pattern-recognition capacities. I thank her warmly for an excellent job.

---

1 Students should note that interest in spiritual matters in psychology is, nonetheless, on the increase in recent years (e.g. Chadwick, 1992; Jackson, 1997).

This text was written in 1999 while I was convalescing after two heart attacks in the October and November of 1998. I must conclude this preface with thanks to my wife Jill for her care and support while this project was being created and to my students, friends and colleagues for their numerous cards, presents and get-well wishes. Many thanks to you all.

Peter Chadwick
Norfolk
July 1999

Definitions of critical concepts as used here[1]

APOLLONIAN: From Nietzsche: A pattern of culture and personality encouraging order and control. After Apollo the Greek sun-god.

ART: The deliberated result of the desire for beauty. In Modern Art also the desire to shock, surprise and in general proclaim the primacy of the aesthetic: art speaking for itself. Also a skill in the production of beauty and of works of the creative imagination.

BEAUTY: A combination of qualities that delight sight, the other senses, the moral sense or the intellect. Qualities such as grace or excellence that give aesthetic pleasure generally.

COGNITRON: A view of person as entirely determined in their behaviour, feelings and experiences by their cognitive processing.

CONSTRUCTIONISM: In social psychology, feminist and gender studies the argument that all 'truths' are relative to particular cultural and linguistic practices and are not mirrors of the world 'as it really is'. All concepts and received truths are therefore constructed rather than discovered and are ephemeral, fluid and metamorphosing. They gain stability only through shared practices and temporary agreement.

CONSTRUCTIVISM: A term originating in Russian art and poetry in the 1920s and later imported into social science. In psychology the view of person as an active agent in the development of their own intellect and personality as opposed to the person as a passive recipient of stimuli and of the products of neurochemical processes. In Kelly's psychology the organisation of one's personal world using constructs: convenient and revisable fictions which may or may not correspond to reality but which give greater or lesser predictive accuracy in everyday social life — more specifically referred to as 'constructive alternativism'.

DECADENCE: In modern times a nineteenth-century movement particularly energised by Baudelaire which emphasised art for art's sake, egocentricity, self-analysis, perversity, personal experience and a preoccupation with sensation and melodrama. Represented in England in the late nineteenth-century particularly by Wilde, Swinburne and Aubrey Beardsley.

---

1. These definitions reflect my understanding of these terms and hence are the ways in which they are used in this text. Please note that psychiatric terms such as 'schizophrenia' and 'schizotypy' give these modes of conduct a concrete and distinctive flavour which does not usually obtain in real life where the boundaries of such categories are greatly blurred.

DIAGNOSIS: In psychiatry an hypothesis about the nature of an illness obtained from observing symptoms, taking the patient's history and conducting various examinations and tests. The validity of the extension of this procedure from general medicine to psychiatry, however, is hotly disputed. Although it is less controversial in the case of psychosis (see Claridge, 1988, 1990), there are many presenting problems which are not fruitfully regarded as 'illnesses' to be 'treated'. (For example is a woman, depressed because of the behaviour of her bullying, heavy drinking, abusive husband best helped by seeing her as 'mentally ill' and in need of medication? Many would say no.) Clinical psychologists, particularly in Great Britain, see the diagnostic enterprise as more of a political than a scientific endeavour (e.g. Russell, 1994) and prefer, in practice, the use of *formulation* to that of diagnosis — where formulation refers to the psychological assessment of a client's problem so as to describe it and understand how it developed and is being maintained. This is argued to be a better foundation on which to plan intervention. It should also be said that even in cases of psychoses diagnostic categories are poor guides to treatment and diagnostic manuals are not therefore particularly helpful tools for clinicians faced with people with these difficulties.

DIONYSIAN: From Nietzsche: A pattern of culture and personality encouraging emotional abandonment. After *Dionysus* the Greek god of wine.

EXPRESSIONISM: An art movement particularly in Germany and Austro-Hungary from 1910 to about 1925 emphasising expression, the turning away from the outer life to the inner and the communication of strong emotion and powerful personal vision. Abstract Expressionism was developed by Pollock and de Kooning in the USA in the 1950s where distortion and fragmentation in the service of expression was taken to the point where no recognisable object was present in the work.

GOTHIC: An alternative to Greek classical style prevalent in architecture in twelfth to sixteenth-century Western Europe but more generally referring in literature to disturbing, romantic and mysterious imagery and theme. The Gothic style in literature was popular in the eighteenth century and is still influential today in the evolution of the ghost story and of things wild and sensational.

HERMENEUTICS: Originally the finding and interpreting of the spiritual truths of the Bible. As imported into philosophy (and thence psychology) by Wilhelm Dilthey (1833–1911) it refers to the general theory of interpretation and the methods and procedures of extracting meaning from texts — where text can be taken to include a client's utterances in therapy.

NATURALISM: A belief that everything that exists is part of nature and can be explained by natural and material causes. Naturalists reject paranormal or supernatural causes such as those suggesting the existence of telepathy, precognition or intervention by demons or saints.

PARANOIA: From the Greek *paranoos* meaning 'distracted', a state of mind characterised by extreme suspiciousness and feelings of threat. Sometimes persecutory feelings can be accompanied by a sense of grandiosity, the latter, however, is more common in younger people.

PERSONALITY: The integration of all the physical, emotional, intellectual and spiritual characteristics of a person which determines their unique style and adjustment to the world and the manner of their presentation to other people.

PHENOMENOLOGY: Knowledge of the appearance of things. More specifically the study deriving from the thinking of Edmund Husserl (1854–1938) of what the essential nature of consciousness is for it to permit experience and knowledge. In practice (in philosophy and psychology) the exact inspection of mental processes in themselves — including extreme states of mind and the experience of the Self.

POSITIVISM: A philosophical system arguing that all concepts be based on observation such that the meaningfulness of a proposition depends on its testability. Positivism is a scientifically oriented form of empiricism — the theory that all concepts are derived from experience and can only be justified by experience. It aims for certainty, assurance and confidence in one's knowledge.

PSYCHOPATHY: A type of personality disorder, more commonly referred to these days as anti-social personality disorder, characterised by irresponsible and aggressive behaviour causing distress to others.

PSYCHOSIS: A general category of mental illness including schizophrenia; endogenous depression; mania and hypomania in which the person experiences delusions and/or hallucinations; suffers from loss of insight, loss of executive control over the workings of their own mind and has difficulty discriminating reality and fantasy. This general term is often preferred, particularly by psychologists, to the use of specific diagnostic categories as the latter have not proved helpful in elucidating causation nor have they acted as reliable guides to treatment.

RATIONALISM: More generally the argument that beliefs must be founded on experience and reason. In the terms, however, of Descartes, Spinoza and Leibniz it is the argument that the general nature of the world can be established wholly by reasoning rather than observation. The term can also apply to those who believe that the nature of the world in itself is fundamentally rational.

SCHIZOPHRENIA: A collection of disorders marked by disturbance in the organisation, integrity and beauty of the personality such that emotional, cognitive and social functioning is impaired, the distinction between reality and fantasy is blurred and the sense of self as a separate coherent reflective entity is damaged.

SCHIZOTYPY: A style of personality characterised by social anxiety; odd beliefs and superstitiousness; unusual perceptual experiences; paranoia and eccentric or odd speech or behaviour.

SCIENCE: Systematic and formulated knowledge of the physical, natural and human world using observation, measurement, experiment and inductive and deductive reasoning. Such knowledge critically tested, systematised and brought under general principles.

STRUCTURALISM: A movement of thought originating in linguistics which has also affected social science. In social science it takes the form of a belief that structures, whether they be biological, linguistic, logical or social underlie behaviour in question and can ultimately be traced to basic characteristics of the mind. For Chomsky e.g. the deep structure of an utterance regulates its meaning which can be expressed in a number of different surface structures. Much, if not all, Piagetian and Eysenckian thinking is structuralist in essence, the structures for Piaget being logical, those for Eysenck being neurophysiological.

Part I
Chapters 1 – 2
Background

1

What is artistic psychology?

The essential tension

The function of art is to make a raid on predictability (Ellmann, 1988, p.304). For Marcel Schwob art is also opposed to generalisation, it describes only the individual, wishes only for the unique. It does not classify, it declassifies (in Jullian, 1994, p.179). These clearly are bold assertions and present a stark contrast with science and here with scientific psychology whose focus specifically is on prediction, generalisation and classification and which has much less interest in the individual in comparison to its interest in the abstract concept of 'human nature'.

Contrast, conflict and contradiction, however, are the triggers of the neural impulses of every subject, and provide that colour and vitality that always precedes knowledge. With no choice, between science and art in psychology (and undergraduates these days in psychology have little choice), there can be no 'essential tension' and hence no real change, merely more facts.

The forgotten 98 per cent

Because the subject of psychology is such a broad church, if I dare use the word, it is necessary at least in introductory courses to give the students a taste of the less empirical and more impressionistic aspects of psychology such as psychodynamics and humanistic psychology. Whenever I have taught Saturday schools or revision weekends, or indeed faced any such congregation of students towards the end of the academic year in whatever university, I have always asked for their attitudes to these more artistic approaches in comparison to those of a scientific nature such as the cognitive, behavioural and biological. The assembled multitude, which can often be more than a hundred students, always prefers the former. Only about two per cent prefer science.

Obviously no academic subject can proceed on a voting basis but this does indicate that there is a liking, a vitality and a need for experiential, more individualistic, and insight-based approaches in psychology that is given little to no recognition by the pre-emptively scientific conceptual orientation. Clinical psychology trainees for example are heavily indoctrinated with the cognitive behavioural approach and notions of the scientist-practitioner model of clinical work to the neglect of all else. This book therefore turns the coin over from these behavioural and cognitive-neuropsychological creeds so evangelically preached in psychology departments up and down Great Britain to present a more person-oriented approach to psychology and to personality study and to give some nurturance to this forgotten 98 per cent of the undergraduate student population.

What I will do in this introductory chapter is outline how artistic psychology differs from its scientific opposite and show how the artistic approach is genuinely useful and necessary as a complementary endeavour in psychology as a whole. Only a taster will be possible in one chapter but the rest of the book will take up the case in more detail.

The fundamental divide in psychology

Science may be exceedingly powerful but it is much weaker than art when faced with the task of capturing the essence, the 'deep music' of the individual personality or when faced with the task of capturing the mood and atmospherics of the unrepeatable moment or unrepeatable experience. It is not surprising that not very long ago grades in scientific psychology actually correlated negatively with success as a therapist (Carkhuff, 1969). Clearly something more than analytical and critical skills are needed to be a healer of minds.

The stress in artistic psychology, compared to science, is therefore more on personal meanings than on facts; on motivation rather than information; more on constructions than causes, and rather than on crisp carefully defined theory more on the telling of a story or on the representation of the labyrinthine complexity of human relationships in a play (e.g. Davis, 1995) — approaches which it should be said can also provide rich and satisfying explanations at times. In artistic psychology, standardisation would be positively crippling and the validity of the unique vision more compelling than 'repeatable findings'. In this context a dedicated destandardiser of mind, R.D. Laing, was very much an artistic psychiatrist.

There are many areas in psychology that cannot with comfort be incorporated under the umbrella of science. The unambiguously scientific schools where empirical methods are most successful and their results least ambiguous are the behavioural, biological and cognitive schools whereas the more artistic approaches where more qualitative and intuitive methods prosper are the largely hermeneutic, experiential, phenomenological, conative and motivational approaches. I speak here of course of existential and phenomenological psychology; psychoanalysis; psychodynamic therapy in general; Jung's Analytic and Adler's Individual psychology; social constructionism; drama therapy; bioenergetics; the broad school of Humanistic psychology with its subspecialisms such as Gestalt therapy, Transactional Analysis (T.A.) and Psychosynthesis, and so on.

Many of these approaches create what are best described as models of experience for the public to rush to try out. We see this particularly clearly in psychoanalysis and T.A. These models, though not established fact, are for many people extremely useful as working heuristics for organisation of memories, personal reflection and as guides to life. Their postulated structures cannot be found in brain circuitry because they are of a different genre to science, they are basically human meaning systems. In this respect they are more accessible than mechanistic propositions, relate more immediately to the emotional and social life of the person and have broader scope for organising experience.

The fundamental common ground in psychology

Having said this, however, it has to be stressed that science and art are not, or at least they need not be, antagonistic cultures. Artistic psychology is not inevitably a hurtful opposite. In both endeavours there is a keen appreciation of beauty and elegance and a combination of transcendental vision with the perception of minutiae (see Koestler, 1964/1989). Both the spheres of science and art thrive on the discovery of new techniques, on new tools, on controversy and argument and all the practitioners critically value the power to abstract essentials and intuit a finished product. Certainly to an extent science is an art and art a science. (We return to these contrasts and overlaps again in Chapter 5.)

It is also important to stress that conventional scientific psychology can learn from the more artistic approaches (Shapiro, 1989) and vice versa (see for example the openness to scientific evidence in Evison and Horobin's work on co-counselling (1990)). There is no justification for the creation of totally separate edifices of knowledge in the more artistic and the more scientific camps. Although overlap research has been done (see for example Kline, 1981; Dixon, 1981) there is a strong in-house tendency in psychology which is (and traditionally has always been) a formidable barrier to cross-fertilisation of ideas in the discipline.

What does a specifically artistic psychology actually involve?

Artistic approaches to the study of mind will inevitably expand the methods and ideas available in our subject. They partake of more subjective procedures such as rhetoric, introspection and insight, case study work and the biographical sketch, conversation, poetry, painting, sculpture, fashion, the story, the novel and dance. So apart from those branches of psychology mentioned above that already are regarded as the more artistic arms of the subject the kinds of things that also would count as artistic psychology would include for example: a painting of 'Conscience'; a novel about bringing up a hyperactive child; an essay on a poet's insights into mind; a garment that represented sadness or power; a story about the experience of behaviour therapy; a poem about the experience of ECT and a prose-poem about a mystical experience, all would stand as having their own identity as artistic psychology if the intention was primarily psychological.

What does this achieve?

Artists of course are not just data collectors for science. They can paint the soul (Munch); the fifth dimension and pure feeling (Malevich); dreams (Dali); the never-before-thought and the unknowable (Magritte). Here we are pushing out the boundaries of what counts as psychology and what counts as art. We will not be just modelling the mind but making it more real. The artistic psychologist teaches us, then, to see those details in people that are already art for one has to face the fact that a person is not only a lay scientist (Kelly, 1955) but a sculptor of his or her own personality and to a degree a dramatist of their life. Is there any reader after all who is not the hero or heroine (or indeed villain) of their own personal story?

Using methods of these kinds, particularly the novel and the biographical sketch, it is possible also to represent at least in outline the historical, cultural, political, economic and spiritual factors that shape the psyche and provide it with its space for expression. The analytical methods of science generally cauterise these issues away to focus a strong beam on the singular phenomenon acontextually. This is a very dangerous thing to do with something as contextually penetrable as the mind — indeed even rock minerals are contextually penetrable!

The story, the novel, the poem are 'kinematic' techniques — they allow a representation of changes over a period. Though certainly not always, science does tend to deal with static snapshots and this can limit its usefulness in comparison to the way, for example, that the story can encapsulate multiple enfolding events over time. In this manner a story can be genuinely explanatory.

Tears in my eyes

This brief preamble may give the reader the impression that I am dismissive of science in comparison to art. Maybe I am trying to undermine science or negate its validity? None of these things are so. I obtain no pleasure from seeing behaviourists castigating psychoanalysts (or vice versa); social constructionists attacking cognitivists; psychobiologists scorning phenomenologists and so on. I would rather we worked together than act like power-barons striving to assert the superiority of our own in-house perspective. An anecdote will bring home to the reader, I hope, the consequences we now have to reap from these cross-field wars that have become such a familiar feature of our subject.

At the end of the 1980s I had a clear-out of some books from my personal library to leave space for a new generation of texts. I do this about every ten years. I (unwisely) took two laundry bags of books to the bookshops on Charing Cross Road in central London to try and sell my collection to the second-hand bookshops there.

Working from top to bottom of Charing Cross Road I entered the first bookshop and told the chap behind the counter what I had to offer.

'I've got all the early Eysenck paperbacks . . . here's Broadbent on empirical psychology; Miller, Galanter and Pribram . . . here's . . . ' but he stopped me in my tracks.

'No, No, I could take all those off you but they'd just end up on the 40p shelf downstairs and I wouldn't be able to sell them . . . have you got any Freud or Jung?'

I had two Freud texts and one of Jung's. I came away with three pounds.

Nipping in to the next shop on my itinerary and quoting different goodies the story was still the same, 'Any Freud or Jung?' The next was the same, and the next. I sold not one more book. Dragging the bags to the corner by Leicester Square tube I stood there, arms and hands aching, with tears in my eyes. But not because I had made so little money. It was because all those hundreds of thousands of man- and woman-hours of research that had been done to fill the space between the covers of those science texts, as far as the general public were concerned, were 'of no interest'. The words 'they'll just end up on the 40p shelf downstairs and I won't be able to sell them' kept reverberating through my mind over and over again. Indeed they still do. In a subject like psychology that after all is about people, the judgement of these very people on what scientific psychology had to offer and had to say was a very sobering and distressing experience.

If rocks were conscious and they regarded what geological science has to say about them as worthy only of some analogue of 'the 40p shelf' one would have to conclude that geological science was not doing a very good job. Clearly it was time for a different attitude to the study of people that respected the richness of personal experience and the importance of meaning as well as fact without sacrificing the standards of rigorous academic study. This book is my personal attempt then to lift us upstairs from the 40p shelf to a place where people will want to read us. This is therefore a very different book to any standard psychological text and indeed could be said to be dangerous — conceptually, morally, and for me personally, professionally. But it seems to me that unless we create a coherent psychology that stretches from genes to spirituality the judgement of the very people we study, real people out there in the street, will forever be a damning one.

2
Artistic leanings in British academic psychology

'Art' appears to be a taboo word in Western academic psychology. Perhaps for reasons concerned with funding and academic respectability specialists will gladly describe themselves as hermeneutic; qualitative; humanistic; transformative; phenomenological; transpersonal or whatever but not as artistic or as artists. In the fields of personality and abnormal psychology there are unambiguously scientific aspects such as five factor or OCEAN model trait theory (Digman, 1990; Goldberg, 1993; Goldberg and Rosolack, 1994); studies of the cognitive underpinnings of clinical psychology practice (Lindsay and Powell, 1994; Brewin, 1998) and social-cognitive theory of personality (Bandura, 1986; Mischel, 1973, 1990) and there are writings on the more self-created aspects of personality such as those of Goffman (1959), Hampson (1988, Chapter 8), Harré (1983) and Harré and Gillett (1994). In this book the approach is more unambiguously artistic and I represent people by stream-of-consciousness writing, musical scores, photographic collages, their own poetry and so on. But between these poles of science and art there is a wide grey area — a grey area seemingly becoming more expansive by the year — of approaches in psychology on which there is no collective agreement on their scientificity nor at times agreement on whether or not they are even aiming for scientific status at all. Many fields fall into this category of uncertain identity and one might describe them, controversially perhaps, as the more artistic arms of our discipline in the sense that they are more subjective and impressionistic and the knowledge they glean is less transferable from one investigator to another.

Psychoanalysis, for example, was claimed by Freud to be, or to be capable of becoming, a science just like any other. Recent research in this vein aims to check and underpin psychoanalytic theory with scientific studies in developmental psychology (e.g. Tyson and Tyson, 1990). Others (e.g. Frosh, 1997, p.35) prefer to make a distinction between positivistic natural sciences such as biology and neuropsychology (*Naturwissenschaften*) — where *explanation* is central (e.g. viral theory of bronchitis), and the more discursive interpretive human or moral sciences (*Geisteswissenschaften*) — where models of experience, meaning and empathic *understanding* (e.g. of a person's jealousy) are central and attempt to locate the endeavour in the latter. Still others (e.g. Storr, 1987) claim an artistic identity for psychoanalysis as it pivotally revolves around the building of relationships — something that cannot be regarded as a science — even if science can help (Argyle, 1996). Certainly psychoanalysis fails the test of scientific status by positivistic standards (Grunbaum, 1984) but attempts to induce the profession to be more willing to disclose its clinical evidence and increase its archival data base (rather than merely presenting conclusions backed up by anecdote) have been made (Spence, 1987).

The recent emergence of enthusiasm for qualitative methods in psychology (Henwood and Pidgeon, 1992, 1994; Banister et al., 1994; Gillett ,1995; Burt and Oaksford, 1999) have provoked heated argument (e.g. Morgan, 1996, 1998). Although qualitative methods (as used here) increase the complexity and richness of the data obtained and give us a fuller, closer and in a sense more 'real' picture of the individual in their tussles with the challenges of life, positivists would complain that the findings are coloured by the admitted presence and influence of the investigator who openly confesses (in this paradigm) to standing in the centre of their investigation, not outside it. Although qualitative researchers themselves complain that this is always the case in science in any research project — and they are simply being more honest in admitting it — psychophysicists such as Morgan disagree and argue that such claims are bogus and the evidence inevitably tainted (Morgan, 1996). This purity may only be achieved, however, in more peripheral processes such as those studied by psychophysics. It hardly applies, for example, in gender studies (e.g. Vetere, 1996).

Basically qualitative methods are an approach to gaining knowledge given the practitioners' assumptions and aims. Perhaps it does not matter whether one regards them as science or art. Certainly such close reading of people at the individual level presents data that are valuable to the therapeutic community and that act as the natural history of experience even if the reliability of the findings is lower than that achieved by more formal and more constrained (and less ecologically valid) methods. The danger of qualitative methodology is that it can very easily be used merely to confirm or demonstrate a previously held opinion. Hence to refute this common charge it is important that qualitative researchers prove that they can *discredit* their presuppositions and produce results that are to some degree surprising. Even a novel, as Thackeray and Proust knew, can be an experiment in which the writing of it twists and turns in unexpected directions.

The claim of psychology as a profession to scientific status has previously rested on its search for the causes of human behaviour. Awareness in recent years of the powerful role of meaning in human life (Bruner, 1990; Zika and Chamberlain, 1992; Power and Brewin, 1997) presents a challenge to this research programme such that psychology could come to regard itself as a hermeneutic discipline — hermeneutics being the art or skill of interpretation (Quinton, 1977, p.380) — rather than a science.

Freud dealt with this dilemma by arguing, in the case, for example, of dream interpretation, that the meaning of the dream was the cause of the dream. Although this now is challenged (Grunbaum, 1984) there seems little reason to doubt that in human life more generally meanings can have causal status. When we come to consider what it is that a person is trying to do in their life the goal and subgoal plans that they erect to mediate their thoughts and behaviour are causally effective meanings. This has been uncontroversial since Miller et al. (1960). There seems little doubt also that certain themes concerned with personal meaning continually emerge in therapy. For example, those concerned with self-esteem; personal power; the future; the actual *existence* of the self and so on (Brewin and Power, 1999) could be empirically studied and quantified and give guidance on treatment and likely outcome. The latter is a problem that psychoanalysts have not solved (Frosh, 1997, Chapter 6). The particular difficulty, however, for the scientific status of a meaning-impregnated psychology is the impossibility of reliably assessing and quantifying extremely personal, iconoclastic and, of course, *unconscious* meanings. Here it may have to be argued that what *can* be achieved is the negotiated creation of a singular narrative for the client or patient that is in many ways self-enhancing, not self-damaging, and that promotes and facilitates growth and an enrichment of consciousness in their individual case. This inevitably has to be an eventuate of the unique therapist-patient relationship (Storr, 1987) and is not, and can never be, transferable knowledge. Hermeneutics, therefore, in all its manifestations in psychology is a Janus-faced entity, part science, part art — if one means by science that is the creation and discovery of replicable, objective, investigator-independent knowledge. If one is to adopt procedures, however, that reveal a unique perspective or that inevitably have different effects on different people — as any novel or painting would — then one's efforts are art, not science.

In both psychoanalysis and in other qualitative approaches there seems no reason to assume nevertheless that investigators will always merely confirm their presuppositions in a circular fashion. Freud himself recognised this could be avoided (for example, in his studies of lesbianism) and indeed in my own experience of supervising (and marking) qualitative projects on the same topic (some with the same data) there is no doubt that a degree of reliability in the interpretations across students does occur. Some students also produce, to them, surprising findings. Inevitably the endeavour is somewhat impressionistic and subjective but the sum total of different investigations of the same topic by different people is informative and enriching and does create novelty. These I find to be useful outcomes of a research process that straddles both science and art in its character.

Social Constructionist and Discourse Analytic methods have blossomed in recent years particularly since publications by Gergen (1985), Edwards and Potter (1992) and Harper (1994). These approaches reject the 'essentialist' position of positivistic psychology that there is a given reality 'out there' or within people to research by standardised methods and argue for a fluid constructed reality based on forever metamorphosing cultural and linguistic practices. Linguistic practices therefore have to be critically studied in search of the stake or 'hidden agenda' that the communicator has in the text they create and deliver. A stake that is usually implicit rather than explicit but that, once discovered, reveals the assumptions and givens that they are perhaps taking for granted in the topic concerned. Researchers in this vein see the replicability of findings in positivistic psychology as nothing more than a result of the researchers working within the same coding framework and claim, as do qualitative researchers in general, that all observations are theory-laden and pre-categorised to a degree that pre-empts any 'raw' seeing of the world.

Researchers in this paradigm are particularly interested in the socially constructed nature of masculinity and femininity (Wetherell, 1996), gender being such a flexible entity that it lends itself well to articulation in the terms of this rationale. The approach has also been used, however, to 'deconstruct', for example, schizophrenia (Sarbin and Mancuso, 1980), childhood (Kessen, 1979) and altruism (Gergen and Gergen, 1983) and clearly offers an alternative way of conceptualising 'the world' and our interpretations of it that transcends that of realism — the exogenic perspective, and of cognitivism and solipsism — the endogenic.

Social Constructionists are generally silent on the issue of whether their endeavour is science or art since the definitions, as they see it, of these enterprises are themselves variable and often tailored to suit the interests and needs of the definer but certainly constructionist thinkers are bedevilled by the relativism implicit in their own position since no general truth claims, can, on this basis, be made or be at all possible.

Although *constructivists* such as Piaget (1959) and Hampson (1988) merely argue for a constructive role in human mentation — in the case of Piaget, for example, the child rediscovers for himself or herself adult thinking via their active manipulations of the world and by reflecting on what they do (Piaget, 1959; Flavell, 1977; Boden, 1979) — the *constructionists* do not make general repeatable truth claims and argue for an entirely constructed and historically and culturally situated nature to all that seems tangible including notions of Mind and Self — which vary, for example, cross-culturally (Lee, 1959; Smith, 1981).

Clearly this is not science, and does not pretend or claim to be so. But what is it and from whence does it obtain its legitimacy? Gergen (1985, p.272) argues that constructionism has an intellectually therapeutic and entertaining role in that its chief aim is to delight and provoke thought. It is not out to prove things or find facts. But really Gergen is quite wrong on this. Constructionism has its impact, for an impact it certainly has had, not by delighting people but by *hurting* them. Indeed if constructionism did not hurt anyone no one would take any notice of it. Undoubtedly the alternative formulations of gender (e.g. Jaeger, 1983, and see also Wetherell, 1996 on masculinity) have presented a viable challenge to traditional exogenic and psychodynamic perspectives on these topics to a degree that constructionist thinking is now taken seriously by many psychologists (e.g. Bruner, 1990; Vetere, 1996) and presents a perspective that is a substantial alternative to more familiar rationales. This does at least demonstrate that one can move away from a positivistic perspective and produce arguments and ideas that are challenging, surprising, enriching of discussion and yet non-factual.

There is little doubt that both people and indeed the endeavour of psychology itself operate in a particular historical, social and economic context such that a merely biological, biophysical or neurocognitive characterisation of mental processes will always be inadequate. Recovery in schizophrenia cannot be traced in terms of biological and biochemical inevitabilities but varies in different social and economic conditions (Warner, 1994). These factors are well recognised by some researchers (e.g. Shotter, 1993; Chadwick, 1996a) to a degree that their role in influencing human experience and both conscious and unconscious processes can no longer be ignored (Henry et al., 1997). Clearly such study cannot be entirely particulate and quantitative but must be qualitative, to a degree impressionistic and subjective and perhaps also to a degree rhetorical (see Billig et al., 1988). It seems, however, that the relaxation in recent years of the stranglehold of cubicle-based, quantitative standardised methodology in psychology, far from threatening to pitch the discipline into chaos, is in the process of producing an enriched and more vibrant subject, a more democratic and indeed more interesting and broadly-based subject more attuned to the interests and needs of its students and more attractive to the general public. Though adversaries abound it is now possible, for example, for researchers openly to discuss ideas on psychology and spirituality (Chadwick, 1992; Watts, 1996); creative flow experiences (Csikszentmihalyi, 1992); the practice of biographical study (Post, 1994, 1996); the study of poems (Rhodes et al., 1995); spiritual healing (Benor, 1990; Hodges and Scofield, 1995) and many other topics of real life relevance and urgency. To cope with this expansion of methodologies and interests and (for better or worse) to give the ideas contained therein a certain professional legitimacy, the Divisions of Transpersonal Psychology (in 1996) and Consciousness and Experiential Psychology (in 1998) were created in the British Psychological Society such that it could now be said that, although controversy over these leanings is far from quiescent, the subject is becoming a multidimensional and multifaceted one in line with the innumerable aspects of mind and human existence with which it has to cope. This book, in extending the practice of psychology into the representation and understanding of people by music, poetry, biographical and autobiographical sketch and photography etc. therefore only completes both a tendency and a democratic trend in the subject that have been ongoing for some 15 to 20 years. Like all departures from positivism it will be staunchly resisted by some but it is my hope that people will recognise the value of extending the territory of psychology into art in this unambiguous way and thus accept a full spectral harmony in psychology from the objective to the subjective, from 'closed textured' to 'open textured' that will finally make it adequate to its subject matter — human beings, in all their complexity. Hopefully it will also show that some topics, such as the beauty of the personality and the idiosyncratic ways of coping of individuals in distress,[1] that have generally been ignored by nomothetic science, lend themselves to artistic study particularly well.

---

1 See, however, user-led research publications by the Mental Health Foundation entitled 'Strategies for Living' (2000) and 'Knowing our Own Minds' (1997).

Part II
Chapters 3 – 5
A personal journey from science to art

These three chapters are partly autobiographical but will also be of theoretical interest to those concerned with how psychology should be practised. In Chapter 3 I voice my discontent, as I felt it in the 1970s, with a pre-emptively objective psychology and then go on, in Chapters 4 and 5, to show how I crafted an alternative philosophy of psychological study via intensifying my own individuality and rejecting a totally standardised approach. As the reader can imagine, this was done at some risk and I certainly suffered terribly at one time from paranoia as a result of the way I was living — something I have dealt with elsewhere (Chadwick, 1992, 1993, 1997). If one lives a life, both personally and professionally that conflicts with and rejects the values of Men, in a world constructed by Men, one eventually will have to pay for it — and this I did.

Scientists and artists, as much research has shown (e.g. Hudson (1966, 1968, 1972); Rump (1982); Post (1994)) are different people. They are different at a personal level, they think differently, they behave differently. Many students who are currently studying psychology may find that they fit the mould of the artistic psychologist or of the 'artist-experimenter' or 'artist-practitioner' far better than that of the scientist even though their department or centre of work gives them little choice but the latter. This is an opportunity to find out about an alternative and of how one psychologist worked his own personal way to it.

Some might say that invective about 1970s British psychology is anachronistic and that 'things are very different now'. I think this would be unfair. There are still a large number of '1970s' psychology departments in Great Britain even today; the libretto may have changed but the music is the same. Such departments probably do not suit either the personalities or the thinking style of most of their students. One converts to their ways, as we will see, only at considerable personal cost.

Chapters 3 and 4 are the most autobiographical of the trio but I think are useful demonstrations of how life and work intertwine and mesh and hence how one's work can eventuate from, and indeed clash with, one's life. Although it is traditional for scientists to stand in the shadows of their creations this is not so for an artist. In writing in this way I am trying to be true to my identity, rather than merely narcissistic, and to illustrate how the ideology of this book originated. Finally I should state that this autobiographical material relates particularly to the period 1963–1990 (see also Chapter 9). The terrible stresses I suffered in Manchester would likely not occur these days. The city now has very active and thriving transvestite and gay cultures and a council extremely sensitive to equal rights issues and to the fostering of the dignity of minority groups.

3
Getting out of science, and why

~

A mood of doubt

I have always loved psychology. As a history A level student at school in the early 1960s, starved of any reference to the psyche in anything I was studying, I began to complain. History, as it was then practised, was only half a subject — it was all battles, wars, bills and laws — it had no real psychological dimension to it at all. Economics was the same — and still is. My teacher dismissed my concerns, as did some of the other boys, as 'irrelevant'. We did not need to know what Hitler and Napoleon were like as people, only their economic strategies and foreign policies. I felt that we did and my concerns remained. I vowed that eventually, when the time was right, I would make the study of mind my central responsibility.

Initially I steered my way through courses in geology at university but, perhaps inevitably, became more fascinated in time by the human element, this time in geological observation, than 'the facts of science'. This was to take me on a trajectory that would eventually mean leaving earth science and moving into the fields of perception, cognition and personality. But, to backtrack a little, for four or five years as a postgraduate geologist I researched in the territory of rock deformation — a branch of the subject known as structural geology. This was a branch on the interface with physics and engineering. Over the years I had reason to mix with geophysicists, metallurgists, geographers, mathematicians and fluid mechanics men and I found the ambience of all these fields, geology included, to be liberal and dominated by enthusiasm and imagination with ideas always put first. Critically — as things were to turn out — I should clarify that geology was largely field- and theory-based with experimentation usually only obtaining after years of observation (to get the field context clear) and theoretical rumination and calculation. The significance of this will soon be apparent.

In 1973, at 27, I shifted careers from geology to what was my first love, psychology, an inevitable move that fitted with the way my work on the human element in geology was going and one that suited the way I was going as a person and matched with my most basic interests. At Bristol where I did a second BSc degree — this time in psychology — the liberalism of old was continued and I worried not. But when I listened to visiting speakers and moved on to lecturing posts elsewhere and travelled around as a visiting speaker myself I noticed that the atmosphere generally in British academic psychology was distinctly chilly. I would not aim this complaint at any singular department, this tract draws on about a dozen, the effect was, as far as I could see, quite general; Bristol had been atypical to the point of being unique.

Hard times in British academic psychology

After researching pretty intensely in what I would have thought was 'real science', where nobody ever talked about whether their subject was a science or not (any more than a woman ever talks about whether she's a woman or not), I found myself now in a subject that seemed intensely self-conscious and unsure of its identity — forever having to both display and prove its scientific credentials (like a man showing designer stubble to advertise that he's a man). This was terribly inhibiting — and produced a discipline that was the most conservative by far with which I had ever had dealings.

It seemed to me very early on that the identity of academic psychology had also been crafted so as to gain credibility via contrast with that of psychoanalysis — just as some men craft their identities so as to be 'nothing like a woman'. Whereas the psychoanalysts talked and talked, but tested and proved nothing, the academic psychologists could test and prove everything. While the analysts were vague and speculative the academicians were precise in method and careful in definition. While the analysts made gross macrotheoretic claims, the academicians would make small microtheoretic claims and while the analysts made feeling central, the academicians would make it marginal. Psychoanalysis was qualitative, they measured nothing, so academic psychology chose to be quantitative and to measure everything. But this was not 'love of the study of the mind' or work with any unified vision so much as a passion for the trappings of science: measuring; defining; testing; proving, however trivial and banal what was proved might be. Indeed 'Mind' itself was little mentioned, and when spoken of as consciousness or The Self was even scorned as irrelevant by the highest authorities in the field!! What on earth was going on here? It looked as if a sizeable percentage of these people cared for the identity of scientist first, and that of psychologist second, if at all. Indeed I sensed that if psychology was declared not to be a science some of them would give up the subject and leave — like a man who would leave a rich wife, who deep down he cares nothing for, if her stockmarket shares suddenly became valueless. Who were these individuals? What were they doing to 'my beloved psychology'?!

A basic distaste or disrespect for psychology would sometimes be revealed in casual conversation and at other times by some people's wish to define themselves as really something else, something more scientific or perhaps more intellectually respectable: I would find a generous peppering of authorities who would claim therefore that they were really physiologists, or linguists, or neurophilosophers, or computer scientists or behavioural technologists or biomathematicians or sociobiologists or . . . *anything* but a *psychologist*! Who were these characters? Who 'let them in here'?!

What is psychology really about?

Of course one has to recognise that psychology, like geology, interfaces with many other subjects — rather like a surrounded European country. Obviously it must try to trade with and benefit from these neighbours. But while metallurgy is not metamorphic petrology, while fluid mechanics is not structural geology, while marine biology is not palaeontology, psychology too is defined not by its methods but by its goals. It may be ringed by powerful intellectual neighbours but, just as geology has its own identity in the study of the rocks of the earth, psychology too has its own identity and human experience is central to it.

Psychology therefore is not computer programming, it is not J.B. Watson's scientific study of behaviour, it is not Gibson's ecological optometry, it is not behavioural engineering or microsociology. It is centrally the study of *mind*.

Many people other than psychologists have studied our conscious and unconscious processes and have much to say about them. Not only linguists and philosophers but painters, poets, playwrights and novelists — even dancers. Psychology is indeed encircled by all the arts and sciences — and not surprisingly so as these are all reflective human endeavours and their content and practice reflects something about human beings — but its identity is still extant. In the 1970s I felt this was like a flickering candle caught in gales from elsewhere. Indeed the people who were the most singularly *psychological* in their content and style were researchers whose scientific credentials were most scorned by the establishment and mainstream — psychoanalysts and humanistic psychologists!

Gradgrind comes alive

'Hard Times' certainly were upon me. So conservative was the discipline that I was hearing rather frequently of lecturers and A level teachers telling their students, 'There must be nothing of *you* in the essay, stick to the facts!' Essays would be criticised for something these right-wingers liked to call 'theoretical speculation' (as if this was valueless). Field examples, that is examples from real life, prized as essential evidence in geology (where one had to use all the hints available), were dismissed as uncontrolled findings, as 'mere anecdotes' and were never to be cited. But if psychology was not about real life then what *was* it about? If education was not about 'bringing out from within' and giving the student the opportunity for personal development and self-realisation then what was that about too? What was happening to this subject?!

The nightmare of materialism

Anything that could not be tightly proven by the evidence generated by survey or experimental techniques was taken to be of no value. There was no question now of spending years on theory development, theoretical psychology was virtually non-existent. Testing was central and testing preferably had to be done quickly. Not only was this hard-line positivism, it was *impatient* positivism. The way physicists had believed for decades in the existence of the neutrino — because it was demanded by theory, but had no evidence for its existence then or any idea how they could find it — this kind of thing would not have been countenanced for a moment in academic psychology. In conversation the method of testing had to come pre-packaged with the idea — in geology I remember specialists waiting eight years between the creation of single layer buckling theory, then its refinement and refinement — before *adequate* testing methodology was desired and created. Again, this would not have been 'on'.

What counted as evidence here in 1970s psychology was conveniently defined so as to suit an experimentalist philosophy. Facts were clean facts from the laboratory cubicle, not messy ones from life. This was more biobehavioural science rather than what I was seeking — psychology: mind in life.

As an experimentalist in the 1970s I eventually found myself, working in this ambience, to have drifted essentially into the identity of being a *finder*. I was, when all the trappings were stripped away, basically a fact-finder (where I define facts as what a true theory states). This was really a denial of 90 per cent of what

I was. A finder is an instrument. This is the instrumental masculinity of positivistic empirical science. A subject designed by traditional men for traditional men — and I guess also for people who like to work within tight formal rule systems. This was like being in a bank.

Me? That's a secret

Things central in my life: experience, empathy, feelings, qualitative study, field work and so on were all outlawed by this dedication to the empirically demonstrated fact. Of course one might point out that pretty well all the most important questions one is confronted with in life cannot be answered by an experiment or psychometric survey anyway. I found that there were virtually no students who felt that positivism was in any way helping them to get to where they wanted to go. I was wasting my life. This was watering a cactus.

A corollary of positivism and this 'cult of the fact' was that, since researchers dealt with generalisations on human nature and with people as processors, and since the mind-brain system was seen as something outside of oneself, one's own personality, quirks and desires need never enter the picture. One could always stand in the wings of one's findings. The emphasis was on standardisation of method and replicability of outcome. The result of all this was that staff would remain strangers to their students even after years in a department where one would least expect it. Positivism gave licence for secrecy, distance and non-involvement. Virtue was to be found not in persons, but in techniques and in results. If what you are is irrelevant (echoes of A level history) and might even be seen to get in the way, why talk about it? Incredible though it was, psychology thus became basically an impersonal subject.

Devotion and deviation

By 1977/78 it was obvious to me that I had to craft a different identity for myself as a psychologist. Nobody was going to tell me that I wasn't a psychologist simply because I wasn't an objectivist in spirit. What basic strategy to my work would emerge I did not know but I kept certain key ideas as central to my quest: life relevance; intuition; experimenting in a life context; working from within; meaning-seeking; psychology out of life rather than psychology out of the laboratory cubicle. If it took years of fieldwork to create hypotheses, so be it. I was not going to slide into the habit I had seen so often of creating hypotheses in a few minutes in the coffee room and then quickly decorating them with ornate and intense experimental logistics. If the hypotheses did not grow organically out of life and if they weren't carefully considered and mulled over, of what use were they? Simply seeming to slavishly follow hypothetico-deductive science was totally phoney if the theorising was so hurried, cursory and banal.

It also seemed to me that it would be better to develop a theoretical superstructure with testing, when it came, just of critical nodes in that superstructure. This was a rather Piagetian idea of course. It was preferable to testing of every conceivable proposition — a procedure that was likely to lead only to a pile of disconnected microtheoretic rubble that would never get off the ground and never coalesce into anything meaningful or life relevant.

But while all these background intuitions were floating around in my mind a central problem had to be solved — my personal and sexual life was in absolute and utter crisis, verging virtually on ruin. In my domestic life I was a transvestite, not an identity that gelled easily with an instrumental view of man — or with the woman in my life at the time. Somehow I had to get myself a life where I wasn't clashing with my environment in every word I said and every thought I entertained. This really was of great urgency as transvestism is not something one does but something one is and as Nietzsche would have expected it reaches to the very depths and heights of one's being.

Clearly a life in positivistic psychology, where empathy, feeling and experience are marginalised to the point of non-existence, is hardly likely to be nourishing to a person whose whole sexual life is founded on empathy, empathy with women and whose being as a feeling person centrally defines everything he is.

Although I have often resisted acknowledging it, there is also something obsessive-compulsive about transvestism. Gestalt therapist Fritz Perls would have said, 'Don't fight it, go *into* it, go to town on yourself!' A wise transsexual told me exactly the same thing. In psychological terms this is known as a paradoxical injunction, don't resist what compels you, do it *more*. Sometimes (not often) this has helped compulsive handwashers and checkers get a grip on their behaviour.

But of course transvestism, for most men, is far from being an agonising source of suffering of which he wants to be rid. Quite the opposite, admitting the paranoia and guilt that can be involved, it is still enjoyable to a voluptuous and opulent degree and surely is to puritans one of the most forbidden fruits of them all.

Protest through subculture

I was obviously becoming more and more discontented over the 1970s, with 'impatient positivism' and the licence it seemed to give to aggressively shut down imagination, enthusiasm and individuality — and hence theoretical elaboration. All life's blood to me. Tight controls on experiments were not giving me rich or representative enough data but there was no journal in those days that was likely to publish much looser studies I had tried (in 1973) involving testing in the field ('sloppy methodology' was the retort I expected). I had also found absolutely nobody anywhere in science with the slightest interest in integrating what they were with their work and with their life. This to me was a pivotal mission of my entire existence. It was also not refreshing to find (later) that even Alan Turing[1] had failed in this quest (Hodges, 1983).

By 1978 I was a dreadfully unhappy man and being what I was sexually prevented me from much open discussion of my plight. I could neither work, rest nor play with any degree of serenity. I was right in the middle of the most extreme example of 'a round peg in a square hole' I had ever come across. It was time to jettison my allegiance with academic psychology and pitch myself into a subculture which was about as far away from positivistic scientism as one could possibly imagine.

---

1 Turing, later in his short life, did have Jungian therapy and may have made some inroads into this problem of reconciling life and work, intellect and emotion. No records, however, of the outcome of these therapy sessions survive.

4
Transvestism as the bridge: two personalities

Deserting into oneself

Life's reward is intrinsic: the purpose of life is to live, not merely reproduce — and one must live one's *own* life, not drag out some false, shallow existence that the world in its hypocrisy demands. Walter Pater taught thus at Oxford in the 1880s and particularly through his influence on Wilde and thence later libertarians such thoughts have shaped the thinking of many in the West ever since.

As a fledgling, however, I made a terrible mistake: I listened always and only to reason. I did not listen to the gentler voice of the heart, the voice of feelings, the real guide to fulfilment. In science feelings, as we have seen, had to be marginalised; the spin-offs of which were countless.

In the 1970s, now a social scientist, I noticed something, as have others (Evans, 1998, p.7), that made me wonder even more whether or not my leapfrog from geology to psychology might send me skidding. It was nothing very portentous, but it was frustrating. Some might say it was utterly trivial, but I didn't think so. I noticed strangely that social scientists can't *dance*.

Why this is, why the personnel move around the dancefloor, as Evans puts it, 'like planks of wood' could probably be a useful PhD topic in itself and, since dance is no inconsequential thing, might well take the student to the very heart of what it means to *be* a social scientist *per se*. (After all, the dancer Suzanne Farrell once said, 'The way you dance is the way you are'.)

It is difficult to avoid the inference that the public and private denial of feeling (Kline, 1988) and of individual style has something to do with this. In psychological writing the personality of the author remains in shadow and all colour and feeling is drained from the rendition. The social scientist must copy (what he or she (wrongly) thinks of as) physics in being standardised in method, style and consciousness. All that is hardly of any use on the dancefloor.

Feeling, art, experience, individuality of style, intuition, all of these rather feminine things appealed to me far more than the nuts and bolts methods that then dominated our subject. But femininity was and is greatly devalued even by some women. It is often said that men also fear somehow 'collapsing back into femininity' (Frosh, 1994; Wetherell, 1996) in their everyday behaviour and fear, virtually to the point of terror, doing or saying anything that could lead them to be labelled as feminine by other men. Being like a woman must be a collapse to a lower plane of existence; it urgently has to be avoided. One really has to wonder whether such men do really like and respect women, whatever they say in public?

As a schoolboy and later as a hard-nosed scientific geologist I always knew that despite the macho ambience of my life I was a latent transvestite — to femininity haters the greatest of all sins. Of course this had to be suppressed in the 'pansie-bashing' atmosphere of the all-boys school to which I went in Manchester and also, it has to be said, in geology: geologists, I noticed, seemed to be particularly scornful of such tendencies. Even at school, though I was totally heterosexual at the time, my hairstyle, which would not have looked out of place on the cover of *Vogue* magazine — and which really was a 'leakage' (Dixon, 1981) of the decorative urge in my transvestism, led me to be labelled a 'latent homosexual' by the school team footballers there. If they'd have known that I was wearing subtle eyebrow and eye-makeup, which I was (more leakage), the persecution would have been even worse.

In 1973 when I moved from earth to social science, I stopped being absurd. I decided to cease suppressing this more ornamented side of my personality — much to girlfriends' (and neighbours') horror — and started to explore I guess what Jung would call my own anima, the woman in man. Neighbours outed me to friends (and beyond) in 1974, pretty well fixing me on this path from then on.

Beforehand, I merely had been mindful to the point of fetishistic about what girlfriends wore but in private, of course, I was vulnerable to the trappings of femininity to a degree where I knew that that door led to a blend of ecstacy and oblivion. In Hermann Hesse fashion it had written on it 'This door leads to slavery to woman's beauty'. I dared not open it beyond a few inches lest I be whirled through it like a leaf in a hurricane.

Throughout the 1970s the door gradually opened to the full. I experimented with transvestism with a mixture of wantonness and dread. Dread of where it was taking me. Rather than seeing myself as developing a gender identity disorder I came to realise that I had a double gender *capacity*. This was not an abnormality — except to the politically and religiously minded — this was a *talent*! And indeed a very creative and meaningful one. No aversion therapy for me. You couldn't explain all this with conditioning theory.

It became clear that transvestism could put the zest back into my life that hard-line positivism had totally removed. I yielded to the field, to the hurricane, and let it take me where it willed.

It also occurred to me as a spin-off that one might come to understand others better if one intensified (rather than denied) one's own individuality. The opposite of the standardising approach. This was an idea I would subsequently find had been subscribed to by both Carl Rogers and Oscar Wilde. If British academic psychology of the 1970s was simply not my style I would have to create my own style, alone, with no map. My first venture was to live out this double gender capacity — it would hardly endear me to the local rugby team, but they deserved a spit in the face. In my imagination I was beckoned by avenues of beautifully dressed girls to join them in the delights of the female world. But where on earth, I quailed, as if tingling and trembling, would all this lead?!

The anatomy of the feminine

Living as a woman is hard work. Men may be transformed easily into women on a video screen by computer graphics techniques but in real life the transformation, if it's to be really convincing, is a very tricky exercise. Apart from the obvious differences in the breasts, genitals and hips and shoulders, and of course body and facial hair, a woman's waistline, for example, is much higher in the overall plan of the body than is a man's. The bridge of her nose is also wider; her cheekbones fuller, more rounded, more prominent. Usually her chin is less square; there is no Adam's Apple bulge; her eyelid-eyebrow separation is greater than a man's; her features are smaller; her teeth larger; her skin smoother and finer-textured . . . and so it goes on.

As a transvestite or transsexual, if one wants to get by ('pass'), and hence not be 'read', not only at night but in the daytime (which is a great deal harder) one has to be mindful of all these differences and of course many more (smaller hands, slimmer fingernails, plumper lips etc.) and pore over the makeup and fashion pages of women's magazines into the early hours — to say nothing of the time in front of mirrors practising different makeups, clothes and walking styles. Passing as a woman though male is, I can tell you, a darn sight more difficult than creating any of the visual tricks one can find in perception psychology. This is indeed the ultimate illusion (see pp. 26–7) and I suppose, some might say, the ultimate and most sinister deception.

Are you man enough to be a woman?!

In 1978–80, man enough or not, I lived as a woman on and off for about 18 months in various parts of London and had stretches of nine to ten days or so now and then continually in the female role. I took the name 'Linda' which seemed to suit my appearance. All of this is known in the transvestite/transsexual scene ('TV/TS' scene) as 'going full time'. From all this experience on the other side of the fence the reader might be intrigued to know how I found life as a woman compared to that as a man and indeed which I thought was the better life. I was in a pretty good position to judge this in those days as my own gender identity and body image, at least by 1977/78, was split 50:50 between male and female. Unlike a transsexual (or a straight man) I felt I had both the mentality and, in a physical sense, the hands, legs, face etc. to live either role (see Figures 4.1 and 4.2) rather than preferring one. To see which suited best I had 'simply' to try them out side by side. I am not physically big, I had the walk, the look, the gear, I was single, I could do it. Talking about it in therapy would have been of little use — and anyway I did not see transvestism as a suitable case for the couch.

Over the gender fence

A woman's life in some respects is a lot more colourful than a man's. I guess most people accept this. The range of styles and colours of men's clothes is positively scrawny and dull compared to those for women and of course this was even more so in the 1970s. With the aid of a bewildering range of hair dyes, wigs, makeup techniques and scarves a woman can also totally change her image from shoulders up so she has plenty of opportunity for artistic licence merely by being the sex that she is. Relatively speaking a man's physical appearance, particularly shoulders up, is virtually in a vice in which he can wriggle around a bit but hardly express or create.

Things are noticeably better now than they were, say, in 1977, but for any expressive man, such as I was, just being a man was limiting. Many of us artistically inclined, and indeed artists such as Francis Bacon, took to transvestism and where the 'standards' for men were most cramped and regulated, as in the north of England, retailers would report that transvestism was more common.

Figure 4.1   Model deception — the author *en travesti* as 'Linda', 1979.
Photo: John Bryant

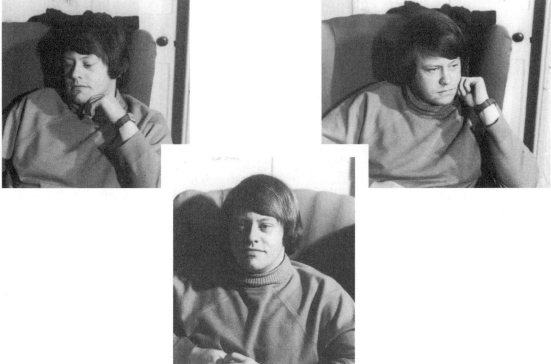

Figure 4.2 'Let not buzz'd whisper tell' (Keats). The many faces of Peter and 'Linda', late 1970s. Photos: Above John Bryant, below John Bromley

The single largest contingent to the local transvestite club in Massachusetts, USA, is from Massachusetts Institute of Technology.

With this freer expression visually came greater licence for expression of softer emotions, something really vital to me. In comparison to the relatively po-faced behaviour of men it actually became OK to have quite a mobile face, to be very caring, and to smile and laugh even at trivia. As a man it was mainly ascerbic humour that would provoke real guffaws. Be too expressive and you risked being seen as 'soft' or even 'queer'.

As a woman I found it easier and virtually automatic to be more friendly and altruistic with people. I even found myself showing more consideration for others in the way I climbed stairs — which I did more slowly and gently. As a man I would rush and stomp up them as if it was the SAS raiding the building. Again, as a man, if one is 'really friendly' one does risk being seen as 'poofy' and even as 'on the pickup'. A man must be stiller in face and rather stiffer and colder in manner unless there's some sporty, aggressive or heterosexual theme to justify 'excess' (or unless he's drunk).

I came to notice that a lot of women's body language and general mannerisms were not as genetic as I'd thought, but simply due to the encumbrances one has as a woman. For example with long fingernails I would pick up cups and knives and forks differently and slightly more daintily. Physically there was no choice, I had to. Similarly I sat down in a skirt with a sweep of the garment unnecessary when in trousers. Again this is a practical thing not anything 'inherent'. I also found it is no use rubbing your face or chin roughly and carelessly if you have an itch there — not if you're wearing foundation — or the whole lot will come off all over your hands. Itches on the cheek, if foundation is on, have to be just pinched or gently touched. It's not 'being ladylike', it's just practical.

For better or worse, appearance is just so important to a young modern Western woman. Because of that I found that if I was in a restaurant, say, I would also touch my face and hair a great deal more often as a woman than I ever would as a man. Waistline and hair style became major topics, I once found myself talking for about 20 minutes not about attribution theory but about my fingernails.

Alas I was a darned sight more attractive as a woman than as a man. Still, it was motive to go out more and until finances prevented it (and until to a degree I wearied of it) I was out in the clubs, discos and pubs of the day at one time almost every other night. Obviously the narcissistic gratification of all this was quite delicious. It was also good to find that whatever image as a woman I had for that day or evening, people were noticeably more friendly and took more time with me.

If I was crazed through lack of art in the monochrome world of 1970s psychology, transvestism had pitched me right into a world of iridescent colour. Decadently I came to live in a world of silks, satins and scents. I gave up smoking partly because it spoiled the image (and the fragrance). I became a purveyor of perfumes, one man giving me seven bottles as a gift. It was all a far cry from theory, cold fact and mechanics. A mind starved of poetry, dance and colour has to right itself, we all have to compensate, and this was my preferred way. Disco, Tennyson and lace.

But of course apart from the good things, the sad things and the irritants there was also the decadence. Live like this and you're bound to be accused of it.

In a way what I was doing was harmless and just playful but as a transvestite I did not only live as a woman above ground in everyday society but, inevitably, in the underground in a realm where every Judaeo-Christian edict about sexual behaviour was broken by the second. This was something else. More on this in a moment.

A woman's down-side

As Chevalier d'Eon de Beaumont (1728–1810) once said, 'Beauty is a woman's portion', but other than beauty and its pay-offs, what was a woman's lot in the late 1970s? Was it *all* 'quite delicious'? Not really. Life as a man, if not better, was easier if greyer. The only work I was offered in the woman's role, as a temp', was cashier or secretarial work and, informally, bar work. I only did the latter. I did some glamour modelling, which was fun, but the actual range of opportunities otherwise was very limited and the pay appalling. Although in shops, assistants would tend to you more and see you as more knowledgeable, it mattered little if one always had to buy the cheapest.

Though on the dance floor I was at ease, social science training or not, walking home at night was a completely different proposition. Men in cars would screech to a halt even on 50 mph stretches to make 'offers' (maybe they did it to any blonde in high heels) while others would crawl the kerb assuming I meant 'business' if I was ever out so late alone. Indeed long blonde hair seemed to be a lightbulb to a moth here. There was also the occasional 'gun in the back' frotteur — here an attractive skirt or attractive hair were lightbulbs. With all these irritants my general manner was 'aloof' but they made you feel vulnerable and of course your space is invaded without assent. A lot of men see this kind of thing as 'flattering' but the behaviours are forced upon you, they are basically attacks. The underground may be decadent, but at least it's all by mutual consent.

So, above-ground culture has its well-known iniquities. But what of the veiled world of alternative sexuality such as I was also inhabiting? Here I had to cast aside diagnostic manuals and north-of-Watford sexual righteousness that saw what I was doing as psychopathology and misdeed, and live in a circle where what I was practising was at least insisted on and at worst inconspicuous.

A walk on the wild side

Art is dangerous because it opens the mind to new possibilities. Though we carelessly assume (and science proves we do) that what is beautiful is good (Dion, 1972; Dion, Berscheid and Walster, 1972) there are other, more cryptic, more subterraneous avenues of thought; avenues that link beauty with sin, with the 'surely impossible' and even with death. In the realms of sexual outrageousness we can easily venture into these darker areas.

Oscar Wilde never believed that to yield to temptation was a sign of weakness. He said, 'I tell you there are temptations so terrible it needs strength, strength and courage, to yield to them.' There was many a cavernous club, often down steep dimly lit steps, with front doors that opened and shut quickly, where one could see the truth in this at every other turn. Men with tongues around stiletto heels; women with tongues around ear-ringed ears; men, backdated to childhood, prettified in baby pink satin dresses, delighting in the joys of 'uncle's lap'. Beauty and power; beauty and youth; beauty and *sin*.

But of course sin is highly poetical, shame is not (Lady Wilde). A man with his face buried in the copious folds of a woman's yellow satin skirt; a transvestite prostrate before his whip-wielding leather-clad Madame; a perfumed lesbian and a transsexual with legs entwined. All to the doctrinaire are irredeemable sinners, their gods false, their pleasures corrupt. But here in underground caves yellow satin decadence is expected; here Beardsley Yellow Book drawings capture the music of the moment, and with no eyes of the scornful to see, on common and vulgar faces, there is no shame.

This was the life: no limits, no taboos, nothing considered shocking, no barriers to absolute freedom of expression. This is how you find yourself: via the jolts and jogs, confirmations and disconfirmations of social life. In living on the edge, like this, 'Borderline living', one dispenses with being anything in particular and lives at the level of the flow of feeling or, even deeper, as a pawn to the fountain flow of one's unconscious processes. This is 'process living', transcendental living, close to the preternatural, where *anything* can happen.

The down-side

In art one always defers to beauty. With Nietzsche and with Wilde we speak of beauty as the higher ethic. 'It is better to be beautiful than to be good,' said Oscar, 'but it is better to be good than to be ugly.' Alas, as Camus knew (1942/1983), if one wagers on the flesh, one knows one will lose. People get old, the flower fades, only the beauty of objects, clothes, paintings, has some fixity — at least if not a painting of Dorian Gray. But for the transvestite there is yet another side to this agony of beauty. While the female personality cavorts as I did in a decadent world of fashion, fantasy and food, wines and dines with man and woman alike, is perfumed, powdered and pampered, what happens to the forgotten fragment of the whole, the male personality? For many the executive of the whole outfit, the guy who put this cherub on the road? What becomes of him?

Here the psychologist definitely has some purchase. If one is not too mindful about it, the male personality can start to wither away — in confidence, self-esteem, and life radius. This is something that is involved in the transition from transvestism to transsexualism. This, alas, I know from the inside.

There is plenty of positive reinforcement for the female, the rose, but the bees omit to reward, and may even sting, the male. For example:

'After all, you've got nothing to offer as a man, have you?'
'You *are* coming to the party as Linda, aren't you?'
'You should dress as a woman all the time.'
'You're booooootiful!'
'Peter doesn't dress up as a woman, he dresses up as a man!'

And so it would go on. By September 1979 'Peter' was like a small leaf on the fine blossom that had become 'Linda'. Then, a year later, and quite suddenly and against the odds, it all ended. I went to my bedroom one afternoon, replete as it was with wigs, makeup, garments by the dozen, to 'dress' for a photo session with some other transvestites and I suddenly found myself saying to myself, 'Oh no, not *again*.' It was satiation, burnout . . . total burnout, even burnout of meaning and creative vitality. A couple of months later, in early November, I had my first date with the woman I eventually married and my life as Linda both at street level and in the grottoes of London's clubland was over.

Reflections

I write in 1999. Linda exists now only in photographs — in albums, in magazines, in fact on many a magazine cover. When I look back, it was quite a time. She was even the very first cover girl to appear on a transvestite magazine on sale in the shops in this country — in the autumn of 1978. Some first!

But unlike Wilde's Dorian, I have aged while the pictures have stayed young. It is better this way. To see those pictures age would have been a terrible thing. Linda was an artist's creation, like a portrait but in 3D, she had to stay young. I poured life into her while I could but as Jung said, the anima of a man is no match for his animus — and, anyway, time takes its toll.

Strangely, and contrary to Jungian theory (Johnson, 1987), my wife Jill is nothing like Linda. Linda was no threat to Jill who just laughed in the early days about my transvestism and said, 'Do what you like.' When I have an offer like that I generally don't. When I am told (as I once was), 'I think what you do is vile and despicable', I do, just to fly the freedom flag. But I had had the kind of freedom I needed, for the duration I needed it, it was time to move on.

The critical outcome of my time as Linda was that, cryptic and gradually preconscious though the processes doubtless were, it radically changed my male personality as well. I became less analytical, more relaxed, more socially minded, more open to my feelings, generally softer and more compassionate. I did not yet have the identity of artist, but I was brought to the point where it was more ready and available. I came out of all this in the 1980s as a kind of blend of the Peter and the Linda of the 1970s. This was good, and really in a way is closer to the reality of what I am, and indeed was, even then — beneath the crust of obnoxious 1950s and 1960s male socialisation (my revulsion at which being the source of my gender ambiguity). Transvestism was, after all is said and done, something to go *into* as a growth experience, not a form of pathology to have deconditioned away. It was essentially the instantiation of the rest of the keyboard of my mind and when it had been played, a fuller and richer male personality eventually was formed.

Occasional emergences of Linda occurred throughout the 1980s but as the decade wore on it became increasingly difficult for me to take my body for a woman's body and I could express my femininity perfectly adequately in the work that I did. My softer male personality seemed to work socially a lot better and had a richer life than it had had in the 1970s. It was now the one that worked, rested and played with serenity. By 1990, though I might have rare glimpses of the old Peter, Linda as process, as noun, as spirit, even as dream, was dead.

5
The artist-experimenter identity in psychology

Mind-in-life

The denouement of my transvestism in 1980, amongst many other things, not least meeting my wife, really took tension out of me. From a war-like and rebellious life things now moved to much calmer waters. My concerns about scientific psychology also began to slot into perspective. It was more important to add to it rather than reject it. In 1982 I began teaching psychology to adults for Birkbeck College, the Open University and the City Literary Institute and over the years taught every branch of the subject apart from psycholinguistics. This was exceptionally rewarding work. The students were strong and keen and class discussion was substantial. These were work contexts in which a great deal of exploration of the subject was permitted (and needed) and where a tremendously large number of issues could be mulled over — particularly for their life relevance — with highly articulate and long-lived audiences. My transvestic escapades to unravel the mysteries of femininity posed no problem, and photographs could even be passed round in class — much to everyone's entertainment. This was a context, unlike science, where one could use all of one's experience.

Over the years as transvestic inclinations petered out the artistic drive that had parented them became focussed on art *per se*. Very much a way of being I should have contemplated earlier. This seemed to be a direction that had many implications for psychology and which provoked plentiful discussion. The key words for most artists are 'meaning' and 'expression', for scientists 'theory' and 'evidence'. Arrange these together and I felt we had a psychology securely standing on four strong and essential pillars. The identity I chose to accommodate this view was that of the 'artist-experimenter' or 'artist-practitioner' in a clinical sense. A person sensitive to purpose as well as cause, to meaning as well as fact. In the rest of this chapter I will try to clarify for the reader why I think these are highly useful identities for many psychologists to adopt who feel ill-at-ease in the square box of pre-emptive positivism with its pronouncements to only be a scientist-practitioner. This will take us on a journey which strangely justifies not a view of life in which 'all is matter and fact' but a view which sees will, trust, faith and meaning as the binding cement of everything we do together, from romance to politics, from science to poetry.

Realistic idealism

The twentieth century, at least in contrast with the nineteenth, has seen the butchery of the poetical character, the 'depoetising' of person. Without hardly realising it so many have become lay reductionists, rationalists, evidence-seekers, materialists. But being obsessed with rationality and measurement keeps a person at a very crass level of understanding. We have seen this only too well from the shortcomings of empirical studies of love and creativity and from empirical psychology's silence and dereliction on such matters as freedom and evil. In psychology we need not only an extrinsic psychology based on evidence and facts, an empirical objective endeavour, but also an intrinsic psychology, a psychology from within; psychology as helping one directly to live, a subjective purposive psychology.

The real enemies in the attempt that many people such as myself are now involved in — to create a rich, full, adequate and satisfying subject of psychology — are not positivistic social scientists *per se*. The real enemies are ignorance, prejudice and fear. There are people who fear that if they relax their assumption of the superiority of empirical psychology the subject will slide away into the form of an amorphous blob of worthless speculative trash and mere opinion. That if the quantitative scientific stranglehold is eased 'mad poets' will rush in with revelation rather than realism, the laboratory will give way to the pulpit, charisma will take over from evidence and we will slither into the mode of the political bigot — where things are true if one says them in a loud enough voice. But novels are not irrelevant to psychologists simply because the stories in them involve imaginary personalities; poets and playwrights can display psychological sensitivity that does not deserve scorn or dismissal and artists generally can have an intuition about people that outstrips the capacities of any narrowly focussed analytical thinker. Only by marshalling together the strengths of both art *and* science can we adequately characterise and understand human beings to a truly satisfying degree.

Science versus art

Science is concerned with the description of the external world. Here mind-brain has to be seen as 'out there', external to the self. It is measured and probed by various forms of instrument in the search by the intellect for explanation. And for explanation we need the creation of theory and the collection of fact. The artist, however, seeks to understand things via what he or she *is,* guided more by feeling. The artist therefore tries to empathise with and *be* with that which he or she is studying. While the scientist deals in generalities and broad trends and works in the service of order, the artist has a feel for the momentary and for individuality and works in the service of expression. But both the scientist and the artist have a feel for the importance of minutiae, both require the deep steering of transcendental vision and both value the search for truth and the creation and appreciation of beauty. A theory may be unsatisfying because of its ugliness or singular absence of elegance.

Experimentation

There is no question, however, that in the search for truth one must check. This is generally avoided by philosophers and has indeed led Jean Piaget (1972) implicitly and Richard Gregory (1970) explicitly to call for an experimental philosophy. This of course, rather ironically, was the way experimental psychology itself was born in the 1870s in the 'philosophical laboratories' of Wilhelm Wundt and William James.

Experimentation is a part of life. The nineteenth and twentieth centuries have particularly seen the flowering of experimental art and indeed some of the experimental games and thought experiments of the Surrealists were bordering on the form of psychological pilot experiments (Cardinal and Short, 1970, p.17). It is therefore no paradox for me to define myself as an artist-experimenter. Experimentation belongs to everyone, it is not the sole preserve of science. The artist-experimenter identity, however, gives licence for both objective and subjective study in psychology while still allowing the person to articulate with the activities of those people, so many in number, who practise controlled experimentation.

Cognitive and emotional incorrectness

In the creation of this identity I argue for a new versatility and a new honesty in psychology. I argue for psychology, like art, to be expression as much as a form of professionalism. Scientific training alone is no training for the dualistic crossfire world of meaning. One is trained to expect and seek a best answer or a right answer. In the discursive realm, that simply doesn't exist. Meanings are not facts as predicted by a correct theory. They are of divergent not convergent quality. Scientists, as we see with some evangelical cognitive therapists, easily drift into preaching for a 'cognitively clean' society, for rational living, for 'cognitive and emotional correctness' and for 'logicism'. The artist in contrast is the defender of chance, of the mistake, of the perverse. While the scientist seeks reason and experiment as guides to life the artist values love and coincidence (see Waggoner, 1966 on E.M. Forster). While the scientist studies the machine and the mechanism, the artist studies the drama. It seems self-evident therefore that the key word 'evidence' (and hence 'evidence-based practice') is not the only pillar on which psychology rests. It rests also, as I say, on 'theory', 'meaning' and 'expression'.

Yin and Yang

It is fairly obvious that we have here a direct attempt to complete a 'Yang'-based endeavour with the addition of the missing more feminine 'Yin'. Of course this raises issues of personal taste, temperament and possible prejudice. Some men, as we have seen in the previous chapter, are femininity-fearing phonies, are totally out of touch with who or what they are and have no interest whatever in using their own knowledge of psychology to illuminate themselves (in empirical psychology that is sadly quite a common attitude). It is therefore hardly surprising that they have no interest in teaching psychology in a way that fosters self-realisation for the students! However, my attitude differs from this very radically and I view psychology as a growth and insight promoting subject as much as an endeavour that describes what is the case in the world.

My own development, as Chapter 4 has starkly revealed, is idiosyncratic, if instructive. There are many paths to art and that was merely one of them. In the end we all have to find our own way to a fulfilling life and for someone like me, who (when he did the work) headed his year at school only in History and English (but certainly not in Chemistry and Mathematics), it is not surprising that, after my detour through geology, I would actualise with time an orientation to psychology that was more artistic than scientific. We each have our contribution to make and it inevitably bears our personal stamp and personal biases, even if this usually, in science, is concealed as much as possible. Indeed it is surprising how often evidence and rational argument can be marshalled to bolster personal biases that are left veiled while the researcher feigns a stance of utter neutrality that is rarely genuine (and probably psychologically impossible).

In order to articulate this chapter with the previous one I think it is fair and it makes things clearer also to emphasise that in some ways I am validating the very artistic impulse that moulded me. This is deeper than transvestism. It is the drive to beauty, the drive to create beauty. This is central. In the privations of the north side of Manchester in the 1950s and 1960s my transvestic triflings were my only glimpse of beauty when I was very young. They were my only artistic outlets. Since my biases were towards arts subjects I can appreciate the value of the artistic perspective better I guess than most scientists. But at least here this is open and declared; the reader can see fully the life context and the intellectual context that has helped these ideas to gestate.

Drama within mechanism, mechanism within drama

Valèry once said that the human organism is a machine for producing poetic states (Kermode, 1966, p.91). Like any play, human existence can only be enacted by minds (with a mechanism) interacting to produce the drama of social life. Rather than seeking the laws of mind in general the artist studies the embodied mind in context. This study of mechanism within drama necessarily focuses on the single case or the biographical sketch (e.g. Chadwick, 1992, 1997). At the level of the single case we can see more clearly the interaction of the motivational, cognitive, physiological, spiritual and social factors that have shaped the person. At the nomothetic level of 'mind in general', the dynamic interplay of these factors is often lost as one is studying only an out-of-context abstraction, a generalisation. This plea for a revival of the single case study therefore is also a plea for a total psychology, a 'real' psychology that recognises the multifaceted nature in life of all phenomenon from visual illusion to religious experience.

Measuring an illusion

I am also arguing here for an interaction of analytic and holistic approaches. Analysis must be grounded. Analytically derived rules and procedures always have to be seen in context, a total life context. For example: that something cannot be defined does not mean it doesn't exist. That a theory can be refuted does not mean it is a good theory. That a theory *cannot* be refuted does not mean it isn't true. And strangely: that something can be measured does not mean that it exists either — one can compute the volume of the Impossible Triangle (Ernst, 1986, p.18); the height of an Escher staircase; the angle of convergence of fanning lines in the Zöllner illusion figure, but none of these things exist. Analysis has to be guided and interpreted, one cannot hope to study London effectively if one does it in the blackout with a pencil torch.

The experiment as will

Thinking is extended by experiment. The first experiments in physics were to find things out, to 'see what happens'. But a painting is also an experiment to an art therapist (see Thomson, 1989) and as it was in Picasso's life (Berger, 1980). The writing of a story, for Thackeray, was an adventure. Whether it be the controlled experiment, the field study or the poem, all are ventures to test the unknown, to discover, to extend the arm of thought by action in the world — so taking thought beyond itself. Piaget was as much an experimenter when he wrote, as he did prolifically, as when he tested children. Both endeavours were the development of thought by action.

But perhaps the particular defining quality of experiment is not the obsessional cleanness we so prize in psychology but the prior attitude and admission of uncertainty, the feeling of vulnerability, the intention to discover rather than merely confirm and the will to reach out to reality to be completed and extended. Experiments seen in this light are centrally about affective and conative factors, they are not 'purely cognitive'.

Faith, trust and meaning

The world can be seen as beauty and logic working together. The cherry tree in my garden instantiates both the survival and proliferation logic of plant life with the beauty of plants. Its beauty moves both the birds who feed on it and the many people who have seen it. It is the perfect combination of form and content.

In the next section of this book we look at personality in these terms, as a combination of form and content and in doing so we put the artist-experimenter and artist-practitioner identities to work.

Like science, the endeavour is an act of faith, a faith that the approach will produce coherent and illuminating characterisations, that it will help us to 'make sense' of this aspect of the world, that it will tell us things we don't already know and hopefully that it will, like any elegant scientific theory or experiment, create beauty.

It is always necessary, or at least better, to write case studies, biographical sketches or psychological studies of people that one loves. As Erich Fromm realised (Fromm, 1957), love sees clearly, it is hate that distorts, that even maims the image. Disinterest and neutrality are little better. In this undertaking, as in science, trust is pivotal. One can have no science and no artistic psychology either in the absence of it. And without trust, and love, meaning is bound to be scrawny and cramped.

In these studies that follow I will try and depict what I see as a total real psychology and I hope in so doing demonstrate the value of the single case approach in our subject. As in science — and indeed in poetry and painting — one's intelligence has to take advantage of error and chance. Many leads have led nowhere and many hours have been spent up blind alleys. But in what follows I will attempt a genuine integrationist approach in which factors from cognitive engineering to spirituality find a blend when considered in the embodied context of the individual.

Part III
Chapters 6 – 11
Studies of the beauty of the personality

I will begin here with a working assumption that everyone's personality possesses beauty, some more than others perhaps but that this beauty can be damaged particularly in psychosis and in psychopathy. I am not saying that the person's personality possesses beauty because they keep us entertained but certainly their beauty makes them likeable and able to please us at least to some degree. Their beauty, however, particularly fosters respect. I am not relating the beauty of the person's personality simply to its social desirability — many scales measure that, even lie scales, but to something more subtle and deeper. Learning-disabled children possess distinctly beautiful personalities so such beauty does not require high intelligence. Physically ugly people also can possess beauty in terms of inner resonance as can depressed or anxious people. Like love, the beauty of the personality does not lend itself at all well to measurement but there is no doubt that it exists and is important. Like any artist (see Wilde in Jackson, 1995) I prefer the definition to come at the end of the study, not, as a scientist would prefer, at the beginning but there is little doubt that the beauty of the personality relates strongly to a person's *style* — and hence to their musical, rather than their verbal, effect on us. These five studies I hope will give a hint of the music of these people's being, in the case of Ivo explicitly so, but at least implicitly for the others.

6
Desmond:
the experience of schizotypy[1]

The scene is London's Drury Lane on a Friday morning in November. It's 1992. Des Marshall, a short, slim 51-year-old, and a friend of long-standing, sits deep in a cafe, *The Fair Deal Sandwich Bar*, a cup of de-caffeinated coffee before him, smoking a cigarette without inhaling. I come in after finishing a lecture at the nearby City Literary Institute. It's just gone 11.30 a.m. The cafe is otherwise empty, if not for long. We've beaten the midday rush.

'Good lecture?' he asks, looking up expectantly.

'Not bad . . . existential psychotherapy,' I reply, putting my bags down with a sigh of relief.

'Oh . . . sounds good . . . '

'Just a mo', must get a sandwich, desperate for tea,' I say, moving to the counter.

My mouth is dry and I've had no time for breakfast.

Provisions ordered I settle down for a chat. The staff are frantically buttering bread ready for lunch time. A cistern of water is coming to the boil. An array of trays of delicious sandwich meat glares out of the glass front of the counter.

'Peter . . . my techniques,' says Des rather intensely.

'What techniques?'

'My techniques . . . affirmations, visualisation, closing down . . . '

'Oh yes,'

'They're not working!'

'Not working?'

'No!'

'It could be temporary,' I reply, trying to be reassuring.

Des has always used various 'New Age' psychological methods to maintain equanimity. Now he seems to be in trouble.

'I don't think so,' he replies gravely.

I smile, 'You remember what Bryan Polikoff said at the Royal Festival Hall? Herbert Beerbohm-Tree used to say "Mediocrity is always brilliant, but genius can be allowed a few lapses".'

'No, no, Peter,' says Des, shaking his head and shaking off the compliment,

---

1 This chapter was modified after feedback on the first draft from Desmond himself; from Geoff Garfield; Ivo Wiesner and Simon Blair. In its present form it therefore represents a fair assessment of Desmond in the opinion of himself and of other people who know him well.

'really I tell you, I'm gonna have to go on medication. I can't take it, it's London, it's driving me crazy. The noise, the traffic, the kids, louts, everything . . . it's too much!' As he speaks several lorries go past and a taxi, honking its horn. There is the sound of young women laughing.

'We were doing it this morning,' I say, 'the only certainties in life are change and death. Life's bound to throw things up that challenge your usual ways of coping.'

'Mm . . . I suppose so,' he sighs, obviously not satisfied with this reply either. 'Be anonymous,' I throw back.

'I AM . . . usually . . . I *am* anonymous but *now* people are looking at me. They keep *looking*, Peter, *looking*, I can't stop it!'

'Probably not as much as you think. At our age, Des, people don't look, we're invisible. When Magritte lived in Belgium he used to say that he laid low by looking just like everybody else.'

'No, I can't do it . . . not now, not any more. Some days they avoid me but these days they *look*.'

'Maybe it's your eyes, your eyes are staring a bit,' I observe. Des looks up from his coffee, alerted. My tea and a chicken-salad sandwich arrive.

'Really?' he asks.

'You're hyped up, you look hyped up.'

'It's all the coffee, I've been drinking so much coffee lately and not de-caffeinated like this. It's bad for me.'

'Seems to me you're overloaded though, information overload, you're too open.'

'I *am*, and I can't close down!'

The cafe starts to fill, partly with students whose ten o'clock classes have just finished. More lorries go by. High heels click on the cafe floor. An aroma of tea fills the air. The cafe is abub with chat.

'Dangerous state,' I say.

'You know, it's funny,' Des replies, 'this looking, it all depends on how I am. These days I feel I stand out like a sore thumb and everyone else is just a blur, a mass,' he looks around the cafe, people are lighting cigarettes and talking animatedly. I munch on my sandwich eagerly.

'That's a good idea . . . that's a great idea!' I exclaim through my mouthful.

'Is it? Why?'

'It's attribution theory . . . consensus and distinctiveness. These days I feel pretty bland, very average. But I see everyone else as individuals. Every person I see is an individual and different from the next person.'

'That's the opposite of what I'm saying.'

'*Exactly*, but it's safer. A lot safer. In 1979 I used to think like you do now. It's a dangerous mode. Very dangerous. You can get really paranoid thinking like that.' I gulp down some tea, 'You know we're onto something here, you could use this in therapy.'

'But I DO stand out, Peter!' says Des, slightly desperate.

'I doubt it's as bad as you think.'

'No, when I'm in this state . . . '

'It's like a field?'

'Yes!'

'Then it must be microfeatures of your body language. People pick up on more than they realise.'

'Yes! I'm not at peace. I'm *ready*, sensitive, self-conscious.'

'Perhaps you need to forget yourself for a time.'

'I can't, I can't, Peter,' Des looks down, and slows down. His coffee is nearly finished. I get us refills and acknowledge some students from my own class. 'If you focus on yourself so much, Des, you're bound to think other people are focusing on you as well,' I say, sitting down.

'Aaaah you know me, Peter . . . egocentric.'

'Then you need to be more loving, get more positive.'

'*That's* what I'm trying to do — but it's not working!'

'Then something's blocking your love.'

'It's London, I can't love in this city. It's all noise, money . . . it's so crass.'

'You have to block it out, live your own life.'

'I can't, it's too much.'

'You have to in order to be able to live in a city like this. You know what it's like, Des, it's the same for all of us.'

'I can't. I could before. I admit that. I could! But now it's getting to me.'

'Peace, you need peace.'

'There is no peace, Peter. Camden Town . . . it's raving *mad*! Assaults at the tube station, burglary, I tell you this whole place is caving in! In ten years, God what's it goin' to be like in ten years!?'

'If you can't let it wash over you . . . '

'No way, I've gotta leave, Peter. Maybe try Brighton or the countryside. Somewhere with space.'

'There's a good idea in there,' I chip in.

'Yeah.'

'No I mean it's a really good idea.'

'Yeah . . . why?'

'I'm thinking of boundaries, people like us have blurry boundaries . . . looking over the ocean or over miles of green fields . . . there are no boundaries. You extend everywhere . . . diffuse out . . . fill the universe. Maybe this is why people are more stable in the countryside.'

'That's what I need. I need to diffuse OUT. But when I do in London things go wrong. People notice me, stare at me, I don't want all this . . . this . . . '

'Interfacing?'

'No, not that . . . it's something like that . . . no, I'm invaded . . . I'm losing myself . . . dissolving in everyone else . . . '

'Yeah, mind you Keats was the same . . . like a piece of cheese invaded?'

'*Just* like that . . . I need stillness . . . safety . . . open space.'

I finish my sandwich. Des looks as if he's got something off his chest a little bit. He lights another cigarette.

'Well I don't know,' I reply. 'I know I need a muffin . . . and more tea!'

Des looks down. I order my goodies and sit down. Chairs are clashing, it's difficult to get through. The cafe is packed now, a dozen and more conversations going on simultaneously. Office workers with perfectly styled hair and smart suits now form the queue getting take-away sandwiches and tea. They talk of events. The students at the tables talk of ideas. One leans over to ask me if I can recommend her anything by Camus. I point her in the direction of *The Myth of Sisyphus* and *The Outsider*. But I add a warning:

'Be careful of this stuff. It's sombre. I have a golden rule: don't give credence to any system of thought that spoils the joy of being alive!'

'Ah . . . who said that?'

'I did.'

'Oh! Ha! Does this stuff do that?' she asks, worried.

'When you go a long way into it the atmosphere gets . . . erm . . . well . . . grey skies . . . know what I mean?'

'Ha! Right, I'll be careful,' she smiles and turns back to her friends.

'Peter, what you were saying,' says Des.

'Yeah?'

'I was on Hampstead Heath yesterday.'

'Yeah.'

'I tell you that's what I need . . . Nature . . . the joy of being alive! It was incredible. The greenness of the grass, the flowers, the birds, the peace! You feel you're in the presence of God.'

'Great, that's great, Des, so why leave? Why go to Brighton?'

'I don't know, I need more of that. If there wasn't Hampstead Heath and Richmond Park I couldn't live here you know.'

'It's funny, I'm the reverse. I like lots of people. Oxford Street at Christmas. That's when I'm in my element.' I savour my muffin, its crumbs are falling everywhere.

'God Almighty, Peter!' says Des, eyes like saucers.

'Yeah, honestly, the city, city life, Oscar Wilde was the same. He used to say "Anyone can be good in the country"!'

'Yeah but I need it, Peter! I have to get away from all this. Get close to God. I need it all near me, around me.'

'I need the shops, the energy, the fashions, the window displays, the action.'

'No, no, it's not for me, it's too much!'

'The city gives me ideas, Des, ideas!'

'Yeah, no it's nature for me, you know yesterday . . . I cried . . . I went to Hampstead Heath and I cried . . . just being there . . . feeling it all around me, being part of it . . . wonderful, Peter.'

'And you're the man who when he had a house concreted over the garden!' We both laugh and make to finish our drinks. Des is a bit short of cash, I make up the difference.

'Jesus didn't pay for The Last Supper!' he says, we chuckle, it's good to hear something like that in the middle of the Tory years.

The real-time experience of schizotypy which to a certain, if benign, extent is what we're seeing here in Desmond is something neglected even in major tomes on the topic (e.g. Raine et al., 1995). Most professionals focus on the factor structure of questionnaire responses from such people (e.g. the O-LIFE questionnaire of Mason et al., 1995; Burch et al., 1998; Claridge, 1997, pp.321–4), diagnosis reliability and also information-processing characteristics (e.g. Claridge, 1997). The artist, however, more concerned with the individual, needs to know the details of their everyday experiential life. Whereas some people express themselves in delusions and hallucinations, schizotypal people express what they are in their style of personality organisation. Schizotypal people, who do seem to form a cluster of rather similar style, may have ruminative paranoid ideas, like Desmond, have difficulty modulating attention and cutting out distraction (this we also see here), have unusual (if enriching) perceptual experiences and odd beliefs and can also have some difficulties in face-to-face rapport but most of them do not become psychotic. There is no doubt, however, that as a diagnostic family there are similar patterns in this family, as revealed by factor analysis, as there are in schizophrenic people. There are 'positive types' (characterised by excesses), 'negative' types, characterised by deficiencies, 'disorganised' types and so on, in both families. Des is not withdrawn and emotionally bland, he falls, though without really serious distress, in the category of the 'Positive schizotypal' and this form of schizotypy is addressed by the STA scale of The Schizotypal Traits Questionnaire (STQ) of Claridge and Broks (1984) and Jackson and Claridge (1991). Similarities in the factor structures of schizotypal and schizophrenic people have been reported by Venables and Bailes (1994) and Vollema and van den Bosch (1995) although differences have been reported by Bergman et al. (1996).[2]

Desmond and I have often talked about the borderline zone between schizotypy and psychosis, something he has not crossed whereas I (in 1979) have. Later in this chapter we will see if study at the individual level can provide any protective ideas about how one can avoid a slide into psychosis if one is, in oneself, of this ilk.

Des and I eventually drift out of the sandwich bar, stroll up Drury Lane and walk along High Holborn in the direction of Holborn tube. Des is still sensitive that a proportion of people are looking at him, especially men, he is not at ease. It's lunch time now and High Holborn is crammed with people and high-speed traffic accelerating towards Tottenham Court Road and Trafalgar Square. The pavements are crowded, office workers thread their way into the pubs. Motor cycle couriers roar past. The place is teeming with life.

'Des, I have an idea . . . walk ten yards in front of me . . . then I can see if people really do look at you more than's usual.'

Fortunately he agrees and saunters ahead. We stroll through the crowds of pedestrians. By the time we've reached the corner of Kingsway the verdict is clear. Some people really *do* look at him in an inquisitive way. The discussion continues around the topics of boundaries and body language — and my caffeine addiction. Des is short, today he is walking in a rather wooden way with a very fixed expression. His appearance is more Mediterranean than northern latitudes anyway (see Figure 6.1). Perhaps he really does stand out, at least to some people. Yet there is no doubt that in some moods he is almost invisible and glides through crowds unnoticed. That he likes. At still other times people shun even noticing him and he can sit in a cafe and not be served. I worry though that Des even spends so much time pondering this issue. There are more important things.

---

2 It has to be admitted that the concept of 'schizophrenia' has been greatly criticised in recent years (Bentall et al., 1988; Boyle, 1990) whilst that of schizotypy has remained relatively unscathed. Considerable validational work has been done on the concept of schizotypy (Claridge, 1988, 1990, 1997; Claridge and Beech, 1995 and references therein) such that the concept has strong predictive value at least over a range of laboratory tasks and appears to define a reasonably clear subgroup of people in a meaningful way. This is a good example of a concept taken from life, then to the lab' and then back to life.

Figure 6.1
Desmond Marshall

For the time being though let's move from dialogue to (an old phrase) 'the interior monologue' and hear him now in his own written words. Being a man who is sensitive to the events of his own private mental life to an unusual degree, Des is someone who can open a window onto the private, but as we'll see, productive world of the schizotypal person in illuminating detail.

The journal of an Urban Robinson Crusoe
November 23rd 1994

I am an Urban Robinson Crusoe, I exist on an Island of Urbanity with no Girl Friday. I keep my head when all around me are losing theirs and blaming it on each other. I live my separate reality, I am an independent witness to the chaos and disintegration that abounds around me, the roar of the traffic outside my fifth-floor flat suddenly demands attention from my tired mind.

I force my attention on this piece of blank paper, a scream from the playground in the centre of this run-down estate startles me out of the sequence of words that were slipping through the cortex of my brain, another scream and bellow with a high-pitch cry starts to unnerve me. I am aware of the pressure of the small, blue, betting shop biro on the paper, my fingers start to go numb, with pins and needles running down from the wrist that was broken six months ago.

The hum of the fridge breaks the uneasy silence, the shouts and screams of the playground are playing with my concentration. I lift my aching neck and stare at the grimy stains on the yellowing dirty lino on the kitchen floor, small pockets of dirt, like on a hairy man's back, filter through my eyes to my awareness. I feel guilty that I am unable to gather energy to clean the greasy stains on the gas cooker standing there so majestically.

I feel lost in linear time, the clock seems to have stopped. I go over to see, it is still ticking, 7.15 p.m. I thought I had been indoors for hours but it had only been 35 minutes, it seems so long, so long. My memories present me with pictures that take me back to forgotten times when I couldn't breathe, like a force squeezing the life out of me as if it didn't want me to live, wanting to terminate the existence of this child — I learned later it was called Asthma — and I see a small child kneeling in prayer, asking God to let him go home from the Institution.

November 29th, about 2.30 p.m. Euston Station Cafeteria

. . . Musing if I did right spending £12.50 on acupuncture, the middle-aged lady Chinese doctor didn't seem to understand me, her English 'not velly good', confused. Anyway, if it helps stop the pins and needles in my fingers . . . Felt I did right by having a large tea, paying only 5p extra . . . . unable to go home yet, feeling cut off, my flat seems like a prison waiting to be occupied.

I become aware of the serviette I used to mop up the spilt tea, it's blood red. Suddenly, the woman opposite me attracts my attention — she has blood red lipstick and blood red fingernails. I feel invisible among this anxious, hurried energy that railway stations create. There are five women opposite me, their northern accents waft over me as I gather my thoughts to write. I'm sitting in the smoking section of the cafeteria. I giggle as I notice clouds of smoke billowing around us puffing billies. We look at each other with quick sidelong glances that create a kind of indifferent curiosity among us. The lady with the blood red lipstick suddenly looks at me. I wonder if she has perceived that I might be writing about her, I feel slightly guilty about it. Pins and needles in my hand stop me writing.

A large group of people sit down near me, ignoring me, they are irritated by the high prices, so they are eating their own food, justifying themselves; well, we bought tea in the cafeteria. I become aware that they're all around me, talking across me, startled by what's happening, I get nervous and begin gathering my bits of writing up, growing very self-conscious, intensely aware of every move I make. They start to laugh, I feel their eyes on me as I walk away. Suddenly I become very very visible, I once read somewhere that hell is other people, I walk to my prison.

Images of melancholy and unease

We can see here that Desmond's is a mind that cannot *not* notice things. This is both the strength and the weakness of the schizotypal. One suspects a similar process in James Joyce. The same kind of sensitivity to the fine-grained detail of the external is present with reference to the internal world. Des has a great openness to the preconscious, a process actually studied and confirmed experimentally in schizotypal people by Julie Evans (1997). But it is clear that this permeability often brings unease, fear, melancholy and even despair. This is undoubtedly the world of the introverted writer. As Des's journal continues Hermann Hesse is quoted but without framing by inverted commas. On first reading it is difficult to see where Des's narrative ends and Hesse's begins.

These impressions and images most people block out, merely to make life, and certainly life in the city, more liveable. The schizotypal mind is one of benefits and costs and one has to wonder whether such sensitivity really is worth it. There are pills, pills like haloperidol [3] (which I take), that can or could desensitise people like Desmond. Should he take them? The temptation has often been very great.

But this great perceptual sensitivity, the iridescent brightness (and also persistence of impressions) of the schizotypal's perceptual world obviously has its rewards. Des has no need of LSD or cannabis to intensify his experiences, his own brain chemistry suffices. Red serviette — red blood — red lips — red fingernails — staring eyes — clutter and clammer must get away — back to prison. These associative sequences may in a way be tormenting but this is the stuff of which fine writing is made. Some reach it with drugs, some can do it anyway. But of course there is a price, and madness is never far away.

Staying sane

Desmond's distractibility externally also tends to apply internally. He has paranoid feelings but never entertains *one* worrisome idea for very long, never long enough for it to captivate his thoughts. So a systematised delusion has never taken hold of his mind. Though schizotypal perhaps Desmond lacks the obsessionality or one-track-mindedness to become psychotic in any paranoid way. He may also be too knowledgeable about life itself for any bizarre (and silly) idea to take hold. Perhaps he has too much common sense to go mad. (See

---

3 Haloperidol is a major tranquilliser, sometimes known as Haldol, Fortunan or Serenace. It can also be used in the treatment of tics, persistent hiccoughs, alcohol withdrawal effect, and delirium.

not. The idea of a major persecutory network, basically an 'external locus of control', operating against him never gets a hold — he has done nothing to deserve it and . . . anyway . . . he knows he's a lovable man. Thoughts like that are like an iron fist against the threat of psychosis.

Clean anger

There is also something particularly preventative of the onset of insidious turmoil in Des and that is his 'clean anger'. Some people, when they get angry, just say it, whatever needs saying, straight out, direct. Others, to their cost, simmer and smoulder — generating what Dostoyevsky in *Notes from Underground* used to call (1864/1972) 'the resentment of the stinking bog'. Des is well clear of this territory of emotion and behaviour through excellent self-assertion skills. The fetid, sinister world of 'dirty anger' is therefore not for him.

Mixing with the right people

Des is an introvert and his friends, such as myself and Ivo (Chapter 7) are also centrally interested in the inner life. None of us have much time for people who sit around recounting stories and who talk about nothing but 'the world'. A rich inner life however requires openness to preconscious processes and an enjoyment of the workings of one's own mind. Des's introversion, however, relates to the world of the mind, it does not mean he is socially shy and withdrawn. Des's then is cognitive introversion (Guilford, 1959) rather than the social introversion of Eysenck (1967). It is an interest in internal topics (like psychology) rather than a state of being socially quiet and subdued.

Clearly Western society, certainly in Britain, if less so in the USA, more greatly values both social and cognitive extraversion. To be a sensitive cognitive introvert and be bombarded with nothing but stories in conversation — my experience in 1979 — is boring, invalidating and, of course, reduces one to silence and passivity. One loses any solid 'Self feeling'. But Des has not been forced, as I was, into an alien subculture via his sexuality (Des is heterosexual), he has sought the company of people more similar to himself. People who could relate to and confirm his style and interests not discredit or ignore them. This clearly helps self-esteem and feelings of personal substantiality. Putting oneself in the way of people who clash with and disconfirm one's identity, although challenging — and very much in the spirit of Popperian refutationist philosophy (see Popper, 1959) — is, as I found, very damaging of mental health (see Chadwick, 1992, pp.47–8 also on this).

The happy schizotype

Schizotypy is not necessarily a personality trait with destructive or malign consequences. It may have advantages to such a degree that some authors have spoken of the 'happy schizotype' (McCreery and Claridge, 1995) and of 'benign schizotypy' (Jackson, 1997). These beneficent aspects of schizotypy relate to the access such people may have to profound spiritual and paranormal experiences which can be strengthening and uplifting even when the events of the secular world or indeed their secular situation itself would lead one to expect the person to be downhearted. The same can also be true of some psychotic individuals (Roberts, 1991). As a mystic and prose-poet Desmond has opened a window also on this beneficent aspect of his everyday thoughts and feelings, some stanzas

Kingdon and Turkington, 1994, pp.62–3 for evidence that sheer ignorance can be a vulnerability factor for psychosis.) Desmond also does keep in touch with people. He is like a boat that rocks on the waves of life, and sometimes rocks tempestuously, but if the sway is too great he reaches out, has a chat, goes out with someone, makes a telephone call, writes in his journal. In one way or another he shares and airs his thoughts, and the unsteadiness reduces. He either hears himself talk, sees himself write, or gets another person's reaction. In whatever way he makes use of *feedback*. He doesn't just career over the edge on a mission that he never checks with anybody or anything (see Table 6.1 for the rather useful exercise of listing vulnerabilities and strengths).

Table 6.1

Desmond

Balance of vulnerabilities and strengths

Vulnerabilities	*Strengths*
Intense perceptual life	Self-love
Distractibility	Good sense of humour
Magical beliefs	Extensive life knowledge
Mood instability	High IQ
Interpersonal anxieties	Fluent conversationalist
Paranormal experiences	Self-assertion skills
Tendency to overarousal	Good relationship with God
Extreme self-focusing	Trusting mentality
Concerns over physical appearance	Willing to ask for help
Sensitive disposition	Absence of obsessionality
Single	Good insight
Short	Realistic mentality
Unemployed	Mental discipline
Poor physical health	Keeps in touch with friends
Sleep disturbances	Good relationships with
Difficult childhood (physical illness etc.)	both sexes
	Accepted by peer group when young
Early separation from and poor relationship with mother	Well read, self-educated
	Psychologically congruent friends

Desmond is in his 50s. He has seen a lot of life and he is a good thinker — he knows his own mind. With an IQ of 132 he is intelligent and this probably is protective of mental health to some degree. His score on the STA scale that measures schizotypy (Jackson and Claridge, 1991) at just under two standard deviations above the mean on this scale (but not 2.5 or 3), reflects a personality that probably is not at really great risk of more serious turmoil (see Claridge and Beech, 1995, p.211 on this).

Although Des is a physically tough man and has had, in years gone by, experience of a macho life in gangland, in recent years he has tried to become a more loving person and to put aggression behind him. This surely is protective. It is worthy of comment on James Joyce's life that when *Ulysses* was approaching publication in 1921, Joyce became frightened and sensitive to omens, very probably due to his veiled hostility to various people he had written about in this and other books (their real identities were only thinly concealed). In the summer of that year it is clear from Ellmann's narrative (Ellmann, 1959/1982, pp.516–18) that Joyce was close, the closest he would ever be to becoming psychotic, and had he become so (as did his daughter Lucia) it would have been the fault of his own anger, fear and guilt.

The point here is that Des's adoption of a loving attitude, as best he can, has probably helped him immensely to stay sane (see Table 6.2). It is not surprising, with reference to the dialogue that started this chapter, that he was so shaken that this was ceasing to help him because of the sheer overload and threatening nature of London life — and indeed he did eventually move to Brighton (ironically only to return to a peaceful flat in St. John's Wood two years later).

Table 6.2

Desmond

Typical affirmations used to ease distress*

Be here *now*.

I choose LOVE.

My word is law . . . I erase these thoughts.

This day continues well. I feel successful, I feel strong.

There is beauty in all things.

In respecting all living things, I respect myself.

In peace I understand myself and the world.

I am truly a part of all things. The God force flows through me. I feel secure.

True intelligence is the capacity of the mind to honour the wisdom of the heart.

- All guilt falling from my shoulders
- All anxiety dropping from my mind
- All fear slipping away from my heart
- I erase these thoughts.   *See also S. Wilde (1987)

Discipline and regulation

It would be wrong, however, to neglect the importance of discipline. In his use of affirmations (see S. Wilde (1987) and Table 6.2) Desmond does make a conscious effort to control his own thoughts. This is known as the use of metacognitive strategies. When ego-alien material starts to flood consciousness he has trained himself to repeat instructions such as 'My word is law . . . I erase these thoughts'. He also writes affirmations down on pieces of paper and puts them on his kitchen wall or cabinet to remind him of strong, disciplined, loving ideas. At a more prosaic level we have seen that he tries to minimise stimulants such as caffeine and generally, if not always, avoids alcohol. He also avoids illicit drugs and periodically takes time away at retreats in the countryside. All of this clearly is therapeutic.

Humour and spirituality

Another powerful component of Des's protective armour is comedy and laughter. Unlike myself in 1979 he has made sure that he mixes with people who share his sense of humour and who can share his desire to lighten his load by laughing at it. We do not see any or much of this in his journal but in conversation a joke is never very far away.

It may seem strange to say this but despite his sporadic feelings of torment, Des actually enjoys his own mind. He likes, when all is said and done, the way it works and, like a true artist (see Chapter 12), is frankly accepting of all experiences, both good and bad. At times when his threshold of coping, by whatever method, is being transgressed, if he cannot find a friend to talk to he visits a church. He opens himself up to forces beyond himself. He prays. He talks to God, the greatest of all friends. Des's spirituality cannot be overestimated in its protective and uplifting effects on his life. This sensitivity to the spiritual is a compensatory aspect of the schizotypal person (see Jackson, 1997) and reflects an arena of life perhaps more available to such people than to the standard-minded.

The sorcery of thought

One very common characteristic of schizotypal people is magical thinking. This again has rewards and costs but its costs can be severe. This is indeed a road to both mystical enlightenment and, if the polarity reverses, to psychosis. One thing that Desmond seems to have avoided is the active seeking of *signs* (sometimes called the 'meaning feeling' or 'semiotic arousal') and any tendency, not only to connect, but to overconnect things. For example, if one thinks that 'people are out to get me', it is easy to 'connect' this idea with events in everyday life (a man stares at one from a doorway across the road; a car driver honks his horn as he goes past; some schoolgirls giggle as they walk by). In a threatened state of mind all these events can seem 'meaningful' to the extent that even a headline on a newspaper blowing past in the wind or lying trapped on a sodden pavement can also seem 'magically significant'. Some people have even seen significance of a personal kind in wind direction. This clearly is a very dangerous state of mind but Desmond has avoided it, despite his belief in Jungian Synchronicity (Jung, 1955/1985) by being a strongly *trusting* person. People whose lives have collapsed into psychosis, although they are not alone in this, have often had their trust seriously damaged by abuse — either as children or in their teenage years (the latter happened to me in 1952 and again in 1963–64) — but Des has

of which I feel are worth reproducing here:

July 24th 1995
The sun's rays sparkling, pour through the window pane.
Feeling good, feeling happy, peaceful.
Another day dawns, as morning breaks.
The sun shines, just another day.
My friend is having a nervous breakdown, I am happy.
Another is in hospital having heart surgery.
An old friend of my mother's is dying of cancer.
And I am happy.

November 1989
Another day dawns, the sun shines, the snow falls
Hilary terminates her existence because she cannot bear to be in her body
with her thoughts and feelings.
It's too painful to live.
And I am feeling happy, just another day.
A child dies somewhere in the world of malnutrition.
Swollen belly, eyes vacant.
She succumbs to death that lulls her to sleep.
Just another day and I am happy.

A terrorist plants a bomb that kills a soldier and his child.
And rejoices in the act of violence on other human beings.
Just another day and I am happy.
Remembrance Day in Flanders fields 1914–1918 War.
When humans slaughtered other humans.
Regardless of their beings.
And STILL the poppies grow in Flanders fields.
Just another day and WHY am I happy?

Des has often said that he is consciously aware of the presence of God — though for most people the presence of God is unconscious (see Chadwick, 1997, p.67). This 'access' to the deep ground of the world, the Divine ground, is for people of spiritual orientation a bounteous source of energy and vitality that is protective against the pain induced by profane and worldly events. But is this protection dispositional or are there windows of despondency and melancholy even in 'happy schizotypes'? Desmond's accounts suggest that there are and that the experiential life of the schizotype is a complex mosaic when considered over time in which facets of both the benign and the malign are present, sometimes alternating by the second and certainly by the day. This of course makes the inner life of such people challenging and demanding for them to cope with but it also reflects the intrinsic interest and appeal of that inner life, its basic colour and dynamism, something a cognitive extravert — interested perhaps only in sport, politics and current affairs — would have difficulty appreciating.

Measuring the mosaic
In the closing section of this chapter I will try to see if this iridescent mosaic of the positive and the negative in the life of a schizotypal personality can be actually

recorded by mood inventories. Can we trace it quantitatively over time? I asked Desmond to fill in the mood questionnaires of MacKay et al. (1978) and Nowlis (1965) over a ten-day period, once a day at roughly similar times each day. These inventories are admittedly rather dated but well respected. They assess such things as stress levels, aggressiveness, positive and negative mood and so on. Desmond, being an early riser, chose the mornings to do this. The results are recorded in Tables 6.3 to 6.6. Table 6.3 provides the raw data of affective state from Day 1 to Day 10 (the inventories were completed over two weeks in March 1999) and it can be seen at a glance that Des, despite the relative peace of St. John's Wood, where he now lives, is in a near-chronic state of high stress and high arousal. This alas does not seem atypical of schizotypals. His concentration and anxiety levels are also very high (see the scaled rank order data of his affective states in Table 6.4). Depression and aggression, however, do not feature very strongly in his mental tapestry at this time (Table 6.4). His most changeable feelings — as assessed by the scaled standard deviations of his scores — are anxiety, arousal and egotism. Though he is quite a high scorer on the former two of these variables they also show considerable volatility, he is therefore quite up and down in anxiety and arousal.

Correlations of his most dominant affective states — stress, arousal, anxiety and also social affection — with other states are shown in Tables 6.5 and 6.6. Most of these correlations accord with common sense except for a hint that when he is not stressed, he tends to become depressed — clearly an unenviable no-win situation — but that when he is depressed he does become more socially affectionate but more anxious. Generally speaking, Des becomes more affectionate socially not when he is 'high', as happens in mania, but when he is calm and peaceful even to the point of being 'down'. When he is anxious he becomes more panicky than aggressive — as shown by the high correlation with startle — his intellect is alerted, he feels unpleasant and sceptical and his activation rises. These general trends are noticeable not only from the correlation tables but from changes over time in Table 6.3. On day 7 for example he 'felt terrible' he said because his word-processor had broken down. The data at day 7 show a rapid rise in stress, anxiety, concentration, scepticism and startle and a drop in social affection and pleasantness. Arousal measures, however, continue at a high level. By day 10 though Des has recovered his calm and the emotional crisis is past (even though the W.P. is still malfunctioning). Note, however, that it takes four days for his anxiety score to drop from 11 to 0 and his arousal score to drop from 15 to 3 (there is a two-day gap between days 9 and 10). This may indicate some difficulties in modulating excitation (see Claridge, 1967). These scores, though snapshots, are in accord with his memories of that time.

The affective changes on day 7 are therefore largely situationally induced; changes, also quite marked, between days 1 and 2 and between days 3 and 4 seem to be largely due to internal processes: it appears that even in a relatively constant and peaceful environment (Des is not working) his life of feelings is quite kaleidoscopic and pleasant feelings (see Table 6.4) do not by any means dominate the picture, in fact they are totally peripheral.

Des nonetheless describes himself as quite happy. He does not take medication because he prefers to stay the way he is. This happiness, however, does not eventuate from just 'feeling good', it seems to be a meta-feeling, a product of reflection on his day-to-day life as a whole rather than a moment-by-moment experience. He does do some relatively light voluntary work at the Centre for the Unemployed and it seems as if his changeable emotional state is quite enough to cope with as it is. Clearly this brief idiographic study lends no support to a sharp cleavage between the cognitive problems of the schizotypal and disorders of emotional volatility as suggested by Jamison (1993). Here the cognitive and the affective appear blended in a spiral of circular causation. Des describes himself as egocentric (see p. 43) but here, the nearest adjective to this, his egotism, ranked only eighth in Table 6.4, comes across as merely that necessary to manage and control his unsettled and capricious affective and attentional processes. As we see in Table 6.4, even his egotism is itself erratic. The tragedy of this is that Des's necessary self-focusing, mutable though it tends to be, makes him vulnerable, as discussed by Fenigstein (1984), to perceiving himself as the focus of other people's

Table 6.3

Desmond

Mood inventory scores

					DAY								
Variable	1	2	3	4	5	6	7	8	9	10	x	S.D.
Stress (19)	16	7	18	5	18	15	19	19	18	18	15.30	5.08
Arousal (15)	15	5	15	13	15	13	15	15	15	3	12.64	4.37
Aggression (12)	6	4	8	2	2	4	3	8	0	4	4.10	2.60
Concentration (12)	12	6	6	6	8	8	10	10	8	6	8.00	2.11
Deactivation (9)	0	6	0	4	2	4	2	2	4	7	3.10	2.33
Social Affection (12)	4	6	0	8	8	6	0	6	8	8	5.40	3.13
Anxiety (12)	5	6	6	0	8	4	11	10	9	0	5.90	3.81
Depression (9)	0	6	2	2	0	2	6	3	6	2	2.90	2.33
Egotism (12)	11	2	7	2	6	8	3	3	3	0	4.50	3.38
Pleasantness (12)	9	2	2	8	4	2	0	0	0	4	3.10	3.21
Activation (9)	9	4	6	4	6	6	6	6	6	0	5.30	2.31
Nonchalance (9)	6	2	2	6	4	2	0	2	4	4	3.20	1.93
Sceptism (6)	1	0	0	0	1	0	4	4	2	3	1.50	1.65
Startle (6)	1	2	2	1	3	2	4	4	2	2	2.30	1.06
Time of day	08.00	07.50	06.30	06.30	08.00	09.00	08.00	09.00	08.00	07.30	12.00	06.55

Mood scores over a ten-day period, Days 1–9 consecutive (March 4th 1999 to March 12th 1999); days 9 and 10 have one-day gap between them. x is mean score. S.D. is standard deviation of scores.

Stress and Arousal are computed with the aid of the MacKay et al. (1978) inventory; Aggression down to Startle with the Nowlis (1965) inventory. Figures in brackets are the maximum possible score on that dimension.

Table 6.4	
Desmond	
Scaled Scores	
Scaled[1] rank order of mood states	Scaled rank order of variability in mood states
Most prominent affective state	*Most variable affective state*
1. Arousal (16.01)	1. Anxiety (6.03)
2. Stress (15.30)	2. Arousal (5.53)
3. Concentration (12.67)	3. Egotism (5.35)
4. Activation (11.19)	4. Scepticism (5.23)
5. Anxiety (9.34)	5. Stress (5.08)
6. Social Affection (8.55)	5. Pleasantness (5.08)
7. Startle (7.28)	7. Social Affection (4.96)
8. Egotism (7.13)	8. Deactivation (4.92)
9. Nonchalance (6.76)	8. Depression (4.92)
10. Deactivation (6.54)	10. Activation (4.88)
11. Aggression (6.49)	11. Aggression (4.12)
12. Depression (6.12)	12. Nonchalance (4.07)
13. Pleasantness (4.91)	13. Startle (3.36)
14. Sceptism (4.75)	14. Concentration (3.34)
Least prominent affective state	*Most consistent affective state*

1 Means (in column 1) and standard deviations (in column 2) are scaled to a maximum possible score of 19 on each variable, this being the highest maximum, that of 19, on the MacKay et al. Stress dimension.

attention, thus causing further distress and added self-consciousness.

Reflections on Desmond

Des has a vacillating and mercurial inner life that I think shows on his face — see the photographic collage study in Figure 6.1. It shows also in conversation, in his journal, in the quantitative data he provides and to a lesser extent in his poetry. All these sources of information tell us far more than would a diagnostic label or manual. This is a man whose mind can only be still via meditation, whose mind usually is a theatre of surprises and shocks, word bursts and jazzing images. The startle dimension on Nowlis's inventory is usually of peripheral, if any, interest in studies of this kind, but with Desmond it is in the foreground of his affective life. In the flow of everyday behaviour he is like a small bush animal, on its hind legs, looking sharply to the left, then the right, then sniffing the air, then down, then up again, left, right, darting forward, sniff, sniff, right, left, then away at high speed, tail held high. This is Desmond, although he is distractible,

Table 6.5

Desmond

Correlations of Stress and Arousal with other affective variables

	Correlations with Stress	*Correlations with Arousal*
Stress	-	+0.347
Arousal	+0.347	-
Aggression	+0.233	+0.062
Concentration	+0.457	+0.559
Deactivation	-0.397	-0.836***
Social Affection	-0.303	-0.342
Anxiety	+0.530	+0.550
Depression	-0.100	-0.175
Egotism	+0.217	+0.561
Pleasantness	-0.452	-0.057
Activation	+0.219	+0.826***
Nonchalance	-0.335	-0.010
Sceptism	+0.617*	+0.045
Startle	+0.560	+0.227

*p<0.05
***p<0.01

when he concentrates he really concentrates as if sending out a laser into the vicinity. When he talks to you, he never seems to blink and when he looks, he really looks.

Both the qualitative and the quantitative, the subjective and the objective studies of him I hope show a complex picture. People are never simple, at least not at the individual level. A dominant feature of him (perhaps less obvious now in the late 1990s than in the early 1990s) is that he seems to be 'in high revs', nervy, quick, agitated, jumpy. His eyes jump, his thoughts jump. In the dialogue that started this chapter the reader might feel that I was being, at least at first, unempathic and unaccepting, but I was challenging him to see if his concerns 'stayed on track' and if he voiced discontents in a similar vein whatever confrontation or evasion I came up with. Usually Des is a moving target, as a streetfighter in days long gone by he was extremely fast and won 80 per cent of his fights. One can sense this vivacity and unpredictable staccato quality in his behaviour even now. This actually has a wonderfully refreshing effect on people who know him. Part of his beauty as a person is that he does not have polished emotions and his behaviour and thinking have a wonderfully unmonitored direct quality about them that endears him to everybody. He is neither secretive nor

	Table 6.6	
	Desmond	
	Correlations of Affective Variables with Anxiety and Social Affection	

	Correlations with Anxiety	*Correlations with Social Affection*
Stress	+0.530	-0.303
Arousal	+0.550	-0.342
Aggression	+0.057	-0.510
Concentration	+0.525	-0.270
Deactivation	-0.461	+0.618*
Social Affection	-0.396	-
Anxiety	-	-0.396
Depression	+0.436	+0.468
Egotism	+0.117	-0.347
Pleasantness	-0.670*	+0.227
Activation	+0.558	-0.402
Nonchalance	-0.585	+0.573
Sceptism	+0.468	-0.107
Startle	+0.751***	-0.274

*p<0.05
***p<0.01

overwhelming, neither bombastic nor subservient, somehow his executive processes keep this bubbling dream factory of a mind on the road in a beautifully tuned way. One sometimes thinks 'Des could be a racing car driver', because in a way that is his life. But the car is his preconscious processes and his track is that he has to get this car through London traffic.

Needless to say, Des is faced with a tall order. He at times tires just of living; seems sad; despairs; feels anguished; like Beckett, 'I can't go on . . . I'll go on . . .' and so he does. Having already set up Self-Esteem groups at the Brighton Unemployed Centre and the Quaker Friends meeting house in Brighton, his latest venture was the giving also of a course at the Swiss Cottage Community Centre with Geoff Garfield on the challenges facing men today; obviously a flavour-of-the-month topic and a challenge in itself that he and Geoff rose to with gusto.

Basically Des has a spring-water beauty to his personality. That sometimes the water runs still is no detraction, it never becomes stagnant. Even in sadness one senses the latent vitality there, even in laughter one senses the depth. Des always feels that whatever the agony there is a part of him that is 'basically OK' and this he sees as his spiritual Self. This then is a glass mind that one feels one can know and yet one that always surprises, that always confounds predictions. For many people Des is their 'favourite person' and it is this strange blend of personal effervescence and directness coupled with a despondency that has a collective quality about it — as if he is being sad for the world — that is a dominant opposition in his personality and a contrast that is particularly engaging.

Science tends to be one-sided and to seek simplicity and economy. But when we study the individual beauty of the personality we come up against contrasts and contradictions and we find that nothing is simple and that to capture economically is crass. But with Desmond it is perhaps in these oppositions that one finds the essential tension and life-giving conflict that energises this protean, versatile and volatile soul. He is enigmatic and uncommon but whatever the threats and the challenges, the disappointments and the losses, his tail is always held high.

7
Ivo:
witness to the preternatural

This is a chapter essentially in sound and vision. A previous prose study of Ivo appeared as Chapter 7 of *Schizophrenia, the Positive Perspective* (Chadwick, 1997) but here, with his permission, I have chosen to represent him instead by poetry, music and by photographic images. The poetry and musical score are created by Colette Meury, a London-based singer-songwriter, arranger and vocal coach and long-standing friend of Ivo's and the photographs were taken by Jacqueline Parker, a professional photographer in Brighton.

But to give the reader at least some background information: Ivo Wiesner is a German-born spiritual healer and musician who came to this country in 1990 and moved to Brighton (from London) in 1996. Ivo's interest in the spiritual was catalysed by the fact that when he was younger (he is now 39) he was a voice-hearer. It should be stressed, however, that as discussed by Romme and Escher (1993) there are many people who hear voices who show no distress about their voices and who are well-integrated, sane and well-adjusted people. We also now know that voice-hearing is far from a rare phenomenon in the general population although it is more common in slightly clouded states of consciousness as when one is falling off to sleep — the so-called hypnogogic state (see Sidgewick, 1894; West, 1948; Romme and Escher, 1993 and Ohayon et al., 1996).

These early experiences were also coupled with the effects of an episode of extraordinary psychokinetic phenomena that occurred after his father's death in 1966 in a car crash (see Chadwick, 1997, pp.75–6). Glasses in the family home imploded; some became sliced in two; photographs in the house changed colour and balls of blue light hovered over his father's grave. All of this not surprisingly prompted an interest in Ivo in the paranormal and the supernatural. To study such topics seriously he took to recording spirit voices in empty rooms (a technique pioneered by the Swede Friederich Jurgenson) and to reading related British and American literature on kindred phenomena.

Alas Ivo found German culture antagonistic to the preternatural and to spiritual healing and spirituality in general and so he decided to move to Britain where his interests were catered for by, for example, the Spiritualist Association of Great Britain and The National Federation of Spiritual Healers.

In Germany Ivo had also obtained a degree in classical percussion and was for a long time a working musician. In Britain some of his more dormant musical talents were seriously recognised — for example his abilities as a pianist and as a composer and arranger. Recently he was talent-spotted by a record producer from Boston USA and has now had the pleasure of recording two albums: one on piano and one orchestrated album with a contract for a third orchestral album.

Since 1988 Ivo's work as a healer has also snowballed and despite the demands of his present life as a musician he still holds healing clinics in Brighton once or twice a week.

The purpose of the present chapter is to attempt to capture the beauty of someone's personality more effectively than it might be done in prose or by measuring instruments. Ivo's personality could be described as 'ambient' and in his creative work he produces calming and uplifting music inducing inner peace via its harmonic richness and wealth of pattern. He sees it as essentially spiritual in nature and it could be said that he himself in his personality embodies both his work and his philosophy in a particularly congruent and well-blended way. In what follows, this 'music' to the personality, usually lost in trait and Repertory Grid description (and completely absent in psychiatric classification systems), will be the central quality that we will try to capture and convey. It is obvious that this is no easy task. Ivo has a certain graceful integration of sense and spirit that of course is unique to him. He is characterised by great peacefulness yet great energy, seems to float as he walks yet seems as if he could walk for ever. This in a way is the power of peace and harmony, the strength of holism and the reach of spirituality. These spectral qualities to the man could easily be lost or dimmed by prose and by numbers. It is my hope that here we will preserve them, fragile and diaphanous as they are, so that they can actually be retained on the printed page.

Figure 7.1 Ivo Wiesner

Figure 7.2 Ivo Wiesner

A friend of mine

Here he is just like he ought to be
and he brought the sun with him
Just like a friend who's always there
he hears you when you call his name.
　　　With the touch of his golden hands
　　　he can take our pains away.

Here he is just like I thought he'll be
just when I needed that friend,
when love seems larger than life itself
and makes me feel so small.
　　　I know he's been there and far beyond,
　　　he's walked on the other side.

Here he is just like I would want him to
and music keeps our hearts in tune.
　　　There have been days I have seen him fly,
　　　on other days he seems to carry
　　　the whole world on his shoulders,
　　　but somehow he always travels light
embracing life on his search for perfection.

(IVO) –A FRIEND

4

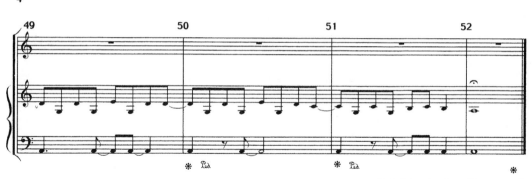

Total 2 minutes 10 seconds

es

8
Jill: coping with, and beating, 'hard-core' depression

The social and cultural setting of the late 1970s was so different from what it is today that youngsters reading this may find it almost impossible to imagine what it was like to live at that time.

The 1970s has sometimes been described as 'the decade that taste forgot' but that is complete nonsense. In fact the 1970s was a tremendous decade in which to live and in which to grow up. A survey around about 1977 in which the public were asked: 'Do you think people these days basically look after themselves and don't care about others?' produced a 70per cent 'No' response. Three years into the Thatcher era the same question evoked a 70per cent 'Yes' reaction. Although the second half of the decade was a time of Labour Socialism (and hence one might expect of 'collective consciousness') it was also a time of tremendous self-expression and individualism beyond anything which is possible today. It is quite wrong — and this is something Oscar Wilde realised — to assume that individualism flourishes best when individualism itself is emphasised. All that flourishes then, as we now know only too well, is selfishness and greed. Individualism flourishes, and truly flourishes, when people care about one another. In the late 1970s it really felt as if people did.

At around the time when I met Jill, who I later married, social life was dominated by 'discomania'. The film *Saturday Night Fever* was released in this country in March 1978 and before long there were seven times more discos in the United Kingdom than cinemas. Discomania was all about colour, glamour, passion and self-expression. The fashions and styles were incredible, it was a brief period when everyone became a little crazy in their own personal way. There were no Aids or HIV threats, *anything* seemed possible. Disco, while it lasted, was really main-lining on sugar. Of course it couldn't last, at least as it was, but while it did last it was a unique time. It was glitz, colour and shine: satin hot pants; satin skirts; satin trousers and trouser-suits; there were glitter fashions; floral fashions; feather decorated outfits; black PVC outfits; heels were high and faces painted; nobody needed drugs to have a good time (though drugs there were), the music and the ambience did it all; everybody was 'going to town'.

On the down-side the economy was in serious trouble. If one was unemployed, as for a time I was, the Department of Health and Social Security payout was only about £26 per week for a single person and the government — with no North Sea oil at that time and determined not to fund property racketeers — would pay only £12 per week towards rent, no more. As it was difficult to rent a room in London for less than £22 a week — the amount I paid — that left only £4 a week on which to live (!). Needless to say, dole was pretty well unbearable and petty theft was rampant; really one had to work, even if only in temporary jobs or of course cheat the (ridiculous) system as many people were forced to do in order to eat.

Nonetheless if the days (and one's digs) were terrible, the nights were fantastic. The disco dance halls, certainly in London, could be breathtaking; London pubs were peppered with colourful drag acts; sexuality became very free and easy and, inspired by androgynous pop stars such as David Bowie, it became quite 'in' to be bisexual.

Contrasted with this was the ever-present shadow of The National Front, then the fourth largest party in the country with its racism and its Mary Whitehouse attitude to sex and the even more sinister shadow of The Yorkshire Ripper. Though most people forget this now, in 1978 and 1979 Peter Sutcliffe had not yet been caught. Every man in the nation, even in his happiest moment, knew in some dark recess of his mind that he was a suspect, and every woman that she was a potential victim. The stench of *The Exorcist*, released in Britain in 1973/74, a film that for a long time swelled church attendances, was still in the air and a number of films on the theme of Satan and Satanic possession followed it throughout the decade. For a time The Devil was big business.

At around this time I had the uncanny experience of meeting endless people whose name began with 'J'. My best friend (John) in the transvestite scene used to prefer to be called simply J and soon women of the same initial followed: Jill; Jeanie; Alana J; Julia; Judith; Jennifer; Joanna: I thought it would never end. Four of these women: Jill, Jeanie, Alana J and Judith were keen dancers. Indeed Jeanie had been named (officially) as 'best dancer' at one of the major London discos at the end of the 1970s. Jill had been in the disco scene long before *Saturday Night Fever*, in fact since 1972 — and indeed was in the troupe from which Arlene Phillips chose *Hot Gossip*, a dance group of tremendous talent (and sensuality) that decorated *The Kenny Everett Show* in the early 1980s.

'The winter of discontent' in 1978/79 featured strikes and spiralling wage demands. Taxes were high, we were in debt to The International Monetary Fund and there was a perception that union bosses were running the show. Of course the radical Conservative government under Margaret Thatcher took over in 1979; she refused even to talk to union leaders when they asked to see her; taxes were slashed; the IMF loan paid off; free market capitalism began to reign and both university and National Health Service funding were quickly cut.

I met Jill in a freezing cold day hospital at Charing Cross Hospital in the autumn of 1979. She was a nurse and was there recovering from a mild bout of depression; I was there recovering from a severe bout of paranoia. To save money the hospital management had switched off the heating. It was clear to us all that times were changing.

Although I was in a grievous state Jill said that she found me 'interesting' and 'different'. At an informal day hospital party we began to chat. Over the course of the following year I gained the impression that this young woman was unique in remarkable ways. She was the only woman I had met up to that time who really wanted to do something *creative* and she saw my transvestic activities also in that light — something that was a considerable relief.

Most transvestites test the women we are friendly with to gauge their reactions and feelings to what we do. In the 1970s I had been both bi-gender and slightly (if only playfully) bisexual. I would recount a typical week to them: 'On the Friday I went out for a drink as a woman with a man; then on the Saturday I went as a man to a disco with a woman. On the following Tuesday I had an evening with a man with me as a man and then on the Sunday I went out to a party as a woman with a male-to-female transsexual' (all of this was true). Judith smiled, Jeannie laughed, Julia recoiled . . . Jill? Jill thought it was 'fantastic and hilarious'. I had found my mate.

Jill and I had our first real date as a couple on November 12th 1980. My decadence was fading and I was moving back to the territory from which I'd come in 1974 — straight sex. If there was any woman I really could love it was this one.

In our first four and a half years together (we married in 1983), Jill's depression totally lifted. She was unemployed and I was a PhD research student at Bedford College and a part-time tutor with Birkbeck and the OU. We were very poor but very happy. I had had money and no love; now I had love and no money, it was better. But depression, or an early version of it, had been an intermittent problem for Jill really since she was six when she first noticed that she was very self-conscious when speaking and remembered thinking 'what is the point of it all?' Remarkable though this philosophising was for a child of such tender years it did not presage well for the future. Later I was to say often that she would have done well in a Paris cafe in 1938 pondering existential issues and challenging everyone with nihilistic confrontations. It was true.

Strangely, with a totally accepting and extremely feminine wife, my transvestism sunk like a stone only to reappear for fun at dinner parties with close friends and the like. Perhaps it had all been part of youthful rebellion and a way of cocking a snoop at the crassness (and cruelty) of standard-minded masculinity. Since Jill had also done lingerie modelling it was obvious that she could wear bewitching clothes *for* me, there was no longer any need to do it myself.

But while she was easing me away from counter-culture sexuality — and thus also easing away any basis I might have for paranoia — the initial anti-depressant aura of our romance was starting to fade as was the ambience of the 1970s dance scene with its glitter and high jinks. When she went for psychotherapy in 1984 to give her extra and renewed protection all the therapist did was open 'cans of worms' that made her depression a dozen times worse. She quickly terminated therapy but it had done its damage; damage it was to take 11 years to repair.

The original damage done to Jill, however, seemed to be much earlier than this. She never seemed to have related closely to or bonded well with her mother — a rather common complaint of the 'J girls' as I called them — and her mother was a cold woman who never seemed to have energised Jill with the real zest for life that one usually sees in the very young. While her fellow tiny tots were full of joy, fun and laughter, Jill was left wondering what the point of it all was. The discomania of the 1970s had been a powerful antidepressant as was our time together when we first met — but as the Thatcher years began to bite the complexion of the country changed. We were living under an Economic Tyranny, it was as if the nation had lost its soul. In health and education the bite was particularly painful. Jill did not feel well enough to take on the many new stresses

Figure 8.1 From resignation to hope. Jill (above) in depression and (below) coming out of it.

of nursing; I sometimes didn't have enough money even to buy the paper on which to write my lecture notes and research money and full-time university posts, if you were over 35, were almost totally absent.

Nonetheless Jill was nothing if not realistic. She took a job in charge of subscriptions in a publishing company in the city and the structure to her day and week seemed to help. It also helped our income. Being part of the commuter crowd to the City of London also made her feel as if she was 'where the action is' and for a time she took to 'power dressing' and seemed to be getting by. The weekends, however, were often times of pandemonium with sobbing, crying, suicide threats, occasional physical fights and an atmosphere of utter despair. Despite it all Jill would marshall her resources and get out of the front door to go to work every Monday morning, even if tears were in her eyes. Her will was incredible: how she held the job down — often with the stress of insults from impatient customers — I really do not know. The antidepressant her G.P. had prescribed (Prothiaden) was of minimal help and induced sluggishness as a side effect. Our sex life collapsed and at times I wondered what had happened to the woman I had fallen in love with and married — particularly when I looked at her face contorted in psychic pain and saw her snarled lips uttering obscenities and mocking phrases. Who was this woman? Where had Jill gone?

There were a number of occasions when I had to leave her in a distressed state simply to go to work. When I rang home at the coffee break, if there was no reply I would have to cancel the rest of the class and come home in case she had overdosed. The students were understanding. Luckily she never did. On one occasion we lay in bed trying to talk her feelings through and I became impatient. I received a kick in the head for my sins. This is what depression is really like.

The philosophy of the depressed does have a kind of logic to it: it is a form of existential nihilism. The glass is not half full, it is half empty; talking to a depressive about the wonderful things in the world is like talking to a bank manager about saving up for a bus stop — the statements don't *mean* anything. Jill once said, 'If I had a positive thought now it would make me *sick*.' The world of the depressive is a world of utter meaninglessness; it is a world with no soul, no purpose, no real point. It is empty, grey, blank, cold. If there is a God He is totally indifferent. People are only machines, beauty is merely subjective, it doesn't actually 'exist', the future and hope don't exist. We are born, we live, we die. Life is merely passing the time until death. There is no Heaven, only Hell, and Hell is right here, right *now*. Indeed the logic of the depressive is the logic of the naturalist and the positivist — except that they don't really face its emotional consequences whereas the depressive does.

Jill's depression waxed and waned from 1984 to 1995. She tried psychotherapy, counselling, cognitive therapy and several antidepressants. She never had ECT. After about 1988 the acting out in her condition began to calm as if she had gotten something out of her system (so she said) and from 1989 to 1995 her depression was a quieter and more spasmodic affair of milder sadness but no tantrums. We have to see now how this dreadful problem was beaten and what qualities of her own personality came to her assistance in defeating it. It is worthy of note that Jill never took to hard drugs, alcohol or even tobacco. She beat it very much from *within* with few props. My feeling is that if Jill could beat this evil sickness then there is hope for us all. This was a hard-core depression that took planning, patience, resolve and will to conquer, but conquer it she did.

Solutions are individual and sequential
Everybody has to find their own personal unique way out of dark nights of the soul. The business is 'person healing' not 'mind engineering' and there are no panaceas. Also healing factors that are not helpful at one time can become helpful later on, when things have changed and the occasion and situation is right. Issues and problems therefore have to be faced one at a time and taken in order, one cannot attack the problem with a single static blanket solution.

Structure to the day
Jill (and her G.P.) noticed that she was more unwell when she was unemployed and easily sank into a lethargic, defeatist and aimless way of life. Being in work seemed to help however difficult it might be to maintain it. She started with office work for four years, moved on to caring for elderly people as a care assistant for three years and then graduated to a full-time nursing post in a nursing home. In between jobs she either attended day centres, day hospitals or did GCSE or diploma courses in English, French and Mathematics — always to give interest, reward and structure to her day.

Increasing self-confidence
Jill was never too confident about either her intellect or her (bespectacled) appearance. Her esteem was therefore lifted greatly when she scored no less than 142 on a Mensa IQ test and also when — of all things — she purchased contact lenses. The lift to her image and self-image from these two seemingly innocuous events was really considerable. Without glasses she felt that people took her more seriously and she felt that she had more presence and self-respect. Eventually getting back into nursing work also lifted her self-esteem and made her feel that she was making real progress as it implied that she could take on more stress and still cope.

Catharsis — and its limits
Venting her anger from myriad vexations in her past did seem to help — but it took a long time (four years) and was also on occasion dangerous. At one point I started to see myself as a battered husband so I said to her something my mother had said to her abusive alcoholic father: 'If you hit me ONE more time I'm gonna hit you back.' And I meant it. Sure enough about two weeks later a row broke out between us in the kitchen and Jill started to hit me. I hit her back with two punches on the top of her right arm. They were very hard punches and hurt. The arm was badly bruised for weeks but all violence between us stopped and never resumed. Jill seemed to respect the limit and the event, if anything, seemed to help her come to terms with her effusiveness.

Clearly this kind of thing cannot be done in formal therapy — when Jill had threatened violent behaviour with her damaging therapist in 1984 the woman had simply warned that she would 'get the police' if she made any move of that kind. Sometimes in turmoil one needs the space of *life* not that of the consulting room.

Money
Poverty is no therapy for depression. As my own income climbed (very slowly at first) from a mere £2,500 a year in 1983 to £23,000 a year in 1993 the increased

freedom and absence of serious financial pressure definitely seemed to help. Alone it would have made little difference but in itself the rise made her feel that at least we were 'getting somewhere' from our dishevelled states in Charing Cross Hospital in 1979. This was particularly so since most of the other people we had known at that time were sadly still unemployed and walking the streets in jumble sale clothes nearly 15 years later. This gave us some sense of movement and a feeling of progression, however superficial advances of this kind might seem to be.

Doing enjoyable things

Merely 'having a good time' is also no therapy for depression unless what one is doing relates to deep concerns and motives. Jill's dancing was protective while it lasted as her love of dancing had stretched back to her early childhood and gave licence for creative expression. Getting our cat, Mimi, in 1993 also tapped Jill's wonderful protective feelings and, as a cat lover all her life, took her away to some degree from her self-concerns.

Jill when she was well also had a great love of literature and reading great writers such as Shakespeare, Colette and Lawrence over the years started to put a sense of meaning and quality back into her life. Art was defeating nihilism and it was wonderful to see.

In addition to this she reached out even from within a void to pray. Though at times there seemed little or no point to it she did it anyway, particularly repeating the Lord's Prayer at times of utter anguish.

Cognitive therapy

The most effective form of psychological help she obtained was cognitive therapy. Although she had motivational problems at the time and didn't do the homework that such therapy traditionally requires, the sessions with the therapist did make her feel that it was at least possible to view events and situations in a different way, in a less negative and more constructive manner. This was helpful, it made her feel that in principle life was not necessarily so negative, empty and meaningless. It was typical of Jill not to blame other people, myself included, for her distress. She took the load on herself and fought it with her own strategies and resources. She never at any time in this whole dreadful period made other people feel that we were pushing her down.

SSRI medication

By 1995 Jill had gradually eaten away at and smashed the foundations of her depression. Her negative thinking was no longer so automatic, we had escaped from poverty through the work that we both did, she was finding things to give her pleasure, not least cuddling Mimi, God had helped her via her prayers enough times to shatter her belief that He was indifferent and, somehow, with a will of steel, she had stayed in work and coped with it for a number of years. When she was tried on Lustral (Sertraline), an SSRI, late in 1995 the final blow at her depression was delivered and after a week or so the drug began to work. The last vestiges of her distress faded away and at long last she found that she was free of it.

She has never looked back. Now she is a full-time working nurse earning nearly £20,000 a year (not an easy task for a nurse), she loves her work and has a totally new life to look forward to.

Looking back it was particularly through drawing on the most beautiful aspects of her personality that Jill made her own contribution to beating this problem. Her love of art and literature; her protectiveness feelings; her faith in God; her persistence; her patience — something she also demonstrates in abundance with the people she works with; her absence of blaming; her ability to enjoy simple things; her intelligence; her strength in confronting issues head-on, all of these things were critical. Also her willingness to ask for help was far from trivial; her willpower in avoiding soporifics such as alcohol, her wonderful intuition and of course her basic lovableness that despite it all was never totally shrouded by her depression were all essential ingredients to the problem being solved. Indeed Jill's lovableness kept all of us who knew her there beside her in the faith that eventually the real Jill could return and shine through this imposed mask of torment. And of course eventually it did.

Reflections

As a psychologist-husband I had always placed my greatest faith in cognitive therapy especially after therapy of an uncovering kind had proved so disastrous. But this, though to a certain extent confirmed by events, blinded me for a long time to more obvious things such as Jill's wish to be rid of spectacles and her need for a cat. I also at times relapsed into the rosy belief that love would conquer all — without always recognising that that love had to be translated into specific actions that would directly impinge on the problem (for example accompanying her to work and back on occasion to help her get by and, of course, buying her surprise presents. These were things I might well have done more often.)

Jill is the centre, the core of my life. One of the things that facing challenges of this kind increases is respect. Psychiatric patients often feel that they command no respect because they have 'broken down' while others have not. But really the onset of such problems is not, for the most part, controllable. The problem that the person has to overcome teaches one enormous respect for them — and of course gives them self-respect, something inevitably protective for the future.

Depression reaches to the depths of one's being and taps one's greatest resources in order to be conquered. Contrary to usual approaches to depression (e.g. Ellis, 1962; Beck, 1976, 1987) I would advance that it is centrally beauty that destroys it as much as the reworking of one's emotional cognitions. The picture of the world and cosmos that scientists of the twentieth century have provided us is a scenario typified by meaninglessness and pessimism. Depressed people are only too aware of this. It is remarkable that art, beauty and spirituality all played significant roles in alleviating Jill's despair sufficient for cognition and biochemistry to deliver the knock-out blows.

The world is beauty and logic working together. We see this in any theatrical production and we see it in nature. Here we see it also in the act of defeating depression. Jill's triumph over her lifelong curse is a testament to the power of art and beauty working together with reason and mechanics to defeat the evil of cyclopean realism. It is true that even today Jill still takes Lustral. A psychoanalyst might say that this is not ideal and that really she is not 'cured'. But this is not the point; the point is, as I say, that *the problem is solved* and it was ameliorative factors from the biochemical to the psychological to the spiritual that solved it. Jill herself does not accept that Lustral was 'the solution' but points instead to all the groundwork she did in the 1980s and early 1990s as the real foundation for her recovery. It would be wrong to think that she has become more self-deluding so as to be happier (although this is a common strategy). It would be fairer to say that her perception of life is richer and broader than it was and in a deeper sense more accepting of the imperfections of the world.

9

'Me and my Mummy': the ocean and the fish

Gleaned from old diaries/ideas notebooks of 1963, 1976, 1985, 1995 and 1999. On events largely before 1971. In 13 sections.

One

I blame my mother a lot you know. I'm always blaming my mother. I don't know why I do it. I don't know whether my mother had anything to do with it all, I mean the transvestism, going crazy and all that. Shrinks blame mothers a lot for things. So when I'd read some psychology I did. I really laid into her, blamed her for everything. It was terrible. We'd have screaming rows all day and all night. Terrible it was. She wouldn't accept the blame for anything at all. Said psychology was a dreadful subject for 'turning a boy against his mother'. I don't know. My mother was a bit of a nutcase. She was. Shouting, always shouting, insulting you, banging doors, throwing things. She had a real problem with anger, a real problem. It used to put me off her. The only time I heard a pleasant sound come out of her face was when she sneezed. I remember thinking that when I was about 16. I actually thought that. She was always shouting and moaning and insulting and everything. She was horrible at times. A real viper, she really was.

Two

Today, for a lot of the time, I was 16. I felt — and thought — like I did when I was 16. Quite frankly I'm not far from that now. But at times I was talking like a kid again, thinking it then saying it, like I used to in the old days. Just being me as I was before the Mind Murder at school. All the bullying, all the horrible things that happened. But you could understand it. Anything big-headed and they used to get you. I mean there was this dance at the Kings Hall in Aberystwyth. I'd be in my second year. It was 1965. I was combing my hair in the gents and I'd got it looking really good. I really had. The hair was all I'd got. Anyway this lad came in and saw me and the hair and said 'Oh yes! Very nice!' The thing was he really meant it. He wasn't taking the piss. Maybe just a little bit but not really. I was walking out when he said this. You know what I said in reply? I mean I didn't make a joke out of it and say 'the hair's all I've got' which would have been true. No, I said — with my nose a bit upturned — 'I've got a choosy bird!' and walked out. I mean what a *pratt*. I mean what a damn poser. How can anybody *say* something like that? I was crazy, I really was. I mean *really* crazy. Sick in the mind. I'd go high. The lad's compliment sent me a bit high — after all the insults at home compliments always did send me high in those days — so I'd say or do something to get higher still. So I said 'I've got a choosy bird'. And then I felt a bit sick about it. But it was too late. I'd said it. God what a pratt. What a poser. I mean how prattish could you get? And there I'd have my chest stuck out, my hair about three inches high. I'd have cuban heels on. I'd look six foot one and all I was was five foot eight. God it was so pathetic. I cringe to think of it now. I can tell you I do.

That was at Aberystwyth. Just after school. But I'd been the same at school in Manchester. Chest out, hair inches high, posing a bit, talking to people side on. I tell you why it was. What it was really all about. It was this ugliness. God I was *ugly*. I just couldn't stand it. I'd look in the mirror for hours, combing my hair, looking at my side with hand mirrors, all to try and look *good*. Everybody else looked alright. I looked awful, just awful. Honestly. It made me feel awful — and inferior. Really inferior. I thought if I could maybe look a bit better — with the hair — and a bit taller and tough looking. God it was so pathetic. But inside I was scared. I can tell you I was. I was always feeling scared all the time. I thought maybe if I looked tough and tall and all that I'd be safer. I guess I did feel a bit safer when I looked like that. But not at school. The lads got at me. They never hit me cos I did weightlifting, but I never hit them. Though I should have. They were taking the piss all the time, it was terrible.

And my mother at home shouting and criticising and moaning. It was all very Manchester. Moanchester. Taking the piss, taking the piss, calling me a puff, 'hit him with yer 'andbag!' Nordcrest said. 'Go on yer big puff!' Sid Whittle said. All the time, going on and on. It did my head in. I couldn't do anythin' about it. I'll tell you why. It's crazy, I mean it's *really* crazy. You wouldn't believe it, you wouldn't, but it's true. The thing was I had eyebrow makeup on — to darken my eyebrows. I thought it would make me look a bit better. It did though, a bit. I wasn't quite so ugly with it on. But I mean what a bloody poof. What a thing to do. This was Manchester . . . an all-boys school . . . in 1962. Christ. A few boys suspected I was doing it but nobody knew. Not for sure. Not Sherwin or Nordcrest. Or Sid Whittle. They didn't know. It would have been suicide if they'd have known. Trouble was if you do that you have to keep on doing it or people really will notice if you stop! I had it on for three years, every day, every single day. And because of it I couldn't get into a fight. If I'd have got into a fight, say with Nordcrest, it could easily have got smudged — and then people would see and shout out 'He's got makeup on!!' and then they'd know and think . . . well . . . you know. It would have got even worse. I reckon I'd have had to leave. Honestly.

I tell you I was sick. I was. Really sick. My mother suspected I was wearing it but she wasn't sure. You can see it in this photo. [Figure 9.1]

I mean without the hair, the makeup, the chest, I looked so revolting. I *had* to do something, just to look normal, just to look O.K. Eyes too close together, ears stuck out, cheeks sunken, teeth all irregular. I looked *horrible*. I heard this girl on a bus say to her friend after she'd looked at me, 'Hey Jennifer, I've just seen the ugliest face I've ever seen' and all that. It was true. I had the ugliest face *I'd* ever seen. It was true. It pissed me off so much it nearly did my head in. All I could think about was how ugly I was. It's a bit like what the shrinks call 'body dysmorphic disorder'. I don't think anybody knew anything about it then.

Figure 9.1 (Left) The fish rides a bicycle. (Right) Chest out, hair high, eyebrow makeup just detectable. At 16 in 1963 and suffering, in total silence and ignorance, from body dysmorphic experiences.

Three

So I'd have all this shouting at home and then I'd have to go into that bloody awful school every day with all those piss-artists. But you think 'well this is just life, this is the way it is', you don't know any different, you just get on with it. It's funny, you can't describe it. But this one night I went out with my girlfriend. Gwen she was called. And *she* was moaning at me all night as well. I couldn't stand it. I broke down with her and started crying. She was pretty good about it though. Said the things she looked for in me weren't the things the lads at school looked for. Said I was alright. Said I was nice. No one had ever said that. I mean really. No one had ever said anything even like that to me . . . ever. Moanchester.

I told my mother a bit about it, not much. It's a silent nightmare this kind of thing at school. She said 'clock 'em one!' But I said I couldn't, but I didn't tell her why, the makeup and all that. I said 'the thing is if you *don't* do anything, they take the piss even more, and if you don't do anything *then*, they take it even *more* and *more* and it goes on and on and never stops'. And she said, really softly, 'Yes Peter, you know why don't you?' and I said 'No, why?' and she said, in this real gentle voice, 'It's because you're dealing with *muck*, that's the way muck behave'.

Four

That's where it all started, I mean where the core of it started, me going crazy and all that. Manchester. North Manchester Grammar School. 1963–64. I'd never have gone crazy if all that bullying hadn't have happened. There were two ringleaders, Sherwin and Nordcrest. But Nordcrest was a good guy really. I worked with him on a vacation job after I left school. He was alright. Sherwin was sick. I mean Sherwin was sick like I was sick but in a different way. He used to get this big kick out of hurting people, other boys. If you were a bit shy and inoffensive, like I was, he'd pick on you, pick on you really bad, one lad ended up at a psychiatrist's. I mean there was this time after the school sports. I'd pulled a muscle in the 220 and had to hobble the last hundred yards. Albert won the race. He'd probably have won anyway. I might have won. I don't know. But anyway we were all sat in the history class waiting for Mr Guggenheim to turn up. Sherwin was sat opposite me across the gangway and he went into one of his routines. He said 'everybody knows you threw the race Chadwick'. I said 'Whatd'yer mean! I never threw the race, I pulled a muscle!' and he came back with 'Naw, you threw the race, everyone thinks it. Mr Ward reckons you threw the race.' O'course I was getting really hot under the collar. And it went back and forth like this and I was getting more and more angry and everyone in the class was giggling until I was almost shouting at the top of my voice 'I didn't!!!' and then Sherwin burst out laughing and banged the table top fast and hard with his hand. But the thing was you could see. You could see how he was enjoying me being hurt and all that. His eyes were bright, his teeth were gleaming, his face was flushed with joy, it was like he was electrified, like electricity was going through him he was so full of *pleasure* at me being humiliated. In fact the only time Sherwin ever used to come alive like that was when he was hurting or humiliating someone. That was how he got his kicks. I tell you there was something wrong. There was something definitely wrong with him. He scared the life out of me. I reckoned he was crazy.

I think the worst thing really is the way people you know, people you thought were friends . . . they join in. If you're a poof they join in with the lads. Like

Cochran told Sherwin and Nordcrest every single thing he knew about me that was embarrassing and would get a laugh. Just to get in with them. Like this time I bought this girls' comic *Julie* every week for 3 weeks to get a big picture of Cliff Richard that was in 3 parts. I wanted to stick it on my bedroom wall. Cochran thought that was a huge joke, 'what a poof, buying a girls' comic!' and all that. And everyone was saying Cliff was a poof in those days. But then he turned all religious-like and it died down.

I mean you end up not trusting anyone. This lad Dave Hobson knew I had a thing about girls' clothes. I'd told him. It was risky but I had to tell someone. Anyway when all the lads were really at their height of piss-taking I really thought Hobson had split on me. He was in with some of them by then, I thought he'd told. But Baz said to me that he hadn't. I found out after I'd left school that he hadn't. They didn't know. I'd thought they *did* know. But they didn't. I reckon I could have got really badly worked over by that lot if they'd known. Manchester lads were like that. They were funny in the head about anything poofy. A bit sort of mad.

Thing was you couldn't be soft in any way. It was the same at home. You couldn't admit a weakness to my mother or she'd *agree* with you and stick the knife in a bit further. You learnt pretty quick to show no weaknesses to her, and it was the same at school. Any weakness, like posing, or being a bit soft, and they'd get you. Sherwin would get you. I remember he stole my ruler once, just to 'test' me, just to see what I'd do. I didn't do anything. I thought it was pathetic. And the next thing I know he was stood there outside the window of my classroom *grinning* at me, mocking me with this sick evil grin that made him look like the devil. Sherwin had upturned eyebrows that looked sinister and impacted eye-teeth on both sides that looked a bit like fangs. God he looked evil, sort of sick and evil. It made me shudder I can tell you. I didn't do anything. That was a disaster in itself. With Sherwin self-assertion was everything. As far as he was concerned — if you weren't assertive you were nothing. He used to think like that. Funny really. Very Manchester. I never got my ruler back.

Five

Yeah, I reckon my mind was murdered at school. It was murdered. It was pretty badly beaten up at home though in a funny sort of way. My mother was sort of on my side, sort of, but she did me in anyway. It's funny. Thing was the two places, I mean home and school, weren't really separate. Or not really that separate. I mean my mother was always going on about the Chadwick family. God she really hated them — especially for disappearing after my father died when I was a kid. And they'd always seemed to have treated her all arrogant-like, as 'not good enough for their darling George' is what she used to say. Anyway I was brought up to think that the name Chadwick was like a dirty word. If I did something selfish she'd sneer at me and say things like 'Yer a right bloody *Chadwick!*' and 'go on yer bloody *Chadwick!*' and all that. Christ it used to put the shits up me. As if I was some sort of . . . I don't know . . . like I was tainted with some curse or something. God it was awful.

Anyway there was this time when I was about eight when I had to stay at the Ormrod's house across the road for about a quarter of an hour before going to school. I think my mother had to go out at 8.30 or something so I was sent over to the Ormrod's 'till about ten to nine and then me and the Ormrod kids, Kenny,

Stuart and Margaret, would go to school. Anyway it looked as if the Ormrods got a bit fed up with this. When I'd arrive at the door Margaret would shout out 'Chadwick's here!' with this really horrible tone in her voice. I got really upset after a time and told my mother 'I don't want to go to the Ormrod's any more, they call me "Chadwick", I don't like it'. Of course it was just bringing back the sort of horrible stuff my mother said in the house. But I didn't connect it all up then. I was only eight. Anyway when all the piss-taking started at school cos of my hair, and posing and stuff like that (the hair was copied from Cliff Richard so that was a big problem), the Ormrod's told Nordcrest about all this, the 'Chadwick' thing cos it showed how soft I was and what a poof I was, just being upset that I was called by my surname. Anyway the next thing I know is that Nordcrest has put this around the district and I get people shouting 'Chaaaaadwick!!' from passing cars and from buses as they go by and all that. All the time. And I mean then I got home and I say this to my mother and all she does is put her nose in the air and walk off with something like 'Yes, yer a right Chadwick' and stuff like that. I tell you it was fucking well doing my head in! God Almighty what a shithole that place was. It was just driving me round the bend it really was. I tell you, you end up trusting *nobody* and you end up thinking people are real swines, real *bastards*, you really do. It only lasted, this Chadwick thing, for about a fortnight though, I mean out in the streets, then it went on to something else, like calling me 'Cliff!' and stuff like that. That went on for two years though. They seemed to really like that, the people round where I lived.

Six

Anyway that was all when I was 16 and 17. I suppose you *can* get your mind murdered. I don't know, I suppose when I left school and got to university I sort of thought 'it mustn't happen again'. Of course when I started really going into transvestism it did. That was the end of me. After home and school, and then it all starting *again* I was on the way to the nuthouse.

But when I first went to university I mixed with Baz, Baz Walker. He'd been one of 'the lads', they were all footballers, the lads, or most of them were, nearly all of them were when I think about it. They were all in the First XI soccer team or the First XV rugby team . . . yes they were. Only Farringdon wasn't, he was on the second XI. Anyway Baz was one of the lads but they'd actually picked on him. Nothing like what they did to me but it'd upset him. So when we both went to university we talked about it a lot. That was good. It was good to talk about it to someone who'd been there and had had it rough as well. But I reckon Baz — Barry was his proper name — did a rebuilding job on me really. He sort of helped to rebuild me in a way where things like that wouldn't happen again. I stopped wearing eye makeup and started talking different — and thinking different. More rough. More Manchester. Mind you Baz also got me in touch with feelings and got my anger going. He got me *feeling* about things. Stopped me denying and pretending — like pretending that Sherwin hadn't hurt me and all that.

But Baz also got me *thinking* about things. Mixing with Hob (Hobson), Tich, and Chris Buckley and Jeff Bullen never did that to me. They weren't *psychological*. I suppose I didn't ever think about anything properly until I started to think about things psychologically. That's when I started, I guess, to think at all! I don't know, it seemed to do me good. I can catch things in my mind as they flit across it now that I couldn't then. Then I'd deny, or pretend, like pretending I 'wasn't bothered' when Sid Whittle made some snide remark and all that.

I was thinking today of those horrible last two years at school. And I thought, in the subway — if it happened again, if I was back there, it would be just the same. And I started to see how vile those boys were who persecuted me. What horrible people they were. Because I'm not like them. I didn't know what to say to them or how to react to them. I'd never met people like that before. And I was thinking, if I was being *me*, not the 'me' that Baz created, I wouldn't know how to react to them even now. I don't think like that, all sick and mean and aggressive. I'm just not like that. All full of hatred for 'queers' and full of snide nasty remarks. I really reckon those people were horrible. I don't know. I suppose at Aberystwyth, with Barry, I thought I'd better learn their wavelength so I'm not that vulnerable and fragile ever again. But it wasn't me, the way I became. It wasn't anything like me!!

There *was* something inside me though that my mother cultivated — a kind of armature inside me, hard, unfeeling, a bastard, especially to George, my brother. I was horrible to George. I reckoned at the time that the persecution at school was a punishment sent by God for how horrible I'd been to George. Perhaps it was. But my mother seemed to like me having this hardness, being mistrustful of people. She couldn't stand weaknesses. She used to say 'You've got to be as hard as nails in this world!!' with a sneer on her face. She really meant it. She looked a bit crazy when she said that, I can tell you.

When I look back on it all it was all the terrible shouting. All she ever did when I was between six and ten was to *shout* all the time. I was terrified of her. I remember when I was about nine and I spilt a can of red paint all over the back yard and my brother came to the back door and saw what I'd done. And I knew he'd split on me cos George always split on me, always told my mother . . . everything. And I flung myself at his feet and shouted 'George!! Please don't tell Mummy!! Please don't tell Mummy!! PLEASE!!' God I was so terrified of her. Anyway he turned round and just said 'Mam' very softly and she came out and cleared up the mess. She didn't say anything.

Seven

Anyway like I say I was really scared. I was scared all the time. I had to somehow stiffen myself to take it all. I stiffened myself inside, like that's why I said I got this armature inside me. I think that's what she wanted, for me to be hard. That's why she did it. She said she wanted to make me hard. And of course I masturbated a lot, to feel better. It made me feel better, if only for a few minutes. I was always thinking about girls.

I don't think I could really work my mother out. At times she was really nice. She really was. I couldn't work her out. It sounded from what she said that she'd had a horrible life and been let down a lot by people. My father had let her down and she'd had a lot of bad luck and illness. George was also ill, from a brain tumour. So I saw her as being angry and bitter at the world, at Manchester, at the Jews who'd sacked my father when he was ill — and he'd died the next day, but she was angry at my father as well, at the Chadwicks. My mother was angry at everything! And then she'd have a go at me if I was . . . I don't know . . . not up to scratch. Always saying 'Don't be a mug', 'don't be easily led', 'yer swine!' 'yer-a-pair of rats!!', I mean she really did say that. I was a rat. George was a rat. God I hated her at times, a lot of times. But she could be really nice. She was always pleased when I did well. But somehow I always felt . . . I don't know . . . there wasn't much to me. She'd say 'No, yer not up to much', things like that. You daren't show a weakness, not ever, *never*. But . . . I suppose really she was a loving mother. There's not much love in Manchester. It's far too important to be hard. Love doesn't get much of a look in. But I sort of thought my mother loved me, sort of. But she had very high standards, so she said, so I was never good enough. No, I was never good enough.

There wasn't a lot of nice people about. The ones that were, were all women. I liked nice people — and nice dresses of course. There wasn't much else nice around. But then when all the piss-taking started at school over my poofy hair and all that I started to pick up that people, or men, thought nice people, if they were men, like Cliff Richard, they were queer. And that made them the lowest of the low. So you were sort of a better person if you were mean, and tough, even nasty. It made you a better person. At least you weren't queer. I mean it was HORRIBLE. Because I wasn't like that but I thought if I'm nice, like at school, people will say I'm a queer. It was HORRIBLE! Horrible, *horrible* people. So I stopped being nice, in fact I thought being brutal, like brutally honest, was real tough and manly. I think that's why I took to science. I was horrible to Barbara, this girlfriend I had, really horrible. She chucked me. I didn't want to be called a queer. I didn't feel it. I wasn't queer. I wasn't.

Eight

My mother wanted me to be a hard wide-boy. But really I'm soft and naive. I am really, that's the truth, soft and naive, I think she hated that. Hated my sensitivity. Hated me for not being worldly wise and a wide-boy. She really wanted me to be a wide-boy, I think that was more important to her than anything. I was a terrible disappointment to her in some ways . . . not up to much, like she said. She never called me a poof though, that was something.

Nine

What's weird is that I find it hard to know what I really think deep down and to tune in to what I really am. It's funny. I've never felt loved and accepted for what I am so I don't hardly know what it is! With my mother I was always having to be 'better', to be better, to be hard, to 'grow up'. As I was I felt she thought I was nothing at all. She wanted me to be successful. That was a big thing. To be a hero or something. But then she could be really nice. Somehow I felt that she loved me, but at the same time I was never 'good enough'.

When you're never good enough you're always RUNNING you know, running towards something. I would run everywhere. But you can't get there, to the tape, because you're not 'good enough'. You're never good enough.

Let me tell you. Let me tell you something. My mother always hated me calling her 'Edie' when I came of age. It went right through her when I said it, as if I'd shot her in the bloody back with a bullet. You could tell. She once said . . . no . . . this was what she said when I first did it . . . she said, 'You've got a long way to go before you can call me Edie'. God I really hated her when she said that. It was like a wave of hate hit me, it really did. She said a lot of things I hated her for. She was like that. Full of snide remarks. I said to her in reply, 'What's the matter with you?! Ian Cochran was calling his father by his first name when he was 14 or 15, maybe earlier!!' and she came back with 'Ian Cochran's a completely different boy to you!' and something like 'You can't hold a candle to Ian Cochran!' and stuff like that. I mean I nearly did my bloody nut I can tell you! Ian Cochran was the bastard who'd spilled all the beans about the *Julie* comic to Sherwin and Nordcrest and Mike Madden and all the lads! Jesus Christ I nearly went bloody *berserk*! I could see it all, Cochran stood in the corridor in the sixth form block where all the mean guys congregated spouting all his 'funny stories' about me with his nose just a little upturned like he did, with his round face and his cheeks a bit red and specs on and Sherwin and Nordcrest and Madden stood there drinking it all in with smirks on their faces like a load of tossers all stood there with leering looks loving every blasted second of it. God how it makes you throw up! Stood there sucking it all in to their stupid heads like starving thirsty men desperate for a pint, licking their lips with it like they did, all for a laugh! All to humiliate someone. Me. All to humiliate me. And there's my stupid mother spouting praise and glory about Ian Cochran, the BASTARD! I tell you that's the kind of stuff that sets you up for going over the edge. Sets you up for going crazy. It's not twisted chemicals and funny brain structures and all that, it's stuff like that. And then you hear something on the radio like 'Wonderful World' by Louis Armstrong and you go and laugh your head off. You'd cry otherwise. And you think 'Come and live in Cheetham Hill for 20 years, go to North Manchester Grammar School and live with my mother and then go out and try and sing that song . . . go on you bloody fat FOOL!!'

Ten

Anyway . . . my mother was full of stuff like that. She used to say 'Why can't you be more like Barry Smithers?' and 'Why can't you be more like Kenneth Ormrod?' — that was the other bastard who'd set me up for the 'Chadwick' incident in 1963. There she is singing his praise and glory as well! God I can tell you these people were all bloody mind-wreckers, they really were. I hated her so much when she came out with stuff like that. Funny thing was it never seemed to cross her bird-brain from one side to the other that saying things like that might harm me in any way. It was as if she thought 'If it hurts him, good, it's too bad, he's got to be better than he is' or something like that. Mind you I don't think she thought much about what she said or did anyway. But God when I started calling her 'Edie' — I was about 22 or 23 at the time . . . it really went through her. She used to stiffen up like a rattlesnake. I mean if you call her Edie then you think you're on a par with her. My mother really didn't like it me thinking I was on a par with her! She really didn't like it . . . not at all. She always had to be the better one, the higher one, someone higher than me that I had to look up to. God I really hated her for that. It was so damned arrogant. Your son's 23 years old and you still can't let him call you by your first name. God what a damned big head she was. And if I complained about things like that she called me a vile person and not fitting to address his mother by her first name. You couldn't win, I mean you couldn't even draw level. You were always behind and down. An inferior, a child. And no way could you complain. God I really hated her. And then I'd get called a 'hateful son' and some vile person, and then psychology would get all the blame for having changed me from the 'nice boy' I used to be. That was the same 'nice boy' she'd called a rat and a rotter and all that stuff. I tell you my mother was a real nutcase, a *real* nutcase. A mind-wrecker.

I reckon she could have done with some help. Sherwin needed help. Nordcrest used to blow things up like into a cartoon, but he was alright. Nordcrest was alright. But my mother . . . in a way it was sad. I mean it's obvious the only thing she could hang onto to feel good was being a mother, up there, with her little boy, me, down there. She had to be up there above me looking after me. When it was obvious that I didn't need looking after by my 'mummy' she had nothing at all left to live for. It was terrible, terrible. She was a mother and that was it. When she couldn't be up there looking down on her not-good-enough-yet son she started to die. I mean she did. She got a recurrence of breast cancer from 20 years back and before you knew it hardly she was dead. In a way I killed her by growing up and not needing her any more. It was awful.

I tell you situations like that are dreadful. Because, like me, you feel you've killed your own mother. I always felt that. They live through you. And when you break the psychological umbilical cord they just wither away and die. I mean she'd said so many vile things to me to convince me I wasn't 'good enough' and that me and George were 'rats' and all that stuff that by the time she died I hated the bloody *sight* of her! It was dreadful. I was glad to be rid of her. God what a screw-up it all was. It got my mind all mangled up.

Anyway in about the last year before she died she started referring to herself *sometimes* as 'Edie'. Like she sent me this card and signed it 'Mum' and then crossed that out and wrote 'Edie'. It was as if it was a real BIG thing and she'd been really conflicted about it and gone this way and that in her head but had deigned in the end to sign herself 'Edie'. It nearly made me throw up I can tell you. I mean why not just damned well let go?! What's mother love all about I ask you? Oh I don't know . . . I'm not a mother . . . I haven't carried someone in my tummy for nine months . . . but Christ Almighty is that a reason to suck the bloody LIFE out of the kid?! I mean . . . Christ . . . oh I don't know. I really don't. You get these people and they're vile to you to put you down all the time and then they can't understand it when you're not 'loving' with them! And then she'd criticise me for not being a loving son! I mean *Christ*!!

I tell you these shrinks they blame going crazy on parents being 'overinvolved, overprotective, critical'. It's not that. It's the bloody patronising attitude that does it. They try and keep you like a little baby or a little kid that needs his mummy all the time. I mean it makes you feel inferior, like you can never join the adult world, like you're always a bit helpless and a bit stupid, like a kid, like the world's a terrifying place and you need 'mummy' to protect you and all that. It really screws you up, it does. In the end it's as if part of you's grown up and a part hasn't like a part you *have* to keep as a kid so they can look down on you, cos they need someone to look down on and mother and protect and look after and all that stuff. I tell you it makes me puke up. You sort of have to preserve their . . . sort of bolster up their thing . . . cos if you don't they'll cave in and fall to bits. God it's . . . it's just awful. I can hardly stand thinking about it, to tell you the truth.

The thing is it poses as something really good and all virtuous, which if you're five it is, but when you're damn well 23 it isn't, it's *evil*. Yes it is, it's *evil*. I really mean that. Because you can't completely get out, can't get into the world. It's weird. I can't describe it.

Anyway in the last year before she died I felt sometimes I was getting through to her. She once said 'Oh go and live your life! *Forget* your mother!' That was really good — and for her really far out. She'd never said anything like that before. That cheered me up, it did, it definitely cheered me up. And like I said she was starting to sign herself 'Edie' now and then. So I suppose it could've been worse. A lot worse. I've heard of people who had it worse than this. Crikey.

Eleven

I felt lousy when I went to bed last night. I mean I thought I could have a heart attack or something after going on about my mother like that. It was like she'd reach out from beyond the grave and kill me for what I said. But then I thought . . . it must be me. I feel it's unfair in a way. In a way it's fair, but in a way it's not fair. It's funny. The thing is you have to look at the big picture . . . sounds like a politician on the telly doesn't it? But it's true. People say a woman's heart is like an ocean. I don't reckon a man can get his mind round it but you can see it, but you can't break it down and analyse it, it's an ocean, it's too big, and it's a gel. That's always a problem. My mother had her own problems but she was just trying to be a good mother in her way. I mean it all came out really twisted and really screwed me up but it was her way. The way her ocean sort of worked.

I mean I don't feel bitter any more. I mean I'd be really happy if my mother had met some friends up there in Heaven or wherever you go. She didn't have any friends, none hardly at all, not regular ones. And she needed to mix with her own kind, the kind of people she admired, the wide-boys like 'Our 'Enry' she used to talk about. I think he was her brother. 'Ooooh 'Enry' she'd say with her eyes in a dreamy state . . . 'Wide as the hills' she'd say and she'd be all dreamy about him. Used to make me sick if you want to know, but there it was, that was the way she was. But . . . really . . . I hope she's got some friends . . . that would be awful if she still had no friends. But you can't describe it . . . it's the way of a woman. This ocean thing. It's even a bit spooky . . . I reckon.

Gwen was an ocean . . . not so much as my mother but an ocean. Denise was an ocean. She was another girl. I don't think any of the others were . . . not that much . . . maybe Maureen. It's spooky. I reckon men don't like to think about it . . . it makes you feel inferior as a sex, it does, if you really think about it.

Twelve

But anyway the main thing is that my mother's happy and has got some friends now and got some other interests, not just me or looking after George. That's the important thing, I'm sure God's sorted that out.

I reckon there's something spooky about women. There's something spooky about transvestites. It's the femininity thing. It's more powerful than . . . I don't know . . . I don't think anybody understands it, not properly.

Edie was two personalities you know . . . Edie Angel and Edie Witch. I could never figure out which she was. In the end you just have to accept it . . . she was both. But in the end I got so I couldn't even *touch* her. Like as if she'd electrocute me. It was like she'd let out a yelling SCREAM if I was to touch her. God it was awful. I kept away from her. I mean physically, like as if she was some kind of electrified plug or something.

Oh I don't know . . . I've got to stop this. Thing is I don't like thinking that much about my mother's good side. For some reason I don't like writing about it either . . . like as if she's said so many snide things to me why should I build her up? Why should I talk of her nice side? But it's funny . . . she could be a really angelic person. She was always angelic with professional people, and it looked as if she meant it, as if she had this great glowing respect for them, she really did. It wasn't put on, she meant it. I think that had a good influence on me. She wasn't just greasing, she did think a lot of them . . . and it looked as if they thought a lot of her . . . I reckon our headmaster Mr Sibson thought a lot of her . . . they had a lot of chats.

Thirteen

I don't know, how do you talk about an ocean? Before I got into psychology I suppose I was just a bit of a docile nice kid, a dutiful son and all that. The type Sherwin would get a kick out of beating up. But when I got into psychology it made me notice things I hadn't noticed before. She really hated psychology, it terrified her . . . you could tell . . . she hid my books. She'd burnt my father's psychoanalysis books when *he'd* got into it in the 30s. She put them in the bin and burnt them! The lot! She was like that. She'd do something like that. Like driving through the red lights of life I used to call it. She did that a lot. She'd seen this film, *Red Headed Woman* with Jean Harlow. She used to mention it. Jean Harlow was like that in the film. It had a big effect on my mother . . . when she was a kid.

But you can't put your finger on someone like Edie. I suppose my mother and I were close, in a way. Not as close as this therapist I had thought we were but pretty close in a way. Maybe closer than most boys and their mothers. A lot of transvestites are like that, we attract our mummies to us I reckon. I reckon it works that way. It's that way round.

All those horrible things she said? . . . In a way it was all gas . . . all a fetid kind of candy floss. I mean she'd never said a single good word about my father ever since he died when I was a little kid. Not *one* good word. And when I said to her when I was about 24, 'Well you've taught me my father was a no-good rotter!' she suddenly went all wide-eyed and said 'Oh no, your father was a wonderful man'. I mean what do you *do* with someone like that?! I mean what are you supposed to *think* about what they say about *anything, ever*?! You listen to all this stuff for twenty-odd years, and then at the end she says she didn't mean *any* of it! Thousands of hours of it. Thousands of remarks over twenty-odd years pumped into your brain like a battering ram and then you're supposed to chuck it all out!! You can't do it . . . I mean . . . what can you *say*?! . . .

But I'm trying to be positive. I really am. It's like . . . the ocean is good, it *is* good . . . but all the fish you find are contaminated . . . d'you know what I mean? . . . it's difficult. I keep trying to grasp the 'good' ocean and all I get are smelly fish . . . like my smelly feet. It's awful. It's enough to screw you up in itself.

And yet somehow I feel she had my best interests at heart. She struggled with a lot of illness. And George was ill. And she never had a go at me for being a poof or being into that kind of thing . . . women's clothes I mean. And she never tried to sabotage my work . . . always encouraged me. She chased off a few 'unsuitable' girlfriends but she only wanted me to get married when I had my head screwed on. Which in the end I did. So that all came out alright in the end.

I think that's it. I reckon you have to look at the big picture, the grand intention . . . and then all the bits look different . . . or at least you can look at them differently. She didn't want me to have a 'ruined life' like she was always saying hers was. And she was prepared to do anything to ensure that . . . if it meant getting rid of 'unsuitable' friends, 'unsuitable' girlfriends, throwing insults . . . all the stuff. But in the end she was a great motivator. Really good. She really was. It was all in this great oceanic cause of giving me a better life than she'd had. Edie never thought much about what she said or did. She just did it. I suppose there's a beauty in that, in it all I guess. A bit like a kid when you think about it.

'Mother love': can any man ever understand it? She was protective; she was encouraging; devoted; tireless in her everyday duties as a mother; a lot of people hated her for how she'd do anything to get me a good education . . . she had to take all that . . . there was a lot of snide stuff from women she worked with . . . she had to take all that. And she did it for me, nobody else. Anything to give me a better life, as if *her* life depended on it. Almost spooky it was if you think about it . . . like as if she had a 'cosmic mission'. Really weird.

But in the end I knew she was on my side. In 1971 before she died she said 'You can get married any time you like now'. It was arrogant but on the other hand she'd let go I guess, but a few months after that life slipped away from her. It was like as if when she let go of me she let go of the will to live at all. It was a terrible devotion. And a devotion that I didn't thank her for. That made it even worse. It was dreadful. To give your life, and for it not to be recognised. She must have felt worthless. I felt worthless, and ungrateful. The terrible devotion of a mother for her son. A devotion so terrible that for him to have life he must break free . . . and yet if he does he kills that which loves him. Mother love begins . . . I don't know . . . as something beautiful, then it turns into something patronising . . . yes . . . and destructive, finally it turns into something pitiful and tragic.

Wherever you are now Edie . . . get yourself a life, a second life. You've got another chance, go for it. Forget your son. Forget me and George. Get a life. You deserve it if anybody does. And one thing . . . cheers . . . *mate.*

10
Trevor: flower
of defiance

An asset without a name

Tahiti lies at the heart of the Polynesian islands, a group of islands of similar culture, art and religion that form a triangle the size of Western Europe with Hawaii at its peak. There is a feature of Tahitian society that confuses Europeans — this is their recognition of the *mahu*. The *mahu* is their equivalent of our 'transgenderal', the transvestite or transsexual. In Tahiti the *mahu* occupies a near-sacred position (Sweetman, 1995, p.275) combining as they do both male and female characteristics. But of course in Western society there is no such degree of acceptance. Generally every village in Tahiti has a *mahu* and they enjoy the same respect and esteem as anybody else. In our society, however, it is often the case that they live, or become themselves, only behind locked doors and drawn curtains.

Trevor Pastaro is a transvestite whose attitude to his situation is realistic. Enslaved to the delights of femininity he values privacy and self concealment. The terraced house in which he lives blends invisibly with its neighbours but it harbours, behind a small plain exterior, chambers within that reach to opulence in their splendour.

To the world he presents as unexceptional, matter-of-fact and pleasant. An everyday guy living an everyday life. Nothing could be further from the truth. Dresses, skirts, lingerie and the like, all by the dozen, are arranged in wall to wall displays, allowing of combinatorial play in the creation of the female image of almost astronomical proportions. It would be easy for a psychoanalyst to write scabrous tomes on the likes of Trevor. Is he 'suffering' perhaps from 'mania transvestica'? Is there a hint of obsessive-compulsiveness here? Perhaps there is, but it is slight and productive. Alas with diagnostic manuals ruled by the values of science the divergent sexual and feminine thinking of the likes of Trevor is an asset without a name.

'Rational sex'

Transvestism, Trevor's activity, is a rather shrouded and shielded practice. Anonymous questionnaire returns indicate that its incidence is high, maybe 1 in 12 adult men, and it could be more.[1] Ten times the incidence of homosexuality. It

---

1 Chris Gosselin, personal communication, autumn 1980. This research was based on a sample of 200 males who filled in an anonymous questionnaire on sexual *fantasies* at Heathrow airport. In transvestism and fetishism, fantasy can very easily be made into . . . contd over

is seen by psychiatry and psychoanalysis as abnormal and is listed as a 'paraphilia' in DSM IV (American Psychiatric Association, 1994), literally 'a liking for that which is beyond'.

Science and psychoanalysis of course steer close to Judaeo-Christian religion in their attitudes to gender and to sexuality. Sex has to be essentially or potentially for procreation if it is not to be regarded as in some sense off-centre. This is the standard nineteenth century view, sex as rational sex, sex in the interests of productivity (Gagnier, 1987) very much the attitude to hold in a science and technology dominated society forever mindful of its economic condition. It is also the product of a greater value put on reality adjustment rather than on fantasy and imagination. Imagination, to be sure, is valued in science but only to the degree that it gives us a closer mapping eventually with 'the world'. People of very little imagination *per se*, very much the reverse of Trevor, the 'lager louts' of our shores, are (interestingly) particularly scornful of any degree of abstraction in sex and always proclaim their sexual virtue by 100 per cent adherence to 'the real thing'. Amen to that I suppose. As Oscar Wilde used to say, 'If the lower orders don't set us a good example, of what use are they?' But Trevor is unmindful of this scorn of straights for what he is. He may be a man of little public self-display but he is one of great self-pride.

If one reframes sexuality as just another realm for the free licence of human imagination, the artist's view, then permuting fantasies and ideas sexually, very much Trevor's life, is no different, as in a sense psychologically it isn't, from the symbol-play in the mind of the mathematician. No mathematician is perverted for questing in domains of the imagination far away from physical reality; a pure mathematician is not a pervert for not being a physicist.

In the world of the artist, and the sexual artist is the true designation for sexually motivated transvestites like Trevor, the reign of reverie has been primary since the work of Walter Pater (Pater, 1873/1990, 1885/1985), the source of many of Wilde's counter-culture ideas. In the sexual underground, where Trevor lives, reality adjustment, rational sex and sex as 'productivity' are totally irrelevant. Here behaviour is born of the total creative impulse; this is not 'bedroom as reproduction chamber', this is bedroom as 'the theatre of sex', sex as a medium for symbol-play, enterprise and inspiration.

The hunter

The public well knows of Marilyn Monroe, Sophia Loren, Brigitte Bardot and similar icons. Yet there are many veils over passageways to mistresses of fantasy maybe even more mesmeric than these in some ways. The majority of people will never see images of underground figures such as Victoria Slater or Vanda von Tauscher. Women like Rita Royce and Rosina Revelle are today also unknown because, in the 1950s, they were literally regarded as too spellbinding and irresistible to be shown on a screen. All these women existed behind veils,

contd . . . reality as another person is not required for the completion of the sexual act — hence these figures may well represent activity as well. Of course in all areas of alternative sexuality, questionnaire responses, even when anonymous, may to some degree underestimate incidence. An unpublished study I did in 1978 of types of sexual preference expressed in contact magazine advertisements suggested an incidence of one in six males for transvestism but contact magazines may over-represent those interested in alternative sexuality.

seen transiently, there only for explorers.

Trevor is such a traveller. Though a man of few words he is a scout for femininity. A man who reconnoitres the world of woman. He has had, and still does have, his fair share of affairs and one-night stands. He was married in 1971 and has a grown-up daughter. However the marriage only lasted 18 months. Nonetheless in the last 20 years Trevor has discovered something additional to the joys of penetration, the joys of fusion sexuality.

The blending of male and female

Trevor, also known as Tina, is a dedicated, committed and unrepentant transvestite. He lives in Guildford and works, really beneath his intelligence, as a painter and decorator. Trevor has given over his life to the act of immersion in femininity, immersion in the luxurious sybaritic femininity of satin and silk. When he is not painting he paints himself, when he is not decorating he decorates himself. In his addiction to lustrous materials it is as if he has found a fount of new life. This is a man devoted to the art of alter-ego creation: the construction, animation and embodying of Tina. Temptress Tina, tantalising Tina, enticing Tina. A woman as if indeed from Beyond. A woman with a thousand masks. This is the dissolution of the Self in periodic oblivion then reincarnation, the forgetting of the Me then its resurrection. A possession of the loved one, the archetype of The Temptress, to a degree greater than physical love allows.

Every man who creates an array of female personas has to learn fast what a real woman has decades to learn. Practice makeups different every day have to be applied with the attention to detail of a Dali while shopping for clothes and charity shop visits becomes a way of life. Trevor indeed is indefatigable in his search for 'materials' yet, like any artist, his use of the material is in the service of something essentially spiritual — an opening up of the Self to forces from beyond itself.

It is not surprising that if one desires something with feverish strength one will want to *be* that which one craves. Kinsey and his colleagues, writing on transvestism, realised as much (Kinsey et al., 1953, p.680). In transvestism a man gets inside the space, the space inside women's clothes that usually is occupied by a woman's body and so 'fuses' symbolically with woman.[2] This 'fusion sexuality' *is* the motive behind any transvestite for whom sexual pleasure, even if only in part, is his goal. This is something that outsiders, looking in, do not realise. This is symbolic sex, symbolically 'being' a woman rather than 'having' a woman. The magic of the clothes is what it is not only because of what they look or feel like but because one can *get inside them*. It is their *space* as well as their substance, that matters. Earrings, wigs, nail varnish, lipstick, are no different. One is still on the inside when one displays them. And of course if the display is glamorous, the sexual combustion is all the more powerful. But as Trevor knows and finds, each act of cross-gender creation is unpredictable, each experience novel, each transformation a different touch of magic.

It used to be thought (Storr, 1964) that transvestites, because of the partial feminine identification involved, are half way between heterosexuals and homosexuals. Very few transvestites, Trevor included, accept this. Really

---

2 It is admitted that the image of woman that attracts transvestites is a rather stereotypically attractive one rather than just woman *per se*.

heterosexuals are half way between transvestites and homosexuals. It virtually is impossible psychologically to *be* a transvestite unless one has some heterosexual drive. Woman, particularly beautiful woman, is the spur.

Transvestites, unless they're homophobic, do not always shy away from men nevertheless. Trevor has flirted with male company once. A male totally dressed as a woman may find it natural to respond to a man's advances. After all, making love to a man is likely to intensify the ecstacy of being a desired woman — but this is more 'heterogenderal sex', sex like straight sex, based on contrast (Tripp, 1977) rather than real homosexuality. Most gays do not see it as truly gay sex (based on sameness) and the men who get involved as partners are usually bisexuals or straights. The through-and-through homosexual man finds the femininity of transvestites a turn-off and cross-dressers like Trevor who have dallied with men only very rarely see it only as playful and 'not really meaning anything'.

Although it is true, and much to the disgust of feminists, that many transvestites portray (and desire) a very stereotypically feminine image of woman this is not always the case or true of all transvestites (or transsexuals). Some who spend a lot of time as women — as I did — need not be averse at all to more casual clothes (and flat shoes) while others may even have beards and cross-dress only from the neck down so as to be able to look down at a body they can temporarily take to be a woman's. Still others (more so transsexuals than transvestites) may shun the Barbie Doll image altogether in the spirit of being more of a 'modern girl'.

Is all this pathological?

I have known Trevor for over 15 years and have never really come across anything about him in either role that would lead one to see him as disturbed. He is a quiet man but of utter dependability and trustworthiness. His kindness to those less fortunate than himself is unmatched in anyone I know. He is also a man who values his family, indeed these days his ageing mother would be lost without his visits and provisions. Socialist in spirit he is sexually an individualist yet this individualism has brought him little paranoia and little ostracism from friends. In many ways Trevor sails on regardless of what people might think of him, really as one of the most stable, secure and deep-rooted people I have ever come across. His attitude is not to 'get cured' by a psychotherapist or a pill but to see what he can make out of the talents and attributes he possesses. Many cross-dressers are the same. The present-day spectacular and multicoloured outfits of 'trannies on display' in clubs all over the country are the result of the takeover of transvestism essentially by art and design rather than by medicine and psychology. Theatre has triumphed over the laboratory.

The underground subculture therefore puts a completely different construction on cross-dressing to that of the human sciences but a construction, as we will see, more in tune with empirical findings. One's tendencies are not seen as signs of neurosis or psychosis but are reframed as capacities to be nurtured and fostered, to be used for the general nourishment of one's life. This also is Trevor's view. One is seen not as a case but as a total person with a range of attributes that one is free to deploy to craft one's own future. This is not transvestite as example of sexual variance, this is transvestite as playwright and artist of their own personal drama.

This in many ways is psychologically for the good. In the 1970s the constructions put on cross-dressing by psychoanalysts and other human scientists caused me personally untold suffering. Now we realise that it is healthy and preferable for a person to have a positive view of their sexuality when that sexuality, like fetishism, transvestism and sado-masochism is intrinsically harmless.

There is no reasonable question about it that Trevor Pastaro is a good man. He can create beautiful images as Tina (see Figure 10.1). This is a loving, kind and gentle soul who has no pathological tendencies greater than the average person — and indeed maybe fewer. His mild obsessive-compulsive traits are no greater than one might find in any accountant. If artists, rather than scientists, wrote diagnostic manuals of mental disorder Trevor would not be listed. One might see instead 'disorders' like 'Pathologically Middle-of-the-Road Personality Disorder' or 'Emotional blandness'; 'Insufficient fantasy life'; 'Arts Aversion', 'Reality obsession' or 'Aspiritual Personality'. If we change the values like this the goalposts move round 90° and different behaviours become 'in' and 'out' of the pathology spotlight.

The ultimate origin of fetishistically inclined transvestism in all probability lies in genetic and prenatal hormone effects[3] (see Gosselin and Wilson, 1980; Ellis, 1998). But these need not result in emotional distress. The individual's task is to marshall the tendencies he has been bestowed to craft a meaningful, fulfilling and enjoyable life. Scabrous attacks on cross-gender behaviour are the preserve of those with a political stake in the reification of gender-congruent behaviour, sex-role stereotyping and rational sex. In a massively overpopulated world with decreasing domination of our lives by physical necessity (including the necessity even for intercourse) and an increasing licence for the imagination provided by all manner of technological and inventive advances, it seems far better to recognise and accept that sexual fantasy of all kinds is an activity with a vast and extensive future.

Measuring Trevor

The psychometric study of personality (in contrast with the social assessment of personality) does not (or should not) usually involve value judgements even if in everyday social contexts such judgements do occur (and indeed many questionnaires are value laden). However, extraversion is not seen by professionals such as Eysenck as 'better' than introversion and the emotionality of a nervous individual need not in practice mean that they are 'worse' than the affectively flatter stable person. Many highly emotional people can be more colourful and creative than their stable opposites. (At street level of course such factors may not be considered.) In this short section I will attempt to make the

---

3 Superficially genetic and hormonal effects seem to have little or no direct relevance to what one wears but an indirect effect may be possible. It is feasible that biological factors could increase skin sensitivity or even shift the peak of sexual responsiveness of skin away from contact with other skin to slightly different textures. Fetishes tend to be of smooth skin-like materials such as silk, satin and latex and virtually never of coarser textures such as wool and linen. Biological factors may also influence sensitivity to and empathy for the feminine. Hence although transvestite fashions change with the times a certain continuity is preserved since transvestites generally prefer 'glamorous' fashions and these do tend to feature materials of fetishistic interest.

Figure 10.1 An ambiguous moment, female or male? Trevor as Tina, befrilled, March 1995.

personalities of Trevor and his alter ego Tina rather more clearly defined by assessing them psychometrically. Does Trevor's apparent stability and altruism also show up in questionnaires? Is there a big difference between Trevor's and Tina's personalities? Do such measures give an indication of why Trevor cross-dresses? These are the kinds of questions I will now try to answer.

In this study, actually of three cross-dressers (Trevor, Ron and Denys), I have used the Eysenck Personality Questionnaire, the EPQ, (Eysenck and Eysenck, 1975) to assess dispositions, and two measures, the MacKay inventory (MacKay et al., 1978) and the Nowlis inventory (Nowlis, 1965), as with Desmond, to assess mood and general state at the time.[4] Trevor's data is shown in Table 10.1, p. 102, the others, in Tables 10.2 to 10.3, are essentially for comparison. Trevor comes across as a tender-minded, stable introvert (low P, low N, low E), confirming the intuitive impression. In mood he is quite pleasant and affectionate, as we would expect of him, and this does not change much as Tina. What does change as Tina is that he becomes far more *aroused* in state of mind and more neurotic in disposition as a woman than as a man. In Eysenck's scheme of things (1967) this means Tina is the more emotional and perhaps more colourful one of the pair. Her high Lie score seems to be due to her being far better or more conventionally well behaved than the male self. Overall Aggression score does not change much but at a more detailed level than can be shown in Table 10.1 it turns out that there are differences in the two roles in the way that that score is reached. Trevor is slightly 'defiant' and 'rebellious' in the male role whereas Tina is more bold (Ron/Rita also showed this tendency). Strangely Tina is less forgiving so overall 'Social Affection' score goes down slightly in the female role. The Nonchalance scores are mainly due to scoring on the adjective 'playful' (this is common with the other participants).

It does seem here that Trevor 'dresses' to self-stimulate, not to relax. The price he pays for this is a slight increase in neuroticism but even as Tina he is below the population means for males and females in this trait. Both Trevor and Tina therefore are stable introverts, Tina being rather more conventionally well behaved (even more so than a real woman!).

Is Trevor typical?

The trait and state scores of two other 'transgenderals' are shown in Tables 10.2 and 10.3 for reflection (Denys/Deanna is a transsexual). A paper by Gosselin and Eysenck (1980) should also be consulted on this issue, based on 13 Beaumont Society transvestites. There are only two variables that show consistent and predicted changes in all the four people here and those are Extraversion, which rises in the female role (also found by Gosselin and Eysenck, 1980) and felt arousal, which also rises in the female persona (state measures were not taken by Gosselin and Eysenck (1980)).

The evidence is not consistent, however, that any of the cross-dressers here are dressing to move towards (at street level) what might be seen as a stereotypically more ideal state and personality (high E, low N, low P) as

---

4 I chose to use the EPQ as it is quick and easy to self-administer; important in this context. The MMPI and other questionnaires such as the I6PF would have been too cumbersome. The dimensions revealed by the EPQ are also still topical in current debates as to whether personality is best assessed by 3, 5 or 16 major traits (Deary and Matthews, 1993).

	Table 10.1	
	The Transvestite Double Image	
	Trevor as male and as female (as Tina) **Age: 49 years**	
	Trevor (17.2.99, 9.45a.m.)	*Tina* (17.2.99, 6.30p.m.)
Extraversion(21)	2	3
Neuroticism(23)	4	9
Psychoticism(25)	2	2
Lie Score(21)	8	18
Stress(19)	2	2
Arousal(15)	7	14
Aggression(12)	3	4
Concentration(12)	4	6
Deactivation(9)	0	0
Social Affection(12)	12	9
Anxiety(12)	0	1
Depression(9)	0	0
Egotism(12)	0	0
Pleasantness(12)	6	10
Activation(9)	3	9
Nonchalance(9)	4	4
Skepticism(6)	0	0
Startle(6)	0	0

Extraversion, Neuroticism, Psychoticism and Lie Score from the EPQ (Eysenck and Eysenck, 1975); Stress and Arousal from the MacKay inventory (MacKay et al., 1978); Aggression to Startle from the use of the Nowlis inventory (Nowlis, 1965). Figures in brackets are the maximum possible score on that dimension.

suggested by Gosselin and Eysenck (1980). In Table 10.4 we see how many have moved in stereotypically more ideal directions in the female role and even Denys/Deanna's data (the most extreme) does not reach significance (p=0.180, sign test). Trevor shows merely three shifts (out of a possible 14) in a stereotypically ideal direction (p=0.058 in the reverse direction), Ron only four. Clearly these transvestites seem to dress not so much to be more ideal in their persona but to change in idiosyncratic directions that please *them*. This is particularly so for Trevor and Ron but it is not so clear for Denys.

So *is* Trevor typical? Both Trevor and Ron are more 'closeted' than Denys used to be and hence have less social experience as women. Though the data in Table 10.4 is not definitive it does look as though Trevor and Ron change rather

	Table 10.2	
	Ron as male and as female (as Rita) **Age: 60 years**	
	Ron (26.7.86, 2p.m.)	*Rita* (26.4.86, 2p.m.)
Extraversion(21)	7	11
Neuroticism(23)	2	2
Psychoticism(25)	3	1
Lie Score(21)	3	3
Stress(19)	0	0
Arousal(15)	12	13
Aggression(12)	0	2
Concentration(12)	7	9
Deactivation (9)	0	0
Social Affection(12)	7	4
Anxiety(12)	0	0
Depression(9)	0	0
Egotism(12)	1	5
Pleasantness(12)	8	5
Activation(9)	6	4
Nonchalance(9)	2	6
Skepticism(6)	0	0
Startle(6)	0	0

little as women and dress to please themselves whereas it is possible, but not certain, that Denys changed rather more, had a more socially attractive personalitiy as Deanna and perhaps, at the time of testing, dressed partly to move with time towards a socially more ideal and acceptable persona. Even in Denys, however, a considerable number of changes are, or seem to be, purely idiosyncratic.[5]

Reflections on Trevor/Tina

Most cross-dressing in men is a part-time short-term activity and it is rare for the female personality to have long continued exposure to the world, say over several days. Even Deanna was quite a 'young' female persona. Tina therefore comes into existence sporadically for a few hours and instantiates a more aroused — and hence changed — state of consciousness than Trevor usually experiences.

5 The questionnaires do seem to have given us some information that was not available from acquaintance with these people but questionnaires may reflect to some extent what people *want* to believe about themselves. Hence we must take these findings with caution. It is evident, however, that the qualitative description tells us far more and paints a fuller more well-rounded picture of the individual. It clearly cannot be omitted in personality studies.

Table 10.3

Denys as male and female (as Deanna)*
Age: 47 years

	Denys (3.12.87, 2.45p.m.)	*Deanna* (28.11.87, 12.47a.m.)
Extraversion(21)	0	17
Neuroticism(23)	18	3
Psychoticism(25)	5	6
Lie Score(21)	6	19
Stress(19)	19	0
Arousal(15)	0	15
Aggression(12)	3	6
Concentration(12)	6	3
Deactivation(9)	9	0
Social affection(12)	6	12
Anxiety(12)	12	0
Depression(9)	6	0
Egotism(12)	0	0
Pleasantness(12)	0	11
Activation(9)	0	9
Nonchalance(9)	3	9
Skepticism(6)	6	0
Startle(6)	6	0

*First published in Chadwick, 1997, Chapter 8. Denys/Deanna it must be noted is a transsexual rather than a transvestite.

This arousal increase, however, may not (and probably cannot) be maintained long term. What does tend to be maintained is socially appropriate mood changes such as decreased aggression or increased pleasantness. How Tina would 'settle into the world' then, if she was given the chance, we do not know. Trevor moves in a LESS socially desirable and acceptable direction when he becomes Tina but this would probably change with more social experience. The clearest picture we, or I, have is of Trevor. Though he is kind, quiet and rather shy there is nonetheless an iron streak of determination, pride and defiance in him which keeps him steady in his life, sure of who and what he is, and stands for, and unashamed of the way he lives. Looking through the trees to see the wood we can even see a hint of this in his questionnaire answers. It is in this combination of peacefulness, kindness and determination that I would say in conclusion lies the beauty of Trevor's personality.

Table 10.4

The Transvestite Double Image (continued)

Changes from the male to the female personality
Increase in score(+), decrease(-) or no change(0)

	Trevor/ Tina	Ron/ Rita	Denys/ Deanna	Ideal
Extraversion	+	+	+	+
Neuroticism	+	0	-	-
Psychoticism	0	-	+	-
Lie Score	+	0	+	-
Stress	0	0	-	-
Arousal	+	+	+	0
Aggression	+	+	+	-
Concentration	+	+	-	0
Deactivation	0	0	-	0
Social Affection	-	-	+	+
Anxiety	+	0	-	-
Depression	0	0	-	-
Egotism	0	+	0	-
Pleasantness	+	-	+	+
Activation	+	-	+	0
Nonchalance	0	+	+	+
Skepticism	0	0	-	-
Startle	0	0	0	-
Number of shifts in ideal direction	3	4	10	(14)
p	0.058	0.180	0.180	
Number of changes of any kind	10	10	17	

The future?

Tahiti is a long way from Guildford and Trevor still perhaps some way from living a life outside a diagnostic category. But I have never believed in a racial hierarchy of truth with 'primitive blacks' having the silliest ideas and upper-middle-class whites the most sophisticated and accurate. Trevor is the victim of socio-historical forces impinging on a discipline — human science — that defines the norm by following culture at a safe distance and then (safely) proclaiming its judgements as cosmic inevitabilities. But times are changing: even clergymen are self-outing their transvestism, as are doctor-journalists and businessmen.

Comedians such as Eddie Izzard make us realise, as did Oscar Wilde, that the best antidote to religious condemnation and gender stereotyping is not philosophical debate but laughter. Really the *mahu* is but another harmless example of human variability and one that carries no connotations of disturbance — any more than does slightly unusual food preference. Tomes on the 'profound personality disturbances' of transvestites have found no support when checked empirically (see also Beatrice, 1985, on this) and really are foolish knowledge gleaned from imposing negative constructions *on* transvestism (usually from studying non-self-accepting, guilt-ridden clients) rather than from discovering things *in* transvestism. We enter the new millennium in a state of some professional ambiguity about cross-dressing in men; most clinical psychologists seem hardly ever to receive such a referral, the category is dying. In the years to come Trevor may be seen as 'a hero of the new'; let us hope so, the days of the suiciding transvestite will then be only a thing of the past — a product of scorn and delusion from 'following culture at a safe distance'.

11
Reflections on personality studies

Deep and surface beauty

The beauty of someone's personality reveals itself only slowly. Because this attribute impresses itself upon one over hundreds of thousands of important moments, though one may notice the critical qualities involved, it cannot ever be fully explained or described. This applies also to our attempts to understand relationships. One might say, however, that whenever beauty is particularly prominent in a person's personality, that personality is strengthening, not weakening, of the people around them — even, as in Jill's case, though she was troubled for a long time. Despite her terrible depression her presence in my life generally has been a strengthening one and I wouldn't blame her for any hang-ups I might have.

One might expect then that beauty only reflects very profound features of a person but I think it would be wrong to argue from this that more superficial aspects — their usual self-presentation strategies for example, features of their persona or mask, are irrelevant. This is just not so. It is unfair to say that a person's persona is axiomatically their false self, although it may be. A lot of self-presentation (not omitting making the best of one's appearance) is done in the service of being considerate of other people, eventuating empathy, showing one's social interest and basically being a civilised person. All of these things could well be manifestations of love and of one's real self (and of course people often present so as to signal what is within). Except in very Machiavellian characters self-presentational strategies may indeed be anchored to some degree in the real self.

The beauty of protectiveness

It is probably a truism that women's self-presentation strategies are more sophisticated than men's. This probably is not only because they have to avoid violence and aggression more (a rather masculine way of looking at women) but because of their greater protective feelings and greater empathy. Jill for example works on an E.M.I. unit, a unit for the elderly mentally infirm. Her patients are mostly over 75 years of age, some are over 100. The women are far beyond child-bearing age and all are not able to fulfil the function of guiding the young as most are so demented they can barely hold a conversation or understand a statement of any degree of complexity. In this trading-floor culture of Thatcher and post-Thatcher Britain they could easily be seen as 'a waste of space' — except perhaps for nursing home owners to make a profit from. They are also sometimes forgotten. They have little to no money and in terms of evolutionary theory are in essence of 'no use to anybody' (something they themselves sometimes say). But this is human life, not a geneticist's dream world. The fact of the matter is that Jill loves them. And well she may.

Love transcends the summer-all-the-time existence that the human sciences seem so keen to provide us with. And of course one will search in vain for some cerebrally localised 'love module'. Love is of the whole system, the whole self loves. Love therefore brings the whole self together.

Protectiveness and shamanism

A greater altruism and higher level of protective feelings than one usually finds in standard-minded men is also characteristic of men stereotypically seen as feminine — although it evidences itself also in the most masculine men who, like the SAS and police, protect the country and the community.

We see this very clearly, however, in Trevor as a transvestite and it was very much part of the beauty of his being. Eastern ideas about the 'man-woman' are embedded in a more mystical and spiritual background that has not in this context in any way caught on in the West. This is why transvestites are far more accepted in, for example, Japan and Malaysia. The idea of a being that is part male, part female, has always had religious and spiritual connotations in the East so that such people can even play a shamanistic role in some cultures. This of course throws quite a different light on cross-gender behaviour to that adopted by Western psychology which is dominated by ideas related to aberrant conditioning, Oedipal fixations and narcissistic personality disturbances. Western psychologists have to find something 'wrong' with the characters of transvestites because transvestites do not fit with Western ideas of what a male person should be. The activity is seen then as psychologically ugly. Hence transgenderals of all types may on divorce be denied access to their children, an absurd situation as some standard-minded men who do not have the same disqualification may never have been sent a really serious challenge in their lives at all or had to deal with any really powerful conflicts within and hence be very juvenile. It is wrong then to assume that a straight man will always and necessarily be a better father simply because he is more sex-role stereotyped.

Music as personal beauty

The scientific view of person is that of an organism designed to survive, reproduce and nurture. Their soul is their function. The artist's view of person, however, is as living instantiation of music. A person's life is a flow through time, a structuring of time; to capture the music of the person is to represent them most fully.

The beauty of the personality therefore is very much a musical concept and hence, as Walter Pater might expect, relates very much to the person's style. In this it is extended over time and cannot be embodied in a measurement or any static representation. It is kinematic, it is longitudinal, it is microprocess but it is colour not geometry, it is the taste of the soup not its formula, and most of all it is individual not nomothetic. Questionnaires therefore may measure personality, or some aspects of it, in static snapshot fashion but they cannot give us a rendition of its rhythm or grace.

The particular problem of science in psychological contexts is its tendency to generalise and categorise. There are some things, such as the problem of how depression tends to be cyclical; how mania turns into depression; how self-efficacy and self-esteem feelings can vary so much with time and how delusions can develop and change that require not generalisation but a close reading moment-by-moment study of experience and events: a longitudinal microprocess approach. One finds this to a certain extent in some writers, such as Dostoyevsky and William Faulkner, but one does not find it in psychological science for ethical, practical and financial reasons. Such studies are incredibly difficult to do. One solution is either to use a day-by-day fact-fiction narrative (see Chapter 3 in Chadwick, 1995); an introspective narrative after the event (Chapter 4 in Chadwick, 1997) or a diary and tape-recorder-based stream of consciousness commentary (see Chapter 9 here). Some reliance on introspection is unavoidable and necessary but, though mistrusted by scientists, it has to be said that if introspection wasn't able to keep a clear and reliable track of mental events mathematical reasoning would be impossible. Though introspection has many limitations it is far from worthless (Ericsson and Simon, 1980, 1984).

The classic example of such longitudinal 'close reading' is of course James Joyce's *Ulysses* (Joyce, 1922), a fine example really of the 'schizotypal credit' and the example *par excellence* of the transfer of the stream (and rhythm) of consciousness from mind to page.[1] *Ulysses* is a touchstone edifice for qualitative researchers and hence well worth a read by undergraduate (and postgraduate) psychologists. The account that a person gives to researchers can so easily stray from the finer grained actual experiences (Walker, 1994) and work such as Joyce's is an exemplary testament to how microscopically experience can be studied from within. (It could indeed be that Joyce's schizotypy enabled him to be sensitive to processes usually preconscious in standard-minded people.)

Beauty-in-person therefore expresses itself longitudinally, slowly, musically. Here we are reaching to a twenty-first-century analogue of 'soul', to the wisps of God within, to the colourous ground of being, maybe even to the instantiation at an individual, personal level of the celestial music we met briefly in the Preface. At this level art is at least at the beginning of mysticism and takes us to a point where we can maybe see further than any instrument.

The artist's view of personality

Scientific views of personality (e.g. Guilford, 1959; Eysenck, 1981; Cattell, 1990; McCrae and Costa, 1990) focus on personal dispositions which generate consistency in a person's behaviour over time. The quantitative study of these dispositions or traits is the central task of many scientific personality researchers (e.g. Eysenck and Eysenck, 1985; Goldberg, 1990; Deary and Matthews, 1993). Other scientists stress the importance of personality as involving both self-deception and impression management strategies (e.g. Paulhus, 1986) whilst others (e.g. Hampson, 1988) emphasise the intrinsically social nature of the personality construct and its dependence on self-other interactions and on the perceptions of the other (e.g. Emler, 1990). Process research focuses on genetic factors, learning processes and on the effects of self-perceptions and executive processes in orchestrating a fairly unified view of the Self in action over time.

---

1 Though to a psychiatrist schizotypy may be seen as a disqualification, schizotypy, particularly when allied with high intelligence, can confer advantages in creativity (see Chadwick, 1997, Chapter 12).

Although no extant personality researchers describe themselves as artists or use the phrase 'artistic approach' (see Chapter 2 also on this) it is probably fair to say that alternative strategies within the personality field could be described as the more artistic avenues of study into this topic. In these more artistic modes the quantification of personality is less important in comparison to the facilitation of possibility in person (see Stevens, 1996). The quantification of traits and hence the location of person in 'trait space', whether it be 3, 5 or 16 dimensional in nature is less important than the study of that which most critically makes the person unique and that which resists quantification. To the artist a person with a bland, middle-of-the-road lowest common denominator personality could be seen as having no personality at all. To the artist their eccentricities and oddities, rather than being evidence of pathology, are seen as conveying colour and uniqueness to the individual.

The scientist, psychiatrist and certainly the psychoanalyst, have often pathologised non-conformity. The artist, however, celebrates it. Artists are perhaps, like many British clinical psychologists, naturally subversive and particularly facilitate individual freedom, unpredictability and new possibility. Here quantification, consistency, reliability and predictability are not central constructs or key words in the endeavour.

Although the view of person as an active agent in the construction of their personality is stressed by some scientific researchers (e.g. Kelly, 1955; Hampson, 1988) the agentic nature of the Self has always been an uncomfortable concept for science as it harbours the flavour of free will and is anti-deterministic. The artist, however, is perfectly at ease with this self-constructive aspect of personality and indeed to him or her it is a central ingredient of the artistic approach. The person, as we will see in Chapter 12, is very much the sculptor of their Self and the dramatist of their own personal story. Person is also seen by the artist, and even by the artist-experimenter such as myself, as naturally resisting quantification, systematisation and prediction. This natural 'bloody-mindedness' of Man is a key topic in Chapter 13, but it is important to recognise that such recalcitrance, if it is a thorn in the side of the scientist, it is a joy to the artist.

This emphasis on beauty, on the unique, on the transformational possibilities of person essentially defines the radius of the artistic approach to personality. It does not of course pre-empt the use of quantitative techniques, as we saw in Chapters 6 and 10, but its perspective is such that it does not perceive person as suffering their personality so much as creating it. And in doing so reality, and indeed the past, is a dictionary more than a causal nexus.

Science also is uncomfortable with the historical and cultural context of personality (see Chapter 8 here). Yet there is little doubt that people's personalities (and attitudes) in the 1920s and 1930s were very different from what they are today. Indeed Des, Ivo and myself particularly rebelled against the stereotype of the standard-minded 1950s and 1960s Man and hence our own quests in search of ourselves cannot be understood without considering that historical context (see Chadwick, 1997). It is unlikely, however, that trait studies would pick up such changes over the decades (or for that matter differences across the social classes) as the tapestry of description in scientific personality research is relatively coarse-grained. For the really fine-grained study of personality one has to turn to the artist as such phenomena in science are merely left in the error term of analyses of variance or, more generally, as unexplained variance in the data. To the artist it is specifically this unexplained variance that is the very essence of the personalities of the people under study.

The paranoid distortion of beauty

Neurotic but particularly psychotic or psychopathic/anti-social tendencies can sometimes greatly mar the beauty of the personality. On occasion the disturbance, to take paranoia as an example, may be relatively benign, as we saw with Desmond's concern over his appearance. Jill also became somewhat paranoid that people would desert her because of her depression. On other occasions, as we saw in Chapters 4 and 9, it can be based very much (if not entirely) on real events — clearly if one behaves in such an off-centre manner as I did and does so in full view of the public one can only expect to be talked about. But of course paranoia can go further than this (as it did in my own case), and in doing so reveals a critical point about beauty and about its absence and deformation: the importance of flaws. In the physical realm we see this in Elizabeth Taylor's slight double-chin; in Sophia Loren's overfull mouth; in Barbra Streisand's nose. The 'too-perfect', in its one-sidedness, is not the pinnacle of beauty (as we know from many a glossy magazine cover) and does not embody the world as it is. As will become apparent the pay-off of perfection is not a passport to Heaven but paranoia.

The paranoid mentality

We saw in Chapter 6 that there are 'happy schizotypes', there are also happy homophobes and happy histrionic people. There are some other personality types that do not involve suffering, such as the so-called passive-aggressive — though the people concerned usually make others suffer. Alas there are no happy paranoid people.

Paranoia involves a blend of feelings and thoughts characterised by suspiciousness and a sense of threat — particularly from people. It is an attitude of mind directed chiefly to the future: the dread is of some awful future event — be it betrayal, ridicule or even murder. Of course nobody knows what the future holds and, in a very uncertain and changing world such as ours has become, dread of this kind is common. This is the age of paranoia. Though we must all be humble before the future yet the future does not exist! Here is something that doesn't exist that humbles all men and all women.

At an information-processing level, people become paranoid partly because of their probability judgements. 'I bet that . . . '; 'I can just imagine . . . '; 'You never know what a person like that's up to . . . ' and so it goes on. But in extreme paranoia probabilities harden into certainties or near certainties: 'I *know!*' 'I'm *sure!*' 'It *is* happening!' Even when what is inferred is improbable to the point of physical or technological impossibility the person finds certainty in it. This almost manic triumph over the probable, over the future and over one's internal critic, so to speak, carries a hint of self-aggrandisement.

What is singularly lacking in paranoia is trust. Paranoids fear being submissive, dependent, trusting, being in someone's power. Again there is a hint of grandiosity here: 'I will submit to no one!' One might well imagine that an attitude of this kind likely has its origins in childhood or in teenage years and is founded on disappointment. Paranoids are not necessarily cold people, or depressed, though they can be; to be paranoid one needs to have joined with others, connected, bonded, but not so much to have lost — as in depression — but to have been betrayed. The more 'unbelievable', shocking and surprising the betrayal, the greater the damage.

Freud (1911) initially linked paranoia with homosexuality but not I think for the right reasons. Before the 1970s and 1980s homosexuality was a great disqualification and the fear of 'turning queer' the uppermost fear in many men's minds. This was particularly so in the North of England. My own persecution on these grounds at North Manchester Grammar School in 1963–64 (see Chapter 9) occurred at a time before decriminalisation. If you were 'thought queer', whether it was justified or not, it was amazing how many 'friends' would desert you and feed the chief bullies with any 'information' they might have that might be 'relevant'. In situations like that, teenage boys have to make sure that they are 'on the right side' and there is considerable street credibility to be had from being a queer-basher. Ostracism in these situations can be total and one's sense of trust and reliance on people can be irreparably damaged. Paranoia is an obvious consequence from then on, needing little to trigger it.

The general effect of a training in mistrust is to make the person feel that the world is not a safe place and that one cannot rely on other people for support and sustenance. Paranoids therefore easily become loners, extreme individualists, cats who 'hunt alone and like the night'. Having had any tendencies to a merry camaraderie with people eliminated, the result is withdrawal and isolation — and in serious cases a solitary creation behind locked doors of outlandish conceptions of the world.

Paranoia and bipolar thinking

Paranoia is not something located entirely inside the head. As we saw in Chapter 9, people rarely come to think in a paranoid way for no good reason, and their consequent aggressiveness and touchiness can so alienate others, and indeed turn others against them, that that very paranoia then feeds on its own consequences in a self-confirming fashion locking the person into an aggravating and anguish-inducing vicious circle from which they may never escape. The very thinking style that characterises a paranoid parent can also be subtly transmitted to their children where it may also germinate and flourish to produce cross-generational patterns of the disorder.

It is very characteristic of paranoid personalities, however, that they like to keep all the good on the inside, within them, and all the bad on the outside, and within others. Paranoids can therefore, when they are temporarily in touch with this 'inner good', show not real beauty but all manner of overdone effects from great virtuousness, perfectionism and self-sacrificial behaviour to grandiosity and Messianic delusions.

It seems impossible for paranoids to feel that they can be partly bad, less than perfect, flawed to some degree, and still feel that they are truly lovable. They can only really be worthy of love if they are 'all good' — and they tend to transmit that attitude to their children who they also cannot love for their flaws. If they do bestow love on such people it comes across subtly and insidiously as a favour and not really deserved — indeed as further evidence of how 'marvellous' they are, viz 'I am so virtuous I will love you despite your obvious limitations and weaknesses, but consider yourself extremely fortunate'.

This terrible splitting of good and bad from inside to outside is a form of (what cognitivists would call) bipolar thinking that also feeds on its consequences.[2] If a person has anything bad about them it is very easy for such people to see them as 'all bad' (rather like a homophobe saying 'if you're slightly queer you're *all* queer'). The same reasoning is applied to themselves: 'I must keep badness at bay lest I too be all bad'. Of course the message to their children derives from the same attitude: 'I have very high standards! You must be perfect!'

The paranoid personality is basically a moral stance rather than a cognitive distortion although cognitive distortion certainly it is. Such people have never been loved for who they are, human with all their flaws, and they are incapable of loving anyone else for who they are either. Perhaps they could love Jesus, a personality without stain, and be 'Brides of Christ', but none of us lesser mortals; sadly we are not up to the job or sufficiently 'worthy'. The pattern in some ways is rather pathetic, but it is also tragic.

The tragedy of paranoia

To be partly bad, as we all are, and still be loved is a prerequisite for a sane and happy life. The beauty of the human personality in life therefore is not predicated on the perfection of the Self. Beauty of any kind, in any aspect of life, always arises out of conflict, out of tension, out of opposition. To deny the dark side is evil (see Chadwick, 1996b) just as any Christian would say that to deny the Divine Light is evil. Beauty emerges through life's struggles, not from a sell-out.

In paranoia this dreadful result of never having experienced unconditional acceptance and love reaches a psychologically gruesome solution. A punitive perfectionistic conscience may be jettisoned and externalised in hallucinations and persecutory delusions leading to a hatred of the world in a relentless quest, as Freud said, for innocence.

I have seen this kind of thing in my own desperately unhappy mother and (worse) in paranoid psychotic patients; I have felt its pushes and pulls myself in our home, at school, and as a transvestite-in-the-community. For a time such pressures made me paranoid myself. But, touched by psychosis: if one doesn't have a reasonable understanding of how one's own mind works, one can actually come to be afraid of it. It is necessary to get such things clear in one's head. Malignant paranoia is destructive of the beauty of personality, it replaces real beauty with a rather unsettling 'goodness'. And such people always have a strangely evaluative presence about them so that one can never relax with them and just *be* — one always senses that one is being judged.

In the end of course the great tragedy is that paranoid people desperately want to be loved for who they are as much as anyone else — yet their very machinations to achieve this are alienating, confusing and off-putting.

Just as 'never' and 'always' are the depressed person's favourite words so paranoids also reach out to the periphery of the verbal spectrum. In really malign cases, the world is polarised, feelings are polarised, 'unfairness' is total, inner anger is without limit and their projected conscience is merciless. For some in this state death is a welcome release. In some delusional psychoses we can see the emergence via projection almost of an inner cauldron of the putrid, a copropersonality ('They are all bad') balanced only by Messianic silliness ('I am all good') (see for example Storr (1996) on the many (and always pathetic)

---

2 Kleinians would prefer 'paranoid-schizoid position'.

imitations of Christ). An alternative psychological scenario — more similar to my own case (see Chadwick, 1993, 1997) — is to see persecutory networks as 'all good' or representative of some stereotyped virtue and oneself as 'all bad' and hence evil, Satanic or possessed by him. Which solution to one's anguish is chosen may simply depend on trivia such as actual everyday events — snatches of conversation heard in the street, off-hand comments made to one in the past and so on.

Strangely, the goodness of inferred persecutory communities and auditory hallucinatory voices in cases like this is a lesser kind of good, rather like the 'goodness' of a neighbourhood gossip rather than a saint (see Chadwick, 1998). Perhaps this is because such people are threatening of others' safety as well as possessing some shallow plastic virtue. There is no beauty in the projected conscience of a paranoid person, it is only the goodness of the lowest common denominator personality.

Bipolar thinking is a rather common human strategy, different styles of which we see also in depression, mania and so-called borderline personality types as well as in paranoia. It tends to carry with it a great aggressiveness. It is an avoidance of beauty rather than its embodiment. Let us hope then that there are no 'Messiahs for the Millennium' in the years to come but instead warts-and-all love, *real* love, that accepts the winters of life as well as the summers and that sees beauty in people as a product of their tensions and contrasts as well as of their strengths and commodities.

Writers on personality

As Freud realised, it is difficult, maybe impossible, for any psychologist or psychoanalyst to 'dig under' the mind of a great writer. The section that follows does not therefore involve reductive analyses of Wilde and Dostoyevsky but instead tries to see how they have illuminated the issue of Mind-in-Life, since personality obviously cannot be studied in a vacuum. It is a contingent entity and so must always be seen in a life context. This these writers do.

Great writers are worth studying for many reasons. At inception we can say that they are models of self-acceptance. A person in denial may have difficulty for example creating characters of the opposite sex or criminal characters or have difficulty in generally exploring the phenomenology of mind unconditionally. People secretive to themselves cannot write. Writers also stop one from forcing conclusions, show life in its real complexity and richness, take one away from jagged machine-like thoughts, away from clichés, away from one-sidedness. They take down the fences around one's mind so that one can breathe and expand to one's fullest extent and thus, in a sense, be oneself and find oneself. This is something highly standardised writers and thinkers simply do not and cannot do. Writers laugh at false virtue, at petty suburban commands, at middle-class common sense and at the pose of naturalness. They do not demand that we be more honourable than really we are, merely for the sake of appearances, but that we honour *who* we are and be true to ourselves in our many facets. The writer therefore 'releases' one to dream, to fantasise, to wonder, to build impossible worlds, and craft tales of the impossible that haunt the imagination. This is a far cry from 'finding the facts'.

In the section that follows we examine the views of person presented by two great writers whose works in many ways have already become part of

Western culture and hence have shaped our identities and the way we think, though many may hardly be aware of it. Jonathan Smith also presents a personal view of several more in Chapter 14. In what follows then is the thinking of men who have been brave enough to lead culture rather than follow it and in so doing have facilitated the development and change of persons and helped make us all who we are.

Part IV
Chapters 12 – 14
Writers on personality

The terms 'mental health' and 'mental illness' are scientific concepts borrowed from medicine; but in practice, unlike medical forms of language, they are heavily impregnated with undertones of an essentially social evaluative nature. Mental illness, or the softer term 'mental disorder', is an expression describing behaviour to a degree disapproved of by the middle-class doctor-scientist and psychoanalyst. It has in a (now) secular society replaced in its 'disapproval power' the term 'sin' of Judaeo-Christian religion.

In the three chapters that follow, this scientific legacy is countered with arguments in favour of the value of 'life as art' and person as artist and dramatist of their own personal story. Many a person's life, despite incident and even tragedy (indeed because of them), can be considered an artistic success. The lives of Sylvia Plath, Nijinsky and Oscar Wilde are notable examples. The high drama of many personalities considered pathological by psychiatry and psychoanalysis can be argued to be a quality in their favour. The colour, vibrancy and vividness of such people can give them an artistic edge over what in some cases can be the deadness and blandness of the label-free centre. For Wilde (see Chapter 12) one could even be a failure, nominally, yet still a success artistically. It is after all, *the flaw* that makes a person interesting. Under the aegis of science all deviance, extremism and non-conformity easily become judged and argued away as pathological. To the artist, and particularly the writer, this is a curse and merely a reflection of the 'decent', conforming, leafy suburb, no-trouble-to-oneself-or-anybody-else, middle-class value systems of scientific and psychoanalytic practitioners. The artist must counter this insipid blandness and assert the diversity, colour and poignancy of individual people in all their complexity and evocativeness. These three chapters are essentially in this vein.

12
Oscar Wilde:
the differentiated personality

The truth of fiction

'Being natural is such a very difficult pose to keep up' wrote Oscar Wilde in 1895 (Mrs Cheveley in *An Ideal Husband*, Wilde, 1895/1994, p.519). In the same vein he wrote of how distressed he was in having to bring some 'sordid' realistic considerations into play in a sonnet on Keats (letter to F. Holland Day, August 1890, Hart-Davis, 1988, p.91) and never denied that one of the most distressing 'events' of his life was the death of a *fictional* character (Balzac's Lucien de Rubempré in *Splendeurs misère des Courtesanes*: 'It is a grief from which I have never been able to completely rid myself' *The Decay of Lying*, 1891/1994, p.1077). Wilde, predictably, believed that the first duty in life was 'to be as artificial as possible' (*Phrases and Philosophies for the use of the Young*, Wilde, 1894/1994, p.1244) and was a man devoted to the artifice of art (and of city life) rather than to nature and reality so central to scientists (Ellmann, 1988). 'Life is the only thing that is never real' he conveyed in *The Decay of Lying*.

It is not surprising to find that personality as (what we would now call) self construction and reconstruction was the essence of Wilde's writing whenever the individual was discussed. This was very much a view of Man as Artist rather than Man as Scientist and an artist to be studied in the full context of social life rather than in any controlled setting. The Piagetian image of the solitary Robinson Crusoe thinker was not for Wilde. He did not believe that we should turn to Nature for the explanation of our own sins ('The worst use that Man can make of Nature is to turn her into a mirror for his own vices') nor that Nature's secrets would be revealed to those who questioned her in this spirit (Wilde, 1887/1995, p.169). The person was the product of their own craftsmanship and their life the product of their own dramatic abilities ('I have put only my talent into my works. I have put all my genius into my life' (Ellmann, 1988, p.341)).

Distributed psychology

Wilde has been accused of shallowness in his depth of characterisation (Gagnier, 1987, p.134) but this is to underestimate the sophistication of his psychology and neglects the fact that this psychology tended to be 'distributed' across several characters in his plays ('When looking on a play, psychological interest is everything' (letter to the editor of the *St James's Gazette* 26th February 1892, Hart-Davis, 1962/1989, p.104)). Wilde was indeed seduced with pleasure by psychological conversation (letter to William Ward, March 1887, Hart-Davis, 1962/1989, p.13) and used conversation as a means of psychologising the events he described. The individual characters were puppets to themes not detailed instantiations of them at the personal level. ('There is no action in my plays, my characters merely sit around and chatter' he was to say.) But in these chatterings Wilde was able to articulate some very powerful ideas e.g. 'It takes a thoroughly good woman to do a thoroughly stupid thing' (*Lady Windermere's Fan*); 'Children begin by loving their parents, after a time they judge them. Rarely, if ever, do they forgive them' (*A Woman of No Importance*); 'The amount of women in London who flirt with their own husbands is perfectly scandalous. It looks so bad. It is simply washing one's clean linen in public' (*The Importance of Being Earnest*); 'Who, being loved, is poor? Oh, no one' (*A Woman of No Importance*); 'There is no secret of life. Life's aim, if it has one, is simply always to be looking for temptation' (*A_Woman of No Importance*) and 'The truth is rarely pure and never simple. Modern life would be very tedious if it were either, and modern literature a complete impossibility!' (*The Importance of Being Earnest*).

All of these statements create an image of person as both wise and foolish; pleasure-seeking; chameleon-like; at best frankly accepting of all experiences (*De Profundis*, Wilde, 1905/1994, p.1029) but at a deeper level, centred by love. Wilde's depictions were not of Man the Machine but often convey almost floral images of Man as poet; as adventurer; even as blunderer, bamboozler and confounder of the doctrinaire and the systematiser. They are depictions of person as taking on the dilemmas of life often half-wittedly but fighting through and as inherently complex and challenging in pattern.

Clearly Wilde as astute observer of people is a much neglected topic in psychology. In this chapter I want therefore to present a view, and a much needed one, of Wilde as at least implicitly a personality psychologist. I will continue by discussing the decadent ideology from which his work emerged, then go on to mention some of the techniques and dramatic ideas he used to express significant concepts and then close with a critique and a discussion of his defeat at the hands of the upper-class Establishment — but, it should be said, with the sneers of the middle and working classes also resounding in his ears — in 1895.

The pluralistic person

If Positivism has an opposite, it is Decadence. Oscar Wilde's popular image was indeed the personification of late nineteenth-century decadence (Symons, 1891, p.27) but Wilde related the decadent imagination surprisingly to growth and not degeneration (Haley, 1985). The central feature of the decadent mind in Wilde's writings was its individualism and its tendency to self-plurality. This was in contrast to a static unity of the ego and also to conformity. The key words for positivists in Wilde's time (and of course today) were rationality, realism, conformity, work and progress. By contrast decadents (particularly young male poets of the time) were seen as valuing the imaginary, being disorderly, self-indulgent, passive, immoral and jaded (Haley, 1985, p.215). But Wilde, drawing in his early student years (1879) on Herbert Spencer's thinking, saw the growth of organisms as being towards greater complexity, differentiation, uniqueness and hence individualism. The simple homogenous organism was precarious and insecure in its existence, nature favoured the heterogeneous, the diverse, both at the individual and the collective level. Wilde saw Socialism as potentially facilitating such diversity but only so long as it gave licence for this individualism (*The Soul of Man under Socialism*, Wilde, 1891/1994, p.1174).

Although Spencer had written within a scientific context, Wilde related these ideas to the life of the artist. Since the artist is the supreme individualist all evolution tends towards the development of the artist or aesthetic critic (Haley, 1985, p.222). The ground condition for permitting this was freedom, freedom from authority and hence freedom for the ego or Self to multiply, secreting selves some directly opposed to one another in nature. This was a bugle call for the maximum complexity and organisation of one's identity, an antidote to the steady, reliable, predictable personality required by nineteenth-century Capitalism in an industrial age. Of course with the passing of 'Heavy Industry Man' Wilde seems more modern now than he did even in his own times. It could be said that early twenty-first-century capitalism has no stake whatsoever in people having fixed and stable identities (Hebdige, 1987/1992), the Wildean age of the pluralistic person could well have arrived.

Personality, freedom and will

Positivism and Decadence therefore exist within contrasting intellectual and socio-economic frameworks. Their morality also differs. For the positivist sincerity, steady routine and single-mindedness of purpose traditionally are essential, but for the decadent a healthy spiritual life comes from vitality and multiplicity in consciousness. Simplicity is seen as degeneration and true spirituality advances from realising the imaginary in all its possibilities even to the point of seeking the *impossible*. As Walter Pater said 'Failure lies in forming habits' (Pater, 1873/1990, p.46).

Wilde also propounded the association of decadence with rebelliousness. With no freedom there can be no growth. Hence like Sartre (Murdoch, 1953/1976, p.73) he saw liberty as a deeper concept than will. It could also be said that, in combining reason and emotion decadence is an advance on positivism — with its edicts in favour of the denial of feeling — and is also braver than positivism with the latter's socially safe style, secretiveness and its preference for the closed knowable world. Decadence then is dangerous — as Wilde discovered. The thunder of decadence is a threat to prim domestic living, it speaks of the unchained human spirit beneath the tidy virtue of socialised thought and behaviour and takes us to truths deeper than the provincial platitudes of puritanism and Protestantism (see the contrast between 'provincialisms' and 'Oscarisms' in Table 12.1).

Discipline and decadence

Clearly decadence as propounded by Wilde is a departure from decadence as understood by the mob. A modern sensualist has only one philosophy: 'feel good all the time'. But this is only hedonism, not decadence. Wilde presented as 'necessarily indolent' but this was a pose. In fact he worked hard and regularly into the early hours of the morning (Hunter-Blair, 1938). His most dangerous neglect, as things proved, was not of scientific truth but of the middle classes (Gagnier, 1987, p.59). Then, as now, Wilde was the perfect antidote to middle-class commonsense (see Table 12.1), a common sense that particularly today pervades the subjects of academic psychology and psychotherapy to a stultifying degree.

The picture we have here is of Man as self-creating as he or she self-eventuates. Rather as in mathematics — an early interest of Wilde's — we discover

Table 12.1

Oscar Wilde's reactions to domestic virtues

Provincialisms	*Oscarisms*
'Everything in moderation.'	'Nothing is good in moderation. You cannot know the good in anything till you have torn the heart out of it by excess.'(a)
'You should always tell the truth.'	'If one tells the truth, one is sure, sooner or later, to be found out.'(b)
'Face reality! Face life!'	'Life is the only thing that is never real.'(c)
'Talk is easy, it's *action* that's difficult.'	'It is very much more difficult to talk about a thing than to do it.'(d)
'To yield to temptation is a sign of weakness.'	'I tell you that there are terrible temptations which it requires strength, strength and courage, to yield to.'(e)
'Don't get into debt.'	'It is only by not paying one's bills that one can hope to live in the memory of the commercial classes.'(f)
'Get a good education!'	'Nothing that is worth knowing can be taught.'(g)
'Silence is golden.'	'It is so exhausting not to talk.'(h)
'Don't sit around dreaming, *do* something!'	'Action is the last resource of those who know not how to dream.'(i)
'Have some common sense!'	'Nowadays most people die of a sort of creeping common sense, and discover when it is too late that the only thing one never regrets are one's mistakes.'(j)
'Never put off until tomorrow what you can do today.'	'I never put off until tomorrow what I can do . . . the day after.' (k)

. . . cont'd . . .

Table 12.1 continued . . .

'Actions form habits, habits form character, character forms destiny.'

'Failure lies in forming habits.'(l)

'Let's gossip!'

'Gossip is charming. History is merely gossip. But scandal is gossip made tedious by morality.'(m)

Sources for Table

(a)   Said often in different forms e.g. Andrews, 1992, p.87.
(b)   *Phrases and Philosophies for the Use of the Young,* in *The Chameleon* Dec. 1894 (Wilde, 1894/1994, p.1244).
(c)   The theme of *The Decay of Lying.*
(d)   in *The Critic as Artist,* p.1121.
(e)   Andrews, 1992, p.263.
(f)   *Phrases and Philosophies,* p.1244.
(g)   *A Few Axims for the Instruction of the Overeducated* in *Saturday Review* Nov. 1894 (Wilde, 1894/1994, p.1242).
(h)   Prince Paul in *Vera* (Wilde, 1883/1994, p.696).
(i)   Pearson (1946/1988), p.145
(j)   Pearson, p.195.
(k)   Pearson, p.197.
(l)   Said often but actually quoted from Pater 1873/1990, p.46.
(m)   Pearson, p.210.

as we probe but not in any simple effusive way. Wilde would, for example, criticise poetry emerging from pure feeling (Coakley, 1994) and emphasised the creative artistic value of criticism (*The Critic as Artist*, Wilde, 1891/1994). It was, however, a picture of disciplined decadence (the discipline perhaps from Ruskin) but with discipline now self-imposed and self-valued, not imposed either by authority or by social condemnation. Wilde relentlessly countered stereotypes, his characters bowed only to beauty and their antidotes to the comfortable conformity of others were comedy and surprise via epigram or aphorism. Really Wilde was the supreme advocate of the emergence of the individual personality against the pressure of self-appointed moralists and the 'restraint of the contemporary' (see Wilde's defence of expression in *Dorian Gray* in *The Preface* to the novel (Wilde, 1994, p.15)).

Personality as movement and contradiction

A focus on being rather than becoming can easily decay into a static view of personality, an attempt to give some kind of solid final characterisation to the individual (Knox's 1994 treatment of Wilde errs in this way). Wilde always avoids this and chooses to do so by using kinematic techniques such as the play and the novel (Ellmann, 1988, p.312) rather than, say, the static images of the portrait or sculpture. (In *The Picture of Dorian Gray* we see that in Wilde's hands even portraits change with time.)

Personality was seen then as fluid and of course as self-deceiving (Ellmann, 1988, p.139). Consistency was not a route to truth but an enemy of truth; in *The Truth of Masks* he would stress that strength (not weakness) was to be found in contradiction (Ellmann, 1988, p.99). Truth was also to be found via a favourite Wildean technique, that of *reversal* from the banal (e.g. instead of 'He who hesitates is lost' we have 'she who hesitates is won'). It was also to be found in (not concealed by) *the mask* — Yeats would eventually follow him (Coakley, 1994, p.190) when Wilde said 'Man is least himself when he talks in his own person. Give him a mask and he will tell you the truth' (in *The Critic as Artist*, p.1142).

Wilde centred his interest around *becoming* rather than *being* and in one's venture through life the products of artists were catalysts of action ('The nineteenth century, as we know it, is largely an invention of Balzac' *The Decay of Lying*, Wilde, 1891/1994, p.1084). Life copies art, goes beyond the roughage of nature, and indeed *is* an art. For him poignancy was more important than mere 'success' ('How fascinating all failures are' (in Ellmann, 1988, p.197)) and even if one's life were to be a tragedy — as to some degree was his own — its dramatic import was in no way dimmed and indeed may even be intensified. In this way Wilde liberated the artistic spirit (and artistic criticism) from anchorage in fact and reality and in so doing gave them the scope of the imaginary in which to roam and delight. This was not life as pyramid climbing, this was life as art.

Mind in style and life

It has been suggested (Green, 1979) that the word 'soul' in Wilde's writing, at least sometimes, can be replaced by 'self' or 'real self' (see also Marzillier, 1990). This is a rendition which helpfully articulates Oscar's writings rather more closely with our own as the word occurs frequently in his prose works. (In *The Picture of Dorian Gray* of course it has a supernatural flavour.) Wilde writes (1890a/1995, p.146) with great sensitivity on Walter Pater's much revered treatment of style

(Pater, 1889/1990) that 'behind the perfection of a man's style must lie the passion of a man's soul'. This phenomenon of 'Mind in style' which Wilde describes in that essay (p.146) as the source of 'conscious artistic structure' introduces his, and Pater's, concern with this music, this beauty of the personality as something deeper and more important than its content and measure.

In articulating — as he did throughout his writings — his own personal psychology of life, and hence of Mind-in-life, it is clear that Oscar adduced many psychological truths and insights which pre-dated the writings of Rogers (1969), Fromm (1947), Goffman (1959) and others. Indeed in his willingness to assert the intrinsic validity in life of paradoxical logic and contradiction (*The Truth of Masks*, Wilde, 1885/1994) as well as chaos (letter to Lord Alfred Douglas: Hart-Davis, 1962/1989, p.120) and in his writings on the construction and deconstruction of social life (*The Decay of Lying*) and on the necessity to liberate the artist-critic from anchorage in the intentions of the author (*The Critic as Artist*, Wilde 1890/1994) it could be argued that he went beyond those writers and anticipated thinking more characteristic of a century ahead (Horgan, 1992; Gleick, 1994; Burr, 1995; Morgan, 1990).

Projection

Wilde never used the Freudian term projection but he nonetheless played continually with the projections of his spectators (Gagnier, 1987) and, when attacked, as of course he often was, used this concept to mock them with glee. In *The Picture of Dorian Gray* the youth's sins, other than murder, are never named. Wilde wrote (Gagnier, 1987, p.61), 'What Dorian Gray's sins are no one knows. He who finds them has brought them.' Indeed by 1891 Wilde was becoming adept at creating plays that were Victorian Rorschachs for his audiences. 'It is the spectator, and not life, that art really mirrors' (Wilde, 1891a). The writing of *Dorian Gray* gave him the opportunity to tempt and then chastise: 'Those who find ugly meanings in beautiful things are corrupt without being charming' (Wilde, 1891a). This ironically from a man who had stated in the Pall Mall Gazette in 1887 that one cannot separate the man from the artist and who had admitted in *The Critic as Artist* that the most interesting writing is autobiographical and whose own writings were autobiographical at times to the point of being confessional (see Schmidgall, 1994, p.297). This was a man, like Gide, who never danced on more than one foot at a time. He would use the technique of changing feet with everything he produced but thanks to projection was able to reveal both himself and the spectator as he did so.

The deployment of the 'half wish'

Thanks to Wilde, and to Freud, we know that wishes are not integers. Indeed Oscar, like many writers, would use this accusation of projection to give himself licence to confess with impunity, seemingly disowning his own creations. Within his writings the characters are either divided by their conflicts (e.g. Dorian Gray, Lord Arthur Savile, the Selfish Giant) or they transcend them but at the cost of remaining mere spectators of life (Lord Henry Wotton, Lord Goring). Wilde reminds us that if we really desire to live we must pitch ourselves headlong into the realm of contradiction and live with the relentless crossfire. Those who do not may suffer more than those who accept the challenge (Wilde, 1891a). Yet implicitly he warns (Ellmann, 1988, p.421), as one might expect from a poet (see

Keats, 1818 in Gittings, 1978, pp.37–8), against thorough commitment and opts instead for this device of changing feet and realising the truth of both poles.

The impossible

In Wilde's writings giants exist, iron filings talk to each other,[1] statues can love swallows (*The Happy Prince*, Wilde, 1888/1994) and portraits can grow old.

While science deals with the possible and the soluble (Medawar, 1969) the truly impossible in art 'is anything that has happened in real life' (Ellmann, 1988, p.24). It is not the role of the artist to model reality but to utilise what is impossible in nature. Picasso had a similar view (Berger, 1980). The artist is an inventor of dreams not a constructor of internal representations of the world. The artist therefore leaves realism behind to live in a second nature, the product of human creativeness, in a sense in a world of 'lies' (*The Decay of Lying*, Wilde, 1889/1994). Nonetheless he or she creates, whether it be by fairy stories, plays or novels etc., models to be experienced, creates life-as-story, vitalised by error (*The Critic as Artist*) and even by sin. For the artist, as a man of moods and superstitions like Wilde always knew, life depends for its fruitfulness far more on love than on reason. Wilde once said, of a critic who had chided him for factual errors in *Salome*, '[His was] the truth of the professor at the Institute. I prefer the other truth, my own, which is that of the dream. Between two truths, the falser is the truer' (Ellmann, 1988, p.343).

It was particularly in *The Picture of Dorian Gray*, a tale as Gothic as anything produced by Poe, that Wilde invented, again via reversal from the obvious, the most haunting yet telling of impossibilities: a portrait that ages, and shows the lines of sin on its countenance, while the sitter, for the price of his very soul, remains young, and seemingly innocent. The book could be regarded as profoundly moral, as Wilde (self-contradictorily) claimed when accused of indecency (Pearson, 1946/1988, p.152), but, while the prose inflicts a tropical climate on the psyche, the whole narrative abounds with the outrageous and the unreasonable. The sober middle classes of the day felt ignored and neglected (Gagnier, 1987, p.59) as were 'truth', 'reality' and 'functional value'. This was life, and writing, for art's sake. Against it sagacious contemporaries, such as Galton and (to a lesser extent) Spencer, would have looked singularly crass.

Playing with perception

Wilde was able to make telling literary use of the strengths and weaknesses of perception in its central tasks of giving us parity with the world and enriching our experience. Synaesthesia comes to his aid on seeing Blum's tints when he says they gave him 'a sensation similar to eating a yellow satin dress' (Birnbaum, 1920; Ellmann, 1988, p.198). He also shows us light-hearted glimpses of appreciating, in his typical word-burst manner, context- and state-dependent perception and memory (Godden and Baddeley, 1975; Goodwin et al., 1969) — for example when failing to recognise a man who said he had known him before in Manchester: 'Very possibly in Manchester I may know you again' was his reply. On apparently cutting an old acquaintance he apologised with, 'I didn't recognise you — I've changed a lot'.

---

1 Pearson (1946/1988, p.213) — where Wilde invents a story about iron filings labouring under the illusion that they are choosing to move to the magnet when of course their behaviour is totally determined.

Defensive functions in audition are repeatedly characterised in his descriptions of the inner dialogue of *The Remarkable Rocket* (Wilde, 1888/1994, pp.294–301). For example, referred to by a boy as an 'old stick' the rocket convinces himself, like a grandiose manic, that the lad had said 'gold stick' (p.301). Referred to by a workman as 'bad rocket', the perception is transformed into 'grand rocket' (p.298).

Yet brute objectivity is scorned in such sayings as 'Whoever called a spade a spade should be compelled to use one, it is all he is fit for', while the use of perception in art faithfully to depict nature similarly is derided with 'Views are for bad painters' and 'A really well-made buttonhole is the only link between art and nature' (*Phrases and Philosophies for the Use of the Young*, Wilde, 1894/1994, p.1244).

Wilde's interest in perception lay in how the processes could be moulded in the service of human artifice. Although Oscar valued and respected science as the continual displacer of religion ('Science is the record of dead religions' *Phrases and Philosophies*) his path was the path of invention, not of 'finding'. Recognising in fact that psychology as a science itself was in its infancy in his day, he was to remark, 'And long may it remain so'.

Language, self-realisation and immortality

As we have seen, the techniques and processes Oscar used were deployed in the service of significant concepts. Although he shunned the role of 'the professor at the Institute', and was expressive and stylistic rather than analytic and standardised in approach, Wilde was in truth a theoretician — particularly on the matter of the relations between art and life (e.g. *The Decay of Lying*). Those writings that he collected together under the heading of *Intentions* (Wilde, 1891b) transmit a number of valuable psychological ideas especially on the role of language in feeling and thought; on individualism, and on self-realisation and growth. *Dorian Gray*, his most revealing work, also deals with the topics of repression, narcissism and immortality (Marzillier, 1990) and the manic and hypomanic thirst to triumph over one's own conscience. The latter work therefore tackles an issue faced also by Freud in his studies of paranoia and delusion (1911, 1915): the quest for innocence, and the price it exacts.

Wilde, only a little earlier than Freud, recognised both the insidious and evil effects of relentless inhibition[2] and also the cathartic power of words in the putting to death of pain. In *The Critic as Artist* (p.1149) he wrote:

> Form is everything . . . find expression for a sorrow and it will become dear to you. Find expression for a joy, and you will intensify its ecstacy. Do you wish to love? Use love's litany, and the words will create the yearning from which the world fancies that they spring.

For Wilde, psychic determinist and mind-body monist[3] though at root he was, it is clear from the above that form and not content was to him the secret of life and, psychotherapist though he was not, there is much there that cognitivists and psychoanalysts alike would acclaim.

---

2 *The Picture of Dorian Gray* (Wilde, 1890b/1985, p.41).
3 'Those who see any difference between soul and body have neither' (Wilde, 1994, p.1244).

In the manner of Jung (with whom he also shared an interest in archetypes),[4] the oppositions and contradictions of the psyche were Wilde's roughage. He upheld imagination, in a deep sense, seeking to gaze on 'poetry and paradox dancing together'. For Wilde, influenced as he had been since the age of 11 by the Greek poets Homer and Pindar, the self had multiple possibilities and the imaginative creation of oneself was to be the essential task of life: 'We teach people how to remember, we never teach them how to grow' (*The Critic as Artist*, Wilde, 1890/1994, p.1152). Rather in the spirit of Rogers (Thorne, 1993) he believed that only by intensifying one's own personality could one be most true and most satisfying in one's interpretations of others (*The Critic as Artist*). This he also applied to the actor when he wrote: 'When a great actor plays Shakespeare, his own individuality becomes a vital part of the interpretation' (*ibid*, Part Two, p.1131).

Wilde's insistence in *The Decay of Lying* on the structuring role of art in social life could be said to place art at the centre rather than at the periphery of psychological investigation and thought. He worked, as did such varied thinkers as Chuang Tsu (Murray, 1971), Nietzsche (Schmidgall, 1994, p.310), Jung and Laing in the service of the destandardisation of consciousness, for the efflorescence of the individual personality against all externality and thus for self-definition, the eventuation of that which is within and the discovery of one's own virtue (see also Schmidgall, 1994, Chapter 15 on this).

Although Wilde may have antedated — and thought in sympathy with — many later psychologists it must not be forgotten that he was influenced greatly, in his creation of 'The English Renaissance' (Wilde, 1882/1995, e.g. pp.196–204) by his tutor at Oxford, the deeply secretive homosexual Walter Pater (see Pater, 1990). It was from Pater in his controversial conclusion to *The Renaissance* (Pater, 1873/1990, pp.44–7) and in his novel *Marius the Epicurean* (Pater, 1885/1985, p61) that the concept of experience as an end in itself, and the experience more correctly of *passion* as a fruit of quickened multiplied consciousness (p47) first re-emerged in late nineteenth-century writing after its early instatement in Roman Epicureanism. From those publications, particularly the former, Wilde was to borrow again and again (e.g. Wilde, 1882/1995, p.202; Wilde, 1890b/1985, p.41). But he was to imbricate some of these ideas into *The Picture of Dorian Gray* to such a degree that they were transformed qualitatively into a far bolder and more dangerous tale than anything Pater (though secretly he was delighted by the book) had ever dared to pen. Intellectual excitement and the reign of reverie; the search for new sights, perfumes, faces, whatever; art for art's sake; the splendour of the moment; the distaste for theory when pitted against life; the repudiation of habit; the truth of both opposites and the wish to 'burn always with a hard gem-like flame' (Pater, 1873/1990, pp.2, 46, 110, 144) in a quickened sense of ecstacy (p.47), all of these dazzling innervations to action, restrained rather than hedonistic though the text is, are from the quiet, closeted Pater, not the peacock Wilde. Pater himself lived a very introspective introverted life.

When Wilde was told in 1894 that Pater had died he said, 'Was he ever alive?' In Wilde's own hands, however, these ideas were to be metamorphosed instead into a philosophy for living life itself to a level eventually of decadent plenitude and voluptuousness. It is interesting that only *Salome* among his plays

---

4 *The Decay of Lying* (Wilde, 1891/1994, p.1082).

really meant anything to him (Ada Leverson in Schmidgall, 1994, p.315) and there sensuality reaches almost mystical levels (Ellmann, 1988, p.345). Virtually self-outing in *The Picture of Dorian Gray*, Wilde borderlines between *expression* of his sexuality and *knowledge* of his own decadence as perceived through the eyes of late-Victorian society. As would Pater, Lord Henry Wotton advised Dorian to strive for self-knowledge (p.41) but with the profound shame of the narcissist (Mollon, 1984), the young man does anything but seek knowledge of his true self (Marzillier, 1990, p.171). In anticipation of Wilde's own ruin his quest for Hellenic beauty and 'the fruit of quickened multiplied consciousness' (quickened because it is multiplied (Haley, 1985)) has meant the renunciation of all that is truly corporeal and irreconcilable in himself. The result is the return of that irreconcilable residue — now fully for the eyes of a deriding society — to destroy its possessor in a Bacchanalia of humiliation, degradation and defilement.

Borderlining: perfection born of sin

Oscar Wilde always believed in the truth of both poles (Ellmann, 1988, p.265) and his defeat at his trials in 1895 was both a perfect blend of them and an instantiation of contraries. The fact is that Queensberry, for all his effort and self-congratulation, did not ruin Oscar — Oscar wanted and had anticipated 'Regina versus Wilde' since his student days, it was a crescendo he had long coveted. He behaved 'stupidly'; 'vainly'; 'irrationally'; 'carelessly' because that future called to him as if from across time. Doom, a 'strange fatality' (Ellmann, 1988, p.92) awaited him and warned at a party by the society palmist Cheiro in 1893 that it was coming (not a warning that a man as superstitious as Wilde would ignore) he seemed to somehow relentlessly stride to meet it — breaking every rule of 'good sense' to get there. (Cheiro had said that his right hand was that of a king who would send himself into exile in about two years time. Wilde had walked out of the party on hearing this.) Oscar's was not a life slaughtered before time by the mob ready with fangs long dripping with saliva. On the contrary the ending in a dramatic sense was perfect, a playwright's master stroke. This was a play that would reverberate down the centuries. Going with the action yet resisting it, claiming innocence yet advertising guilt, unfairly treated yet blatantly asking for it, above the whole farcical scenario (and planning *The Ballad of Reading Gaol*) yet beneath it, caught in a web of lies yet completely honest — and finally dying prematurely yet perfectly on time. Wilde couldn't have orchestrated it all better if he had consciously planned it for decades. Instead I would claim that his unconscious and preconscious particularly after Cheiro's devastating reading (the reading was actually done blind with hands put through a curtain) was what gently structured, enabled and in the end permitted it. The enemy, the strange fatality he had feared yet yearned for, met him from the future like an old friend from the past. This was true Borderlining, living the ambiguity, ignoring the obvious and living on the edge, walking the tightrope with no net beneath and, of course, in the end, failing.

'The massacre of the moment'

Tragedian though eventually he was therefore to show himself, it is nonetheless quite easy to become angry with Oscar Wilde (see for example the vexation of Bartlett, 1993, pp.201–4). As he admitted to Conan Doyle (Pearson, 1946/1988, p.150) for the sake of art, sometimes for the sake of a rhyme, he often was untruthful and wrong. He was wrong in saying for example — (Mrs Cheveley in *An Ideal Husband* (Wilde, 1895/1994, p.520)) that science could never grapple with the irrational (see Skinner, 1953, p.55; Sutherland, 1992). He was wrong to say, as he often did, that in contrast to reason, the emotions lead us astray — as we know from the vile fruits of eugenics (Gould, 1981) reason can be the most seductive and misleading of guides. While it is true that life copies art, it is also true that art copies life, and that the relations between the two are complex (Rauschenberg 1990, p.14) — and while people can shape their own future, for many they are trapped by their situation (and also by poverty) and their room to manoeuvre is extremely limited.

With Rogers, Wilde would say (see Jackson, 1995) that a person could not believe in themselves and their decisions if they were not being themselves — and (with Freud) (*The Picture of Dorian Gray*, p.41) that relentless inhibition was demeaning and distorting of the Self. But why these processes had these effects was merely left to the reader's or listener's common sense. It also had to be said that Wilde was no more successful than anyone else with the same dilemma in resolving the contradiction between his psychic determinism and his voluntarism.

We may celebrate Wilde when he says that psychology is the process infrastructure of all plays (letter to Marie Prescott, April 1883, Hart-Davis, 1962/1989, p.50) but we have to remember that these plays often left his wife in tears — and not from laughing ('In married life affection comes when people thoroughly dislike each other' (in *An Ideal Husband*) and 'In married life, three is company and two is none' (in *The Importance of Being Earnest*)). Imagine also her reaction to 'The one charm of marriage is that it makes a life of deception absolutely necessary for both parties' in *The Picture of Dorian Gray* (Chapter 1) and 'A man can be happy with any woman as long as he does not love her' also in *Dorian Gray* (Chapter 15). (These examples are by no means exhaustive.)

It is true: Wilde neglected his wife, let money slip through his fingers like sand, smoked too much, drank too much, ate too much, lay in bed daily until after midday, was overdressed, overeducated, overconfident, plagiaristic, self-contradictory sometimes to a bewildering degree and (of course) sexually scandalous. He had bad front teeth, possibly slight acromegaly (an underactive thyroid some might say), was pedantic about table manners and feigned, in typical Oxbridge fashion, utter indolence in all matters regarding his studies. He was also fat. Yet it is also true that today, despite his many imperfections, Wilde stands tall as one of the most brilliant and colourful personalities of the last two centuries. He may have been categorisable as 'very disturbed' (Post, 1994) but most of all, and despite all his posing, he was a human being of vividness and vitality; a man who lived for trials and tribulations, for intensity, for *moments* rather than by theories or in the service of a planned enterprise. During his productive years he never tired of demonstrating how the creative possibilities of individuals could weave rich dramatic tapestries of life out of simple and basic elements. Often these elements stood in opposition to each other, but in the tension of their contrast and contradiction was always the possibility of an (unpredictable) story — be it a comedy, a tragedy, a romance or whatever. While the scientists studied the threads, Wilde embraced the embroidery and the riot of colour. His own 'therapy' was to launch himself into *life*, provoking growth by the alternating confirmation and disconfirmation provided by the jolts of daily social existence and conversation, to creatively transform the world, rather than by 'consciousness expansion' in the confines of the consulting room, to discover one's own 'space'. If the supreme object of life is to live, in search of 'the pleasure that abideth for a moment' (Wilde, 1994, p.300) we must really ask ourselves whether or not, in contrast to Wilde and his 'life for art's sake' (Ellmann, 1988, p.359) our own obsessions one century on with therapeutically engineered normalisation, integration, mood stability, impulse management and rational living have not made us now quite pale and tepid in comparison?

13
Dostoyevsky:
the underground man

Since the publication of Dostoyevsky's *Notes from Underground* (1864/1972) every nation has identified its own style of Underground Man (Frank, 1961/1988). The concept has indeed become a powerful archetypal literary image but like any archetype it escapes and indeed needs to escape precise definition. In Western, particularly British society, the man of the Underground is to be found, like Desmond, sat deep in cafes and sandwich bars, like myself in cellar clubs and like so many others in flats and bedsitters, behind drawn curtains, embodying the image in the film *Taxi Driver* of 'the man and his room'. Our Underground Man is shy, sensitive, unable to mix easily. He is shunned, misunderstood, quiet yet tormented. A man both above the common herd through his insight and education and yet simultaneously insignificant, an insect, morally depraved, socially skill-less, alternating in company between inarticulateness and verbal diarrhoea. He is a man, and ironically pretty well always a man, not a woman, who cannot mesh with others yet not through lack of feeling or lack of empathy for the human condition, not at all; it is simply that he is stood right by the track and yet miles from the nearest station.

Rather in the manner of Bleuler's original definition of the schizoid personality: he alternates between sentimentality and brutal indifference and then chastises himself for both. He is never at peace, seems unable to be happy, and as Freud observed in Dostoyevsky's writings, bereft of love.

Dostoyevsky is at his most naked in the first half of the novella (Frank, 1961/1988) but it is because of this that his writing is so compelling. *Notes from Underground* is at times close to stream-of-consciousness writing and its density is so high that one feels that one accesses its author directly. What would normally be censored is there on the page, the honesty of Nietzschean tone, at times, is blistering, having read it one feels ashamed of one's own self-deceptions and petty concealments.

It is recognised that the book was written as a satirical reaction and antidote to Nicola G. Chernyshevsky's novel *'What is to be done?'* (1863). This was a Utopian plea for human conduct and the organisation of society to be based on reason, science and enlightened self-interest. The quest of the Underground Man is to assert, somehow, anyhow, the individual willing personality against the scientific nihilistic predictions of a deterministic calculus even if, at the last gasp, it means 'going mad' to refute it. The Underground Man is the artist making a raid on predictability in the spirit of asserting the autonomy of the individual and the capriciousness of the emotions. Though egocentric, his quest is a profoundly moral quest to undercut 1860s Russian nihilism with 1840s Russian romantic idealism. Although mid nineteenth-century the dilemma is uncannily modern. The determinists of the 1860s have their counterparts today. The romantics of the 1840s are reduplicated today in all who assert the autonomy of the individual as a prerequisite for the existence of morality *per se*. Deterministic nihilism while posing as the saviour of society runs the risk of totally undermining it.

The Underground Man, however, delights in polarities and contradictions. He champions free will even unto madness yet finds himself caught in ruts, stagnant, unable to change. He scorns the destructive power of determinism yet seeks, and misuses, power himself. He is the enemy of rational egoism yet he himself is the ultimate in self-centredness, unable to love, unable to be good.

In *Notes from Underground* Dostoyevsky wrote that salvation from these impossible contradictions was to be found in faith and in Christ but this was censored (Mochulsky, 1971; Conradi, 1988). Elsewhere he wrote that the fullest development of the personality was to be found in the dissolution of the I and in the act of living for others (*Journal* 16 April 1864 in Conradi, 1988, p.39). This of course is the mystical refutation of deterministic individualism.

Psychologically *Notes from Underground* can also be read as both a celebration of and a deterrent to extreme introversion. The heightened consciousness of the Underground Man and his extreme sensitivity give him an awareness and insight far beyond that of the lout but at the same time he sacrifices the latter's simplicity and directness. The lout may be stupid but in his ignorance he is undivided and hence behaves 'as a Man'. The Underground Man, aware of all the possibilities, contradictions and consequences is frozen by his complexity and behaves 'as a mouse'.

The lout acts and loves and fights. Because he does not reflect, the scientist might indeed be able to predict him but he cares not. He merely lives and does. The Underground Man, however, is the prisoner not so much of scientific predictions but of his own self-consciousness. Because his world is so centred on himself he cannot reach out and unreflectively give himself to another or indeed genuinely empathise with them. They are either in his power or he is in theirs. He dare not love lest he tyrannise the beloved with the new-found moral superiority of 'he-who-can-love'.

The Underground Man is never named. He is 40 and has been underground like this, we are told, 'for about 20 years'. Yet he proclaims himself a flag bearer of the complexity and messiness of life as it is lived over the tidy conceptualisation and neat simplicity of the scientific determinists. This theme of course is modern. But the Underground Man has a great deal to say and he warns that when others of this genre come above ground, they will 'talk and talk and talk'. This talk, however, when all is said and done, is nonetheless predicated on courage. The Underground Man writes (p.123) 'as for what concerns me personally, after all I have only carried to a logical conclusion in my life what you yourselves didn't dare take more than half-way; and you supposed your cowardice was common sense, and comforted yourself with the self-deception'.

So *that* is what it is all about: courage. Courage to reach to a deeper truth, a truth deeper than the facile pronouncements of the determinist. He writes (p.38) 'the whole business of humanity consists solely in this — that a man should constantly prove to himself that he is a man and not a sprig in a barrel-organ! To prove it even at the expense of his own skin.' To the Underground Man the greatest sin or weakness for a man is that he is predictable by science, an automaton, a piano-key, then he is not a man. Science is seen as dehumanising and were it successful, would leave us with 'nothing to do' but live out our predicted lives like machines. This we must avoid at all costs even if it means curses, chaos and destruction — and were that too predicted — then madness, *anything* to avoid the deterministic curse of reason.

In writing in this way The Underground Man is not merely arresting the caprice of Man, he is fighting for the moral high ground, thrusting upwards to escape the identity of 'sprig in a barrel-organ', fighting for the dignity of humanity. As a man of heightened consciousness his predicament is tragic. He is a part-prisoner of his own education. With the prostitute Lisa, in the second half of the story, he talks of love, as she detects, as if from a book. Her own simple heart is the more loving. For all his high thoughts he is unable to indwell in the most essential of human emotions and weeps that he cannot, no matter how hard he twists his intellect this way and that, even be *good*.

Psychologically the story is a reminder of the perils of education and of the intellect. The story continually harps on the chasm between the refined intellect and the simplicity and brutal freshness of 'ordinary people'. The Underground Man craves recognition for his educated consciousness, fails, then chastises himself for his arrogance. His sensitivity enables him to miss nothing yet he cannot take any advantage of this perceptiveness and is scorned by his peers for his clumsiness and awkward hostilities.

The novella is a tribute to the revelation of the personality via what is available to consciousness. Inferences are unnecessary, the phenomenology, at least in places, lays the soul bare. In asserting the primacy of the will and in shunning the explanation of that which can be seen by that which cannot the text certainly has an existential tone (Kaufman, 1956). Its pessimism, however, is a far cry from the West Coast human potential movement, and given Dostoyevsky's (censored) belief in salvation in Christ it is not a manuscript that is a testament to humanism. The themes are European not Californian with no reference whatever to innate goodness nor (tragically) to self-creation. The Underground Man takes us to a point where we might surmise that self-creation is possible but he is pessimistic and himself remains stuck in spite, petty vanities and periodic self-flagellation. We are left feeling sad, slightly hopeful but mindful of the enormity of this (imperative) task.

The Underground Man, like all Underground Men, is angry, divided, sensitive, pessimistic. He alternates between vanity and self-abasement, between craving the company of others and imposing his will on them. He seeks power, but when he has achieved it, he holds those over whom he has power in contempt. He is not only the neurotic personality of mid nineteenth-century Russia, fighting for validity, he is, in this quest, the neurotic personality of *all* times.

Of course the essence of any novel or novella by a great writer cannot be captured in words. That is part of its magic. But here Dostoyevsky probes to truths about human personality, to the inner man, beyond anything that science or cognition could provide. It is part of the thesis of this book that personality is a musical concept and it is this music that the artist, rather than the scientist, can reach, express and apprehend. It is the way Dostoyevsky writes, the metaphors he uses, the rhythm and grain of the text and the themes and conflicts he describes that together take us beneath the surface of the individual to the magic also of what it is to be human.

14
Stories, poems and personality
by Jonathan Smith

Unlike the scientific psychologist whose work is driven by the values of objectivity, quantification and causal explanation, writers of stories and poems are, for the most part, fundamentally different in all these respects:

- Their concern is to capture the experience, the phenomenology of the subject of their piece. Subjective experience is at the heart of their work. To present 'What it feels like' to be a person figuring in a piece of literature is a primary goal of the writer's quest; when critics talk of the credibility of a story or a character, they are referring as often as not to the degree to which the writer has portrayed the character or story as recognisable; that is to say behaving and responding in ways which the reader could imagine people responding and behaving. The characters are in some way or another following laws of human behaviour as subjectively understood and recognised by the reader, based on their own experience, not as proved to be the case by objective evidence.
- Measurement and quantification simply do not feature as relevant to a writer, whereas they are regarded as a way of sharpening up the precision of objective data and evidence.
- Description rather than explanation is the focus of a writer's craft. To characterise, to give an account of some experience or event, to capture the flavour or taste of being in certain situations is what good writers do so well, rather than explain in terms of specifying prior conditions for it to occur. Their descriptions often will entail or imply a causal sequence, as for example when a character in a story is shown to have built their life in reaction to childhood trauma or hardship; but the pleasure or craft to be found in a story does not depend on the establishment of such causal connections. Rather, the reader finds the whole account credible and plausible, only partly by virtue of the implied causal link. It is not at all *the* point of storytelling to show how some set of circumstances causes some particular effect, in the way it *is* the point of science.

And yet, powerful writing (whether in literature or in the social and physical sciences) shares with good psychology the capacity to illuminate the human condition, to excite the reader and open his/her horizons to new perspectives, to as yet unthought-of ways of seeing or thinking, to capture the imagination and resonate empathically so that the reader either sees the world anew or experiences a newly found validation of what had been hitherto merely a half-suspected or dimly perceived truth.

In novels and plays, writers introduce us to characters and, when they are well-formed and plausibly drawn, the reader may begin to see the world through the character's eyes. We are offered a portrait of a personality and an intimate view of a mind and its thoughts and feelings at work. We are shown how particular combinations of circumstances may result in certain response patterns from the characters. Sometimes those responses may be quite reasonable, sometimes quite unreasonable, but either way we are presented for our consideration a sort of mini-model, or a fictional case history of how a particular person thinks, acts and feels when confronted with a particular set of circumstances. Great writers, compassionate writers succeed in painting their characters in such a way that we understand how a combination of their childhood circumstances, adult environment, and their own inner psychic dynamics (vanities and aspirations, yearnings and rivalries, fears and resistances) all contribute to their current behaviour. We the readers get to appreciate the complexity of human action and, in so doing, to understand and thereby to forgive a little more. Storytelling can humanise us because it can reveal the complexity and inherent ambiguity of life itself and show how the choices characters make are often not straightforward and represent a compromise between conflicting needs, passions and duties. As we see literary characters wrestling with dilemmas of living, so, hopefully, we can regard with greater tolerance the difficulties we encounter facing our own.

Poets can be psychologists, too. Some may simply use the form of poetry to tell a tale which could otherwise have been told in prose, as in epic poetry. Other poems can address what are effectively philosophical problems of meaning and purpose. But there are those whose interest lies in reflecting back to the reader certain aspects of our experiences, or at least, some of our experiences, which the poet wants to highlight and portray sometimes with the effect of presenting a hypothesis, a generalisation, about human emotions or human relationships. The particular gift of the poet lies in their skill in capturing the essence of an experience by using economical and perhaps particularly pointed choice of words.

In this chapter I would like to consider two ways in which literature and personality theories touch each other: first I will provide a few examples of writing which (at least for some readers) manage to capture human experience and the richness of human personality, and I will explore possible 'translations' of these literary accounts into their scientific psychological equivalents. Second I will explore the recent move in narrative psychology which calls for a redefinition of traditional concepts such as 'self' or 'person' in terms of stories or biographical narratives. Here the view is that literary forms, particularly the form of the story, are much more appropriate for describing and accounting for human personality, than traditional 'objective' theories with their emphasis on measured variables and experimental methods.

Managing emotions

The Poison Tree
William Blake

I was angry with my friend
I told my wrath, my wrath did end.
I was angry with my foe:
I told it not, my wrath did grow

And I watered it in fears,
Night and Morning with my tears,
And I sunned it with smiles,
And with soft deceitful wiles,

And it grew both day and night,
Till it bore an apple bright,
And my foe beheld it shine,
And he knew that it was mine,

And into my garden stole
When the night had veil'd the pole:
In the morning glad I see
My foe outstretch'd beneath the tree.

William Blake's poem *The Poison Tree* presents two ways of dealing with anger, the Cathartic, to tell it and to end it, and the Withholding, to conceal it and to have it grow. It is a fictional case study, told in poetry. In the condensed language of poetry, it contains both a generalisation, and a prescription. The generalisation: anger held in unexpressed will grow in intensity and, eventually, turn to poison, and the prescription: express your angry feelings; that way the poisonous feelings will dissipate and disappear. Already we have lost the economy of expression which poetry retains and begun perhaps too to lose some of the impact which Blake's punchy rhyming makes on the reader. We have, however, begun to move towards the language of the scientific psychologist. Before long we will arrive at the neutered impersonal account of anger presented by Hokanson (1961) or Dimsdale et al. (1986), whose research into the link between heart disease and the expression of hostility clearly supports Blake's hypothesis; opportunities to vent hostility do indeed seem to lower blood pressure.

Blake's verses do not simply state that wrath told will end and that wrath told not will grow. It also provides a vivid and image-rich account of the process of that growth. How our fears and tears nourish and sustain our wrath, and how we will go to considerable length to conceal it from the outside world with sunny and deceitful smiles. As a description of the psychology of anger-management, this will strike many chords in contemporary readers, and the fact that Blake was writing two hundred years ago suggests he may have spotted a relatively constant feature of human social/emotional processes. His description of the way fears and tears keep anger alive sound also highly compatible with the view of the cognitive therapists regarding the power of recurrent thoughts to maintain bad and destructive feelings. If we keep running over events and conversations in our minds we keep re-igniting the accompanying feelings, often finding a new slant on the scene which can fuel the flames of indignation and self-righteousness still further.

Parents' effects on children

This Be the Verse
Philip Larkin

They fuck you up your mum and dad
They may not mean to but they do
They fill you with the faults they had
And add some extra just for you

But they were fucked up in their turn
By fools in old-style hats and coats
Who half the time were soppy-stern
And half at one another's throats

Man hands on misery to man.
It deepens like a coastal shelf.
Get out as early as you can,
and don't have any kids yourself.

This bleak assessment of the role of parents on their growing offspring struck a powerful chord with Larkin's public. Both cynical and yet with a reluctant streak of compassion ('they may not mean to'), it hints at the inevitability of parental damage. It is a strangely comforting message in that not only do I not need to blame myself for my shortcomings and misery, but I don't even have to blame my parents ('they were fucked up in their turn') and therefore can neatly side-step any invitation to feel guilty for so doing. Blame and responsibility in fact disappear into the mists of history, and as the responsible agents become vaguer and ever more elusive so does my own impotence become ever more entrenched. There's really nothing I will be able to do about my condition, so I might as well resign myself to it.

Admittedly this stance of passive pessimism is not particularly typical of the positivist psychologist, as represented for example by the cognitive therapist who would attempt to unpack 'misery' into its constituent cognitive parts with a view to replacing them with more adaptive non-miserable cognitions. The inevitability of Larkin's misery again suggests an immunity to any such pragmatic tampering. After all, the misery has been handed down from generation to generation and is not likely to yield to the interventions of a therapist. This is not stated, of course, but implied and is an example of where the evocative power of the story told by the poet is actually misleading. After all, empirical evidence in favour of cognitive therapy is well documented. Nonetheless it represents, again in a stark and memorable form, a point of view arrived at by several psychologists studying child development and particularly attachment processes (e.g. overly permissive parents *and* those who use physical punishment frequently or erratically are likely to have children showing increased levels of aggression themselves, as summarised in Mussen et al. (1990, p.269)). Even Carl Rogers, in spite of his reputation for emphasising the potential for good in human nature, describes how children inevitably learn 'conditions of worth', however benign; i.e. we learn that we are only worthy and acceptable on condition that we fulfil various requirements presented explicitly or implicitly by, for the most part, our parents. Rogers describes this process as largely a universal one, part of the human condition as it were, and quotes Kierkegaard to strengthen his case: 'The basic estrangement in man . . . is that . . . he is not true to himself . . . this is not a conscious choice, but a natural, tragic, development in infancy'. Kierkegaard identifies the estrangement; Rogers adds the role of the parents. Larkin re-states the observation in rather more earthy language.

It is important to acknowledge, however, that scientific psychology has a role to play in debates such as these. We do know, for example from the work of Diana Baumrind, that there are degrees of 'fuck-up' associated with the behaviour of parents. In her work on parenting styles she has shown how certain types of parenting style seem, in European and American cultures at least, to be more damaging than others. In particular the autocratic and permissive styles are associated with less confident and productive behaviour in the offspring than the authoritative style (Baumrind, 1980, 1989). Poetry can be a dangerous medium in this regard. In the hands of a skilled poet such as Larkin, the (partial) truth about the way parents can damage their children's growth can be expressed so evocatively and convincingly that other parts of the truth, i.e. that some parents can actually provide 'good enough' environments for children to retain their capacity for some healthy and constructive growth, can recede into the background. Poetic insight can only ever be partial.

Reactions to death 1

Do Not Go Gentle into that Good Night
Dylan Thomas

Do not go gentle into that good night,
Old age should burn and rage at close of day;
Rage, rage against the dying of the light.

Though wise men at their end know dark is right,
Because their words had forked no lightning they
Do not go gentle into that good night.

. . .

And you, my father, there on the sad height,
Curse, bless, me now with your fierce tears, I pray.
Do not go gentle into that good night.
Rage, rage against the dying of the light.

What do we make of death? Death as the 'last taboo' does not fit comfortably into the world of street-wise catch phrases and cool image-maintenance. The process of dying has not received a great deal of attention from psychologists; bereavement perhaps a little more. Nonetheless, psychologists have written about it, one of the best known accounts being that of Elizabeth Kubler-Ross, who describes five stages which the dying person may go through; Denial, Anger, Bargaining, Depression, Acceptance (1970). Dylan Thomas' passionate plea effectively invites us to throw ourselves fully into stage 3 (anger) and to beware the apparent attractions of stage 5, acceptance ('though wise men at their end know dark is right'). His poem has wide appeal, which suggests that many recognise the need for a rageful outburst at the prospect of the loss of someone loved (the poem was written on the occasion of his father's death). And yet, perhaps particularly in Anglo-Saxon cultures, we learn the norm of self-control, restraint on passion, the value of dignity and private grief; to rant and rage at an Anglican funeral indeed would seem the height of bad manners and poor taste. Thomas' poem speaks to a part of us normally restrained by these socialised introjects and calls us to honour our passion, not to be ashamed of it.

This form of poetry appeals perhaps precisely because it addresses and calls forth those parts of a personality which are normally left in the shadow and allowed only part or in some cases no expression at all. It is not nice to rage, we 'should' have grown up and out of 'that kind of thing'. And yet the strength of the appeal of this poem testifies to the fact that many of us have not at all left these emotional levels of responding behind; that we do in fact need to own up to and express these feelings if we are to become fully all that we can be. In this sense Dylan Thomas is showing himself to be in the same camp as the humanistic psychologists. Both Maslow and Rogers describe the 'self-actualised' or the 'fully functioning' person respectively as someone who has become all that they can be, and both propose the drive towards self-actualisation as a central motivator behind human life and behaviour. Dylan Thomas reminds us that there is indeed a time and a place for raging, and that we need to acknowledge and respect that.

Reactions to death 2

A different account of the aftermath of death is offered by Anne Tyler in her novel, *Saint Maybe*. Published in 1992, the book tells the story of the Bedloe family who inhabit suburban Baltimore. Of the three children, Claudia, the eldest has married and left home, leaving Danny, 25, and Ian, 17. Danny marries Lucy who brings with her two children from an earlier relationship and she soon falls pregnant, giving birth to little Daphne. Unfortunately Ian has calculated that Daphne has come along less than nine months after she and Danny were married, and as he discovers that Lucy keeps spending time away from the home in unexplained ways, Ian concludes that she has a lover somewhere. One evening when Ian has been baby-sitting for Lucy, and she still hasn't come home hours after she promised she would, Ian, exasperated beyond measure, tells his brother of his suspicions: how often she is out, how she comes home 'perfumed and laughing and wearing clothes she can't afford . . . how come she married you quick as a flash and then had a baby just seven months later?' (p. 45). Danny says nothing but drops Ian off home. As Ian hears his brother's Chevy roaring and squealing off down the road, he suddenly realises the car is not slowing down at the brick wall at the end of the road; instead, 'there was a gigantic, explosive, complicated crash, then a delicate tinkle and then silence' (p. 46).

The death hits the family members in different ways. Lucy has three children: Agatha (the oldest) and Thomas from her earlier partner, and Daphne, after she married Danny. Thomas at first keeps forgetting that Danny is dead; three mornings in a row he asks, 'Do you think Danny will fix apple pancakes for breakfast?' This infuriates Agatha who starts to remind him of every detail of that dreadful evening; when Thomas clamps his hands over his ears Agatha presses on:

'"When the phone rang and we didn't pick it up . . . and when the door banged we didn't unlock it."

Thomas said, "Nee-nee-nee-nee-nee!" but she rode over it.

"Mama had to crawl in a window, and she tore her sleeve and was crying . . ."

"Shut up! Shut up! Shut up!" says Thomas.

She just had these urges to be evil to him. She couldn't say exactly why.'

Thomas' forgetting, Agatha's desperate taunting of her younger brother, each have an awful ring of truth about them, a plausibility. How children cope with the death of a family member, how any of us cope, even if the person is only a step-parent, can never be predicted. But in the depiction of this small, domestic breakfast scene, the author manages to hint, lightly, but no less poignantly at the confusion and distress, the denial and the hurtful rage, which can follow in the aftermath of a loss.

Ian, the younger brother, has a more complicated reaction, as perhaps befits a blood relative and sibling, a relationship with some 17 years worth of history by now, and a person whose exchange with his dead brother seems to have been the stimulus which provoked Danny's taking of his own life. Chapter 3 of the book opens with an account of how Ian tries to accommodate the fact of Danny's death, comparing the process to that of 'an amoeba Ian had watched in ninth grade biology . . . [as it] . . . approached a dot of food and gradually surrounded it. Then it had moved on, wider now and blunter, distorted to accommodate the dot of food within' (p.82). He runs over and over the facts and the events of that night, desperately trying on alternative explanations: maybe it was an accident, after all he had been drinking; trying to make himself believe that 'everyone on earth walked around with at least one unbearable guilty secret hidden away inside': maybe if he confessed to his mother, she would forgive him with a 'Why, sweetheart, is that all that's bothering you?' Immediately, though, he realises that if he confessed, his mother would realise it was no accident, and 'if his mother felt any worse than she did already, he thought it would kill her' (p. 84).

These two conflicting thoughts of Ian's, the magical, 'If-I-tell-my-mother-everything-will-be-alright' and the sombre realism of the likely actual consequences, nicely present for the reader the operation of different sides to a personality. The Parent-Adult-Child model of Transactional Analysis could accommodate this description with ease, with the magical Mummy-will-make-it-all-OK' thinking of the wretched Child ego state being superseded by the realistic, logical prediction of the Adult ego state. Other theories of the self, for example those which emphasise the multiple nature of the self, or which talk about Subpersonalities (e.g. Rowan, 1990), would also find their theories well represented in this account of Ian's churning thoughts about his brother's death. The theoretical statements would be unlikely to convey the experience of that inner dialogue in the way that Tyler's fictional story manages to do.

Ian also dreams about his brother: standing in the doorway jingling change and offering to pay him for the baby-sitting for that evening. A few weeks later

Ian calls home from college only to hear yet another piece of devastating news: Lucy, Danny's wife, has taken an overdose and died. The little girl Agatha had phoned to say that 'Mama keeps sleeping and won't wake up'. The final blow to Ian's battered ego comes when he learns on the day of the funeral that Lucy had been seen by a neighbour systematically shoplifting. He finally realises that she didn't, after all, have a lover; that the new clothes he had seen her wearing were stolen, not presents from another man. His guilt is complete. 'Oh God, this is the one last little dark dot I can't possibly absorb' he thinks to himself, and, as he and his parents leave the house to walk to the car, 'Ian felt bruised all down the front of his body, as if he'd been kicked' (p. 100).

This catalogue of disasters may sound barely plausible when presented in this summary form; and yet Anne Tyler succeeds in creating a thoroughly credible sequence of events. The account of Ian's thoughts and feelings sound heart-rendingly likely, as they veer from puzzlement to denial to magical wishes it never happened, to the almost physical sense of battering described above.

Tyler allows us access to Ian's vulnerable and private mental interior in such a way that we recognise ourselves in the play of Ian's poor mind. We can acknowledge how that degree of pain would produce a similar set of mental gyrations in anyone and we end up with a clearer and more vivid picture of a mind at work than we might be likely to do from a more academic and impersonal account of the same processes.

Ian's redemption comes in the form of the *Church of the Second Chance* which he happens to be passing one day and is drawn inside by the sound of a hymn. There comes a point in the service where any member of the congregation is invited to 'step forward and ask for our prayers' Ian does so and ends up confessing to the pastor his part in his brother's death. 'Do you think I'm forgiven?' Ian asks the pastor. 'Goodness no,' says Reverend Emmett briskly. 'You have to offer reparation — concrete, practical reparation...'. The discussion which follows results in Ian accepting that he has to give up his college course and devote himself to the care and upbringing of his brother's children and, during the course of the rest of the book, we hear how Ian does just that and eventually out of this kind of penance he finds his own love. The redemptive tone of the second half of the story takes it somewhat out of the domain of mainstream psychology, although the account of Ian's reaching for the rather simple born-again kind of church community again rings true and is reminiscent of some of the case histories one comes across of the appeal these organisations can have for the damaged and suffering in society.

Abnormal psychology and literature

The portrayal of the mentally ill and disturbed is a far from uncommon theme in novels and literature; the raving lunatic, the dangerous psychopath, the suicidal depressive are all familiar and often cliched stereotypes, and only too often the fictional portrayal of these personalities is misleading and downright unhelpful to sufferers and their families. Sometimes, however, the novelist or writer can capture the feel of the life of the mentally ill person in a way that formal psychiatric diagnosis and theorising will rarely if ever succeed in doing. Sensitive and effective writing can paint portraits which are human and complex enough to be realistic and in some cases the reader can end up being truly educated by a novelist or storyteller. They may find themselves feeling more insight and sympathy than one might expect after any number of worthy lectures from psychiatrists.

Charles Harwell, in his book *Disordered Personalities in Literature*, has collected a whole range of character depictions taken from authors ranging from Dorothy Parker, Jean-Paul Sartre, John Mortimer, through to John Steinbeck, Lawrence Durrell and the Marquis de Sade, and matched each against one of the categories of the DSMIII listing of psychiatric disorders. Harwell's book was published in 1980 and it contains 27 brief character sketches intended to portray diagnoses such as schizophrenia, paranoid disorders, affective and anxiety disorders, psychosexual and personality disorders.

Harwell recognises the complementarity of psychology and literature:
'Each probes the complexities of human perception, emotion and behaviour; each assesses the impact of environment and personal relationships on an individual. Each contributes in its own special way, to an understanding of personality . . . While psychology strives for clinical objectivity, literature portrays characters in all their richness and intricacy . . . Literature presents the fierce emotions that many people experience and some cannot control' (pp. xiii–xiv).

For example: Sally Benson's short story, *Little Woman* describes the coming together and early married life of Penny, a short, petite woman and Ralph, over six foot tall who loves to take her in his arms, guide and protect her. Penny in turn loves to be little and to look up to Ralph. When Ralph goes on a business trip to Chicago, Penny becomes anxious about her security in the house and insists that he call her every night he is away. As the story ends, Ralph is just beginning to appreciate the burden that such dependency imposes on partners:
'He did not notice that the cab had stopped in front of their apartment until Penny's voice gaily brought him back to earth. It was habit which made him pick her up and carry her across the wet, slippery pavement. And for such a little woman, she felt surprisingly heavy in his arms' (p. 246).

DSMIV describes as one of the disorders of personality, the *Dependent Personality Disorder*, and some of the main features of this personality type include: allowing others to make their decisions for them; desperate to avoid rejection; feeling uncomfortable or helpless when alone; difficulty in initiating projects on their own. The character of Penny in this story certainly provides a close match to these traits and yet is presented in a way that makes her identifiable. We feel we know that type, even though we may not have a diagnostic label for her.

Somatoform disorders are psychological conditions which manifest themselves in physical form. The sufferer will experience physical symptoms (pains, paralysis, loss of sight or voice) but there will be no organic damage or dysfunction. The assumption is that anxiety, or some other form of psychological process, lies behind the symptom and in some way fuels it. The symptom in turn will serve to cope with or defend against the inner conflict or unbearable feeling.

Paul Gallico's story of *The Enchanted Doll* is offered as a portrayal of someone suffering from this condition. The story tells of an encounter between a New York physician and an apparently crippled young girl, Essie Nolan, who is forced to spend her days making dolls by her crude and greedy cousin Rose Callamit.

Essie's parents were killed in an accident when she was 15, and while there was some real damage she suffered at the time of the accident, her present condition, listless and helpless, depressed and virtually bed-bound, exacerbated the deformity and had reduced her to a shadow. The doctor falls in love with her, but is soon after dismissed by the cruel Rose who fears the loss of the income Essie's dolls bring. Eventually the doctor finds a way to return and take Essie away to be his wife and everything turns out fine in the end. In the story the doctor recognises Essie's true condition: a broken spirit, taunted and bullied by her foul cousin and, above all, starved of love.

Such a poetic and perhaps sentimental account would need translating into the more detached and formal language of the DSM; a set of physical symptoms with no organic explanation, but which enables the patient to keep her inner conflict at least partly out of awareness. (When the doctor first examines Essie, he asks her to walk towards him; she pleads with him, 'Don't, don't make me'. She cannot bear to face the psychological pain associated with her physical condition.) And yet the story creates a living world populated by virtual people and this creation communicates the state of 'somatoform' illnesses with a vividness and a sense of human compassion inevitably lacking from the psychiatric criteria.

Self and identity as story

Often when teaching psychology, I have felt disappointed when the syllabus has contained references to the self; my disappointment has focussed on the failure of any of the major theorists of 'the self' to construct an adequate account of the thing. Individual contributions have all certainly had something to offer; William James (as is so often the case) seems to stimulate the imagination of students at least as much if not more than most contemporary theorists with his notions of the multiple aspects of the self and the inherently social origins of our various 'subselves'; Assagioli and, more recently, Rowan have extended and elaborated the notion of 'subpersonalities' with the claim that the self cannot be fairly regarded as a unitary item, but that it rather has a range of manifestations.

Carl Rogers on the other hand reminds us of a quite different phenomenological perspective on the self when he describes it as an item of subjective experience:

> ... that portion of the individual's experience [which] becomes differentiated and *symbolised* in an *awareness* of being ... Such awareness may be described as *self-experience* (Rogers, 1959).

From the psychoanalytic tradition we have other versions of the self: Winnicott is well known for his distinction between the 'true' and the 'false' self: the true self requiring continuing recognition and reflecting in the mirror of the mother's face, and the false self being constituted by all the strategies the child has to find to comply with mother's rejection (Winnicott, 1965). While Winnicott is less explicit about a definition of the true self, he does propose one 'essential element' in the true self, namely, 'creative originality'. The 'spontaneous gesture' is linked with the idea of the true self.

A very different idea of self or rather Self is to be found in Jungian writing, where the Self is described as a far less personal entity, but more of an over-arching, organising principle of the potential wholeness of the personality.

However, in Jungian psychology, there is something abstract and universal about the Self which marks it off from other versions. The Self is almost seen as an independently existing psychic form with which the individual has to learn to make a relationship, which in turn is sometimes characterised as the task of a lifetime.

The social identity theorists (Tajfel,1982; Robinson,1986) emphasise the social nature of identity, and how the processes of identification with reference groups in the wider society, and social comparison, all have a part to play in the formation of identity. In this model we build up our sense of who we are partly at least by identifying with and comparing ourselves with various groups of others, whether work colleagues, neighbourhoods, ethnic or religious groups, or of course, family. Erikson's writings on identity attempt a more sophisticated and interactive approach as he argues that the quest for identity involves both inner and outer worlds; for Erikson, identity requires an active organising and reorganising of one's experiences so far into a sense of where I am now and who am I to become in this society. It is a quest which tends to preoccupy during adolescence, but which is by no means always quiescent at other times. For Erikson, identity needs to take on possible themes and values from the surrounding culture, but to make them his/her own. It involves a mutual acknowledgement and construction between the individual and society.

All these versions of self and identity (and of course there are more) have something to offer, each highlighting one or more aspects of the self, and yet none of them seem able to capture the full complexity of what is involved in a person's lived life; a complete 'personality'.

An approach which seems to offer a way of pulling these various ideas together has been developed by Dan MacAdams (1988, 1993) and Kenneth Gergen (Gergen and Gergen, 1983), among others. This is the notion that one possible answer to the questions 'Who am I?', 'What is the self?', could be 'I am a story' 'The self is a narrative'. The concept of the narrative nature of a person offers several features which seem to match the experience of a lived self, what it feels like to be a self and to have an identity.

A story is dynamic; it moves over time, making possible past, present and future. At any point in a story there will be a history and a possibility of a future. Markus and Murelius' work on possible selves highlight the idea of a self containing its own future. They have shown how we carry around (often implicit) versions of 'ourselves in the future'. The movement of stories over time also allows of course for them to be revised, rewritten, for alternative versions to be created. It could indeed be argued that one of the effects of psychotherapy is just that: to help the client rewrite their life story.

A story can be fragmented and chaotic or single-track and highly coherent. So it is with a self. A person's identity can have taken them through a whole range of different careers for example, each of which shaping their identity in particular and contrasting ways, or they may have chosen one particular occupational identity and stayed with it throughout their life. All the projects, relationships and events which go to make up our life may be linked logically and consistently with each other, or may leap all over the place, both metaphorically and physically.

Stories can contain a range of possible plots. Some may have a whole range of subplots each with a rich life of its own, in addition to the main storyline, others are largely the account of one particular sequence. Some of the subplots may be to do with family and relationships, shifting allegiances and divided loyalties; others to do with schemes, plans and adventures which the characters in the story involve themselves in. That is to say that stories vary in complexity, as do people's identities.

Stories can contain a widely varying number of characters. Some are littered with vivid and exciting people each of whom may fill the frame for a short while before vanishing from one's life space, others concentrate on just a few, perhaps only one main relationship around whom the whole story hinges. The characters and relationships encountered during a life very often provide the most absorbing and engaging themes of any story.

What then are stories and how do they come to provide such an appealing model for self and identity?

Telling stories seems a characteristic form of human behaviour. Most if not all cultures seem to do it, even though the forms of storytelling may differ widely, from groups gathered around a night-time fire listening to the solo teller, to latter-day groups gathered around perhaps one twentieth-century version of the camp fire . . . the cinema screen. Such groups seem to have at least one characteristic in common, the desire to have a series of events recounted to them, which above all, captures their attention. Individual stories may serve a variety of functions: some may amuse; some may instruct; others may thrill, but a good story, whatever its function, will leave us with a sense of completion and absorption. That is to say, they must keep us, the listeners/readers, firmly under their spell if we are to find the story satisfying.

Good stories have that effect on us. They take us up into themselves, invite us in and then sustain the involvement by engaging us in the action, the relationships between the characters, the atmosphere and mood.

The Jungian writer James Hillman (1975) suggests that story is an archetype, that we are naturally drawn both to stories we hear which show us how to make sense of events and people out there, and to our own experience as story : 'One integrates life as story because one has stories in the back of the mind (unconscious) as containers for organizing events into meaningful experiences.'

The suggestion is that naturally we seek out some story-like account of our own lives either implicitly or explicitly in order to help give ourselves some meaning. Gergen and Gergen (1983) say we are driven to create some kind of narrative order for our lives. These self-narratives connect up the various phases and episodes in our lives. They have a historical and dynamic aspect and continue to evolve. He points out how they have a 'nested' quality: I have a story of me in a wider social and cultural setting; within that is the story of me as a particular professional; and within that is the story of me reading books and struggling with a recalcitrant computer to write this page.

Dan McAdams is one writer who has recently developed this theme in a number of books on personal identity and the story (*Power, Intimacy and the Story*, 1988, *Stories We Live By*, 1996). Two of his claims are particularly relevant to our discussion here; first that an understanding of story or narrative is relatively universal e.g. that virtually everyone over the age of five knows intuitively what a story is, and will show high agreement as to whether a piece of prose is to count as a story or not (Stein and Policastro, 1984); and second that a story is the best, or most complete way we have at present to conceptualise the nature of personal identity.

He points out how every story (like every person) is in some respects like all other stories; in some respects like some other stories, and in some respects like no other. In other words, while there may be certain structural qualities required of any narrative for it to count as a story (Stein and Policastro, 1984), there are also a number of typical story forms into which most stories will fall.

Northrop Frye, the literary theorist, presented in his book *The Anatomy of Criticism* (1957) four 'mythic archetypes' to characterise four fundamental story forms, each with its own structure and associations: *Comedy*, associated with dawn, spring and birth. Comic stories are not necessarily funny; rather they concern revival and return to a basically secure and benevolent world. No evil or suffering is so great that it cannot be overcome. The bad guys are more rigid and ridiculous than evil and dangerous. The world is basically predictable and controllable and tomorrow is always another day. *Romance*, allied with the noonday and high summer, is the second story type, where life is a quest or a series of quests, perilous and heroic. The goal of this quest may be to penetrate some mystery, to find passion, honour, grandeur. The seeker will be an adventurer, often an innocent hero, showing courage in battle and overcoming obstacles. The dragons are more substantial than in comedy, but will be overcome nonetheless. And yet, suggests Frye, there is a strand of nostalgia often present in romance, some slight ambiguity about the essential nature of life. *We* have left behind the unsullied optimism of comedy.

Tragedy, associated with evening and autumn, brings a reality to pain and loss. They are neither denied as in comedy, nor overcome as in romance. Passion may clash with duty requiring a real sacrifice somewhere. Learning and change always bring loss. The hero, who in romantic mode always runs the risk of grandiosity, is humbled and has to learn the inevitability of suffering. Clear divisions between good and bad, however, are beginning to blur. Clear-cut villains are less easy to identify.

The fourth and final story form is *Irony*, the time of night and winter. The ironic story shows full awareness of the contradictions and paradoxes of living. While the tragic hero heroine can lose themselves in the drama of suffering, the ironic hero or heroine (if such we can call them) retains a certain detachment, taking nothing for granted. Irony 'challenges the urgency and largeness of tragedy'.

Both Frye and MacAdams suggest that these archetypal forms are not merely attributes of stories as told or written, but are actually reflections of universal forms which lives can take. Patterns of living come first, as it were, and stories grow up to reflect these patterns. (Doubtless the influence is mutual, and the stories we encounter in our culture can come to help shape our lives and our sense of ourselves.)

There is an implicit developmental sequence contained in Frye's account, too, which has been picked up by the psychoanalyst Roy Schafer in his book *A New Language for Psychoanalysis* (1976), where he suggests that the work of psychoanalytic therapy is at least partly to help the patient come through the sequence to a point where the ironic stance can be achieved and a certain detachment enables life to be accepted in all of its shades of grey.

Conclusion

Stories and personality therefore have much to offer each other. Novels and poetry can distil an experience for us in vivid and image-ful ways such that we are struck powerfully by the contents and operations of a person's mind. Often, as we have seen, these mental processes captured by the artist have many similarities to the processes described in psychological and psychiatric textbooks, and yet the poem or the novel may leave more of an impact on the reader, and of course be more widely read, than the more formalised statement of the psychological professional. This does not mean that the scientific and detached approach has no place. On the contrary, the very power of literature can be abused to present a misleading and untypical picture of how minds work, and the cool light of objectivity needs sometimes to be brought to bear if we wish for a fully rounded picture.

I have also discussed how the inner structure of stories may reflect the structure of a lived life and the personality which constitutes that life. Perhaps stories have a powerful part to play in shaping and constraining the sense we develop of who we are, our selves and identities. If Story is an archetype, that in turn implies that it forms part of the 'design characteristics' of the human mind; that we cannot but experience our selves and our lives in story-like form, in which case it is hardly surprising that literature and poetry continue to fascinate and entrance. They are holding up mirrors to ourselves.

Part V
Chapters 15 – 17
Applications

15
Implications for therapy

The purpose of this chapter is to discuss further methods of coping with distress and also to discuss how partners and families of depressed people can best help themselves and the sufferer. The arts have a major part to play in mental health care (see Kaye and Blee, 1997) but what I will do in this chapter is to bring both the artistic and the scientific, the intuitive and the empirical to bear on serious mental health problems in such a way as to demonstrate how a blending of these rationales can be effective. This therefore again puts the artist-experimenter and artist-practitioner identities to work. In this chapter we range from the value of cognitive-behavioural approaches to the value of writing and prayer. At the individual level the person must choose their own path to mental tranquillity and it is far better if a range of possible avenues to mental health is put before them rather than them being prised into any particular helping model.

Coping with attentional problems
Attentional difficulties have been a frequent theme of discussion in the Borderliners Group (see p. iv) and of visitors to it. A number of people have praised the value of *meditation* in controlling information overload and distractibility. The repeated practise of meditation has facilitated such processes as (what our people have called) 'selective ignoring', the funnelling of attention, 'discounting' (of meaningful coincidences for example) and 'auditory shut-down' (for example to conversational babble in a busy place). Clearly the control of attention and the stilling of the mind produced by meditational techniques offer promise as a genuine form of alternative therapy.

The above comments refer to intervention at (what is usually regarded as) an automatic level of processing. Training of attention in controlled settings with people with a diagnosis of schizophrenia has been attempted previously (e.g. Benedict et al., 1994). Change, however, has not been substantial. Clearly intervention at this level of processing — what could be referred to as the 'cognitive hardware' level is extremely difficult. Nonetheless as we see with Desmond (Chapter 6 here and Chadwick, 1997, Chapter 6) and with other people we have met it *is* possible to modify automatic cognitive processes of this kind with continued practice and high motivation.

At the level where voluntary processes are usually more effective — the 'cognitive software' level — other forms of strategy become more relevant.

In many of the Borderliners Group and its network of contacts, myself included, we have found the following procedures useful in undermining the evolution of aberrant cognitions:

1. Systematic attack on inferences of there being an external locus of control (e.g. a persecutory organisation) for everyday events. A dismembering of the logic of such an inference.

2. Processing of discrediting evidence for a delusional thought i.e. evidence that does not 'fit'.

3. Search for mundane and ordinary rather than spectacular explanations for worrying events (e.g. 'that car honked its horn just to alert me to its presence, not to mock me').

4. Noticing of *meaningless* coincidences (e.g. 'seven objects on my work table at home are blue — it means nothing') instead of looking for 'signs' and uncanny meaningful coincidences — the latter always rather threatening of sanity in fragile people (e.g. 'I've seen three people today who look like Jesus, he's returning tomorrow to save me').

5. Creative rather than psychotic use of worrying coincidences (e.g. 'how can I use this event to enliven conversation or perhaps in a story' (rather than in a delusion))?

6. Reaction to striking and otherwise worrying coincidences with humour and discounting rather than fear and 'incorporating'.

7. Deliberate avoidance of projection tempting activities such as Ouija boards and Tarot cards.

8. Airing in conversation of evolving paranoid ideas *early on* rather than withdrawing to one's room or bedsitter and building the ideas up into something they're not.

9. De-centring from one's own private world to focus, even if only temporarily, on anything that helps one to forget oneself (e.g. items in the news; other people's problems; developments in art, football, car design etc. etc.).

10. The development of an attitude of self-discipline (see also Deanna on this in Chadwick, 1997, Chapter 8).

11. An orientation towards more positive thinking and towards calmness and peace. Generally orienting oneself towards excitement and the negative can be dangerously damaging.

12. An adoption of an attitude whereby one never lives out a worrying prophecy (e.g. from a palmist or clairvoyant) just for the romance of it. Whatever it is one still has a choice; no prophecy really is certain and one's utter fate.

13. Finally: in any use of a journal or self-analysis notebook (an increasingly popular activity these days) an avoidance of concentrating just on confessing and condemning and an avoidance of concentrating too much on sexual matters to the neglect of other things (see also Horney (1942) on these points). As any good therapist would do, one has to focus on one's strengths and positive qualities as well as one's fears and limitations — otherwise one can write oneself into a morass of self-condemnatory misery. Being kind and charitable to oneself gives a touchstone of hope and helps to build positive schemata in one's mind that can attack and overcome the products of negative schemata.

Coping with paranoia

Paranoia in the context of this book has featured in the lives of myself, my mother, Desmond, and to a slight extent Jill. Gleaning from the experiences of all of these people and others close to us I will try and present concisely some advice on how sufferers and carers can best cope with it.

Controllable/uncontrollable factors

It is necessary to separate out things over which the sufferer has control in their lives from those that they do not. For example they may have less control over the actual presence of voices but they have more control over how they interpret those voices and react to them. This is particularly important if voices are demanding suicide or attacks on other people.

Right/wrong judgements

It is important to separate out those things about which the person could be right (such as the unfriendliness of a bus driver) from those where they are definitely wrong (the milkman is poisoning the milk). It is very damaging to the person's self-esteem to assume that everything a paranoid person says is wrong. Recognising their good judgement when it is justified is actually helpful and genuinely therapeutic.

Foresee difficulties

Try to anticipate problems rather than wait for them just to happen. For example if you are moving to a new area or the person suffering from paranoia is moving to a new job talk over the kind of difficulties that might arise, such the threat of mixing with new people.

Regard thoughts as hypotheses

It is much better to regard paranoid thoughts as hypotheses based on evidence rather than as 'solid facts'. Hypotheses and evidence can be questioned and discussed and hence revised. This is the approach used by cognitive-behavioural therapists. Knowledge about paranoia can also make it seem less threatening and less mysterious and can give sufferers and carers additional hints on coping (see Chadwick, 1995; Fowler et al., 1995; Haddock and Slade, 1996; P.D.J. Chadwick et al., 1996).

Do not collude

Where the sufferer's beliefs are almost certainly wrong it is always necessary to stand firm, say that you accept that they have their beliefs, but that you do not share them.

Don't be confrontational

Telling the person that they are stupid or 'talking rubbish' is arrogant, dismissive and never effective. It damages self-esteem, gives the impression that you do not respect the person or care and is liable to make things worse.

Allow independence

Try not to be overprotective, overinvolved and critical. Give the sufferer space, allow them to live their life and show them respect and love. It also helps to encourage talk about things *other* than the person's delusions.

Don't be all negative

People suffering from paranoia are often intelligent, imaginative and talented people. Their paranoia is really an unfortunate misuse of their imagination. Try to look through their paranoia at the positive qualities that underlie it. Many people have turned their irrational thinking around and eventually made it work for them not against them.

Self-help groups

It is useful to find out, perhaps via the hospital or your local health centre, if other families in the neighbourhood have similar difficulties. Families can help each other, it is not always encumbent on professionals to do the therapy.

Attack thinking biases

It has been found that some paranoia sufferers have low self-esteem at least in certain areas of their personality and tend to attribute negative intent to people outside themselves to absolve themselves from blame and to protect that fragile self-esteem (see Kinderman and Bentall, 1996, 1997). More generally it seems to be true that paranoid people have a bias to jump to conclusions, to be hasty and overconfident in their thinking and to seek data that confirm their beliefs to an extreme degree, at the same time as ignoring evidence that discredits them. American research (Magaro, 1981) also suggests that paranoia sufferers tend to view the world in a very narrowly focussed analytical way and neglect the broad view, the context. They therefore very easily get 'the wrong end of the stick' and focus on minutiae rather than the total picture.

These thinking errors, known as 'cognitive biases', can both interfere with social relationships and lead the person to think in an abnormal way — causing further social difficulties in a vicious circle (see Chadwick, 1992, 1995; Garety and Freeman, 1999).

Insight into these problems is one of the ways cognitive therapists work to undermine paranoid belief systems whilst simultaneously working to improve the sufferer's self-esteem (see also McKay and Fanning, 1987 on this latter issue from the cognitive perspective).

Encourage empathy and perspective taking

Finally: very recent research has focussed on the abilities of paranoia sufferers to put themselves in other people's shoes and take other people's perspectives. Paranoia sufferers do not lack the ability to 'feel for other people' as if they were them and do score highly on some measures of empathy (Chadwick, 1997, p.139). However, this empathic reaching out may be a 'projective' form of empathy viz 'If I feel it then you feel it'. Such empathy may not always be accurate and there is recent evidence that paranoid people have difficulty appreciating others' perspectives when those perspectives are likely to be *different* from their own. This may be one of the reasons why paranoia sufferers misinterpret other people's thoughts and intentions (see Kinderman et al., 1998). A similar deficiency, although to a more marked degree, characterises sufferers of autism and Asperger's Syndrome. It is feasible that clarifying differences in perspective — even in very simple social situations — may gradually help the paranoia sufferer to 'de-centre' from their world and to recognise the independence of minds other than their own. People with these deficiencies for example often have speech with very unclear reference — for example when giving directions or instructions, because they adopt an 'If I know it then you know it' attitude which does not take into account the other person's current situation. When asked therefore where the scissors are they may say 'in the drawer' in a house with over 30 drawers. They may say 'look at this!' about something on the television while standing directly in the line of view so that what *they* are looking at cannot be seen. If these tendencies are recognised as a specific problem, related to paranoia, attempts to overcome them may be more successful.[1]

Coping as the partner of a depressed person

Helping agencies generally provide no support to the partners or families of a depressed person, their focus is the sufferer. What then can such people do to help themselves to cope and to help them ameliorate the sufferer's pain? I will draw here on my experience of living through Jill's depression (focussed on in Chapter 8) and through the experiences of myself and others of hostel living in 1980–81. Other material of value to readers can be found in Orford (1987) and Milne (1999).

Journal keeping

A journal can be a friend in these circumstances. Depressed people are very poor listeners but a journal records everything faithfully and never forgets. Living through one's partner's depression is agonisingly stressful and the mere act of expressing discontents onto the page and *not* at one's partner helps everyone concerned.

Keep in touch with friends

This is a challenging time for friends as well. Keep in touch with them and request their support. Too many partners and families disappear into a closed-in private world and do not reach out to *anyone*. That is not a good strategy. Do not forget that The Samaritans are a willing ear to partners as well as sufferers at these times.

Minimise criticism

Criticism is very damaging indeed to depressed people. It is better to make every effort to minimise or eliminate it. Unlike with a well person it will be of no benefit and is likely only to make matters worse.

Don't be smothering

There is no value to treating your depressed partner or family member as if they are in cotton wool all the time. It will only make them more and more helpless. Establish what they *can* do and what they cannot and notice what areas of their life they do have some control over and where they have less control. Be encouraging but don't treat them like a baby, it will make them sink more into inertia.

Notice what's enjoyable

Depressed people have had things in their life that they enjoyed. They may still find a few things enjoyable. Make a systematic effort to find out what these are

---

1 Drug-induced paranoia is also common, particularly with users of cannabis and amphetamine. It is therefore important to be mindful and informed about the person's legal and illegal drug intake.

and try to maximise their presence in your lives. Jill's depression for example lifted for several days after seeing the film *Staying Alive* with John Travolta on television. Dance features on television were always watched.

Don't copy
It is vitally important not to mimic the depressed person's style of thinking, facial and bodily expression and style of life. Fight for your own independence and difference. Keeping in touch with other people does help here.

Separate the distress from the person
Avoid seeing your partner or family member as a 'depressive' as this characterises them by their distress. Remember how they were when they were healthy and see the distress as an enemy partly separate from you both that you therefore both have to fight.

If you're a man: avoid the 'good time lout' syndrome
With the recent well-publicised rise in young male suicides there is an emphasis on men talking about feelings and problems more than they used to. Working-class men particularly need to do this as 20 or so years ago they were described as very poor confidantes (Brown and Harris, 1978). Having a depressed woman at home interferes with a 'feel good' life rationale. It is very easy for men in this situation to relapse into heavy drinking, staying out late and into infidelity and even violence towards their partner. Violence, infidelity and heavy drinking in men can also be causes or partial causes of depression in their women. This is a very dangerous vicious circle.

Facing depression in the home, however, can sometimes make men grow up, face their personal responsibilities and limitations and realise that life is not a permanent merry-go-round oiled by beer and football. Seeing depression as a common enemy is a good approach in terms of channelling aggressive energies into something constructive rather than destructive.

Depressed people are not stupid
Depression usually onsets after a loss or failure of some kind. It is not a total fantasy but is reality-based. Recognise that the person is dealing with a real issue, they are not making things up and have faith that this problem *can* be beaten. *Never* say that 'nothing can be done' or relapse into acceptance of a hopeless situation.

Take suicide threats seriously
People who threaten suicide are more likely to actually commit it and depressed people — particularly those who feel hopeless — are the most likely suiciders of all. Never regard suicide threats as empty verbiage.

Activity is useful
Couch potato living is not helpful for depression. It is better to be doing *something*, even going for walks or gentle cycling than sitting together night after night in mutual misery.

Spiritual help

Depression strikes a person as if from beyond. It is like a force from beyond the Self and has an evil quality to it. For this reason some people find prayer, visits to church and talks with vicars genuinely helpful. An agnostic attitude is not for all in situations like this and if the sufferer has a faith it should be encouraged not ridiculed. Partners may also find their religiosity kindled by the agonies of this disorder. If this happens it should not be resisted.

Poetry and writing

Language, whether spoken, read, written or heard is a powerful weapon in the fight against depression. Some people have discovered either a capacity for or a love of poetry and literature when depressed. If this route is discovered by the sufferer (or the partner for that matter) it is likely to be a fruitful one.

With obesity, drug use, paranoia and boredom, depression is a disorder of the modern age. Social and cultural pressures, the situation in the home, losses, failures and learned helplessness and attempts to live up to impossibly high standards all have parts to play in its causation. The way a person *thinks* when they are depressed also has a role in maintaining it. With such a multidimensional disorder only a multifaceted approach to treatment and care is appropriate and readers should be suspicious of those claiming 'magic bullet' solutions. But depression can be beaten and indeed the life skills a person learns in defeating it can enrich them and strengthen them greatly in the face of future challenges.

The writer as therapist

There are many people who would rather read than visit the consulting room. That writers are implicitly therapists is a fact of life and the recent burgeoning of interest in poetry as therapy (Philipp and Roberston, 1996) reflects strongly the therapeutic value of the written word and of writing in itself.

Wilde once said that the description can be better than the analysis as it comes to us more directly and a very close description of experience might well consist in itself of an explanation — this was also Walter Pater's view and that of many contemporary therapists.

The writers presented in this volume inevitably have their idiosyncracies. Wilde, but not Dostoyevsky, often uses floral imagery, to him life is *social* life. He never portrays the isolated Robinson Crusoe thinker as does Piaget (and of course as does Desmond Marshall here in Chapter 6). Dostoyevsky's Underground Man of course pays the price for his solitude. Wilde's prototype character, however, is the person with a secret. His heroes all have *secrets*. He was also very politically sensitive, as was his mother of course (Melville, 1994; Banville, 1994) and forever grappling with the spiritual.

Wilde used laughter as therapy. He tried to destroy solemn moralising with humour rather than reason. The senses must cure the soul. Also in Wilde it is clear that society itself was not 'safe'. It was not 'in good condition'. This paved the way for the acceptance of the Freudian id and the Jungian shadow. People had secrets, all was not as it seemed and reason was *not* in control!

There is a certain distaste in both Wilde and Dostoyevsky for theory and certainly for consistency. Most psychologists could be said to have drawn a veil of concepts over the mind, it is refreshing when one faces Wilde and Dostoyevsky to see this mind laid bare and not filtered through the higher levels of the intellect.

This experience in itself is therapeutic. Paradoxically it was Wildean theory that one cannot find oneself via a theory and that theories arrest growth rather than promote it. Jung had a similar attitude. In this respect Wilde and Dostoyevsky release 'intellectic pressure', take pressure off, relax you. This is part of art as healing art. They take the reader to the core.

Wilde also has a tremendous sense of fun. It is so easy to deny oneself pure fun and to be chained by standards, responsibilities and commands. In this vein the Greeks had a beautiful blend of decadence and discipline which must have attracted Oscar.

Dostoyevsky and Wilde were also healing because of their perennial avoidance of the obvious. In Wilde we see rejection of bourgeois platitudes, in Dostoyevsky of scientific crassness. Both of them send safe stereotypes and bland banalities to the pit. They lift you out of ruts, shake you down and put you on the plain, where you can see for miles. In both writers the frames in our minds are taken away, the frames that determine in and out, good and bad, right and wrong. Fences down they help us to see poignancy, intensity and beauty everywhere, even in the most unlikely places — and in a very real sense, help you to love yourself.

Art is centrally about beauty and beauty in itself is healing. The writer is also nothing if not entertaining and as we know entertainment is the therapy of the masses. It is also the writer's job to reveal all the shades and hues of life and perhaps to comment on and reveal what is too minute and subtle to appear in (often quite coarse-grained) everyday conversation and chatter. In doing this we often find ourselves saying 'Ah! I've felt that too!' yet we may never have spoken of it (even in therapy). Considerable tracts of the interior monologues of the Underground Man in *Notes from Underground* and of the character Goldyakin in *The Double* have this 'too tiny to mention' quality. Yet, strangely, to see it mentioned there on the page has a remarkably uplifting quality — as if one feels that nothing in life really is wasted or irrelevant. So-called Super-realist painters such as Otto Dix can have similar effects: their realism is so minute and accurate that it jolts us and evokes quite new, even alarming, experiences. In this way Dix was an inspiration for my own effort in Chapter 9.

This focus on the minutiae of experience is itself also very refreshing as it takes us away from the highly reconstructed, streamlined and polished prose of heavily intellectual writers and returns us to 'raw feels'. This inevitably is invigorating as well as giving us licence to use all of our experience in the enrichment of our lives (to say nothing of the fact that it also inspires our very own sensitivity).

In writing, as well as painting, intelligence has to take advantage of error and chance. Combinatorial play of this kind, though little respected by convergers and fact-finders, is for many people a fount of new life. The act then of organising experience is also therapeutic such that the general exploratory acts of coalescence and amalgamation give a sense of freedom, hope and meaning that working within rule systems denies. One cannot seek oneself in a theory, a personality is fluid, ever-changing and metamorphosing, it is not a structure. Self-discovery and elaboration therefore is more like travel than configuration, it is an act of 'living psychology' rather than 'algebraic psychology'. If one is then confined by one's algebra one can never know who one really is — and, as Wilde observed, one cannot believe in oneself if one is not being oneself.

16
Implications for education

The circularity of positivism

Over the last ten years or so increasing numbers of psychologists have ceased to care whether psychology is or is not a science. Certainly 20 years ago this manuscript could not have been submitted with any hope of publication but today the complexion of the subject, certainly in Great Britain, is in the process of considerable change. What I say below has to be seen in the context of this evolving scenario where, for example, post-modern approaches are now increasingly infiltrating psychology curricula.

People's thirst for meaning is alas not being satisfied by science and many are turning aside to seek alternatives. Positivism bolsters faith instead in a materialistic reality as it relies on information to the sense organs from the tangible world to count as and to act as its 'evidence'. But to then go on to say that the world *is* only matter and fact is not an advance on the assumptions that fuel the system. Positivism also seeks reliable evidence that can be generated 'on call' and be intersubjectively verified. But such phenomena could only be produced by a machine, not by an intentional entity. To then conclude that the world *is* a machine from such a definition of and use of evidence is self-fulfilling. To then go on to discount contradictory evidence, meaningful to religious and spiritual people, of a different genre that does not occur on call — and hence brings the machine metaphor into question — as merely 'fantasy and drivel', is verging on the corrupt.

The limitations of science

Science therefore provides us with a very partial and limited conception of the world. It has next to no understanding of freedom, will or evil, little to no respect for the power of coincidence, little knowledge of the roots of interest and confidence and few tools or concepts really to understand love. It downgrades the world of myth and of dream, has no respect for the power and usefulness of irrationality or of empathy and is seriously undermined by anything it cannot measure. It has little purchase on the understanding of the individual, its truths relating to mass populations, is embarrassed about the way cognitions can be enslaved to emotional drives and can only really function efficiently if a system yields to reductionistic analysis — which of course not all systems do.

Everything that has to be grasped as a totality is problematic for science and the emphasis in science on truth-telling and truth-finding, though productive in the impersonal world, can often be catastrophic in the context of the personal world, where 'the truth' is very often not at all what is wanted or needed.

Science seems unable to be at ease then with 'the facts of life' that some things — such as getting on with people — are more important than truth, that unprovable beliefs can very often be far more motivationally powerful than evidence-based beliefs and that nature cannot be controlled to the extent of giving Man a summer-all-the-time world. Everything is two-sided, tails do not wag dogs, and one does not obtain a full apprehension of the Alps by looking at it through a hand lens.

Science as a 'half-education'

A scientific education also has many serious limitations. The scientist is basically concerned with finding out about the objective world — the world that has a career independent of the observer. Scientists are generally apsychological or even anti-psychological in attitude, resent being studied as subjects themselves, except perhaps as a one-off project and have little interest in psychological biases and distortions in cognition. Science therefore encourages an attitude that is forgetful of and distracting from the Self and leads to an intellectual orientation focussed on finding and problem solving but in such a way that the contexts faced have one unique solution. Such singularity of goal rarely occurs in life.

In scientific work, emotion is a poor relation and hence science students have little to no chance to explore their inner world of feeling. They are encouraged to have a narrowly focussed attentional beam, to hold an analytic rather than holistic attitude, to keep themselves out of the picture in everything they write and to value precision and measurement from an outside-in perspective rather than the empathy and indwelling of the inside-out perspective. The limitations of this, particularly in psychiatry, are self-evident.

The result of this is that a science education leaves the individual a stranger to themselves, cognitively extraverted, convergent in problem-solving mentality and unable to appreciate or recognise the ontological value of anything that cannot be measured. There is also at a non-structural level a certain machismo in science that can contaminate a student's willingness to appreciate or see value in anything stereotypically classifiable as feminine.

A scientific education therefore is not an education of the person. Scientists conceive of problems as existing outside of themselves and they are trained to be problem-solving instruments — as if the purpose of life was merely to obtain an increasingly accurate representation of 'the world', the nature of which is then 'solved'. This is not an education for life at all because in the ebb and flow of daily affairs there is nothing that has 'a career independent of the observer' unless one is dealing with inanimate matter — and at the level of microphysics even that proviso no longer holds true.

Science is essentially half an education. Not only does it produce wooden dancers, it puts little to no demands on the individual to know themselves or to develop social skills, other than in the context of research collaboration, or to have any respect for the world of feelings other than to reduce them to biological or cognitive underpinnings. Indeed science could be done well, even very well indeed, by people who were somewhat schizoid, or even mildly autistic or with Asperger's Syndrome but we have to ask whether or not this cauterisation of the socio-emotional domain is what we want of the educational process. The tragedy is that while spirituality and desire dominate the arts, the values, attitudes, procedures and goals of materialistic science have been imported wholesale into psychology to produce the loveless, godless half-subject so many are today rebelling against.

The artistic alternative

The remit of this artistic psychological text is to create a different ideology for psychology that eventuates from the values prized by artists over the centuries: the value of the subjective perspective and the unique vision; the striving to create and work via empathy; the evocation of feeling, of joy, of surprise and shock; the valuing of the inner life and the prizing of invention and construction over finding and fact. The artist also is free to contemplate and create the impossible and to deal with issues in an open-ended open-textured way.

While the scientist wants explanation, reduction, prediction and control, the artist is mindful also of the importance of letting a phenomenon just be and to feel this stillness and awesomeness in being. This, as Rogers knew, is of the utmost importance in therapy but is an attitude also vital to the novelist and playwright, indeed to any artist. In this sense the *reduction* of scientific psychology stands in contrast to the *equivalence* of artistic psychology.

The remit of this text, however, is not merely destructive anti-scientism. Although it is true that an education in science is only half an education this also is true of an education in art. My purpose is to complete the gestalt that is psychology as a subject and to leave it 'fully rounded' and richer, a discipline that values the subjective as well as the objective, intuition as well as fact, empathy as well as intelligence and experience as well as mechanism. While we have a plethora of information about populations, some small, some enormous, the case study or biographical sketch lies in neglect in scientific psychology, the personal anecdote is considered almost worthless and the personal journey deemed interesting but too singular to count as evidence.

There is little reason, however, why the ideologies of science and of art need not dovetail together, they are complementary rather than antagonistic. Certainly in the love of experimentation and the striving for beauty there is common ground. In a previous work on schizophrenia and schizotypy (Chadwick, 1997) I used both artistic and scientific methods to characterise and explore the space I set myself. There was considerable agreement in the conclusions reached by the two approaches. Certainly the mixed-method approach and the willingness to entertain the more artistic procedures, such as used in this book, would broaden out education in psychology very considerably from its scrawny nature in the days of behaviourism.

Education is not simply about being more critically minded. Being able to design a clean experiment or spot a confounding variable will also not get you through life. We need less of the distant and cold attitude encouraged by science and more classes where students are encouraged to write of their own experiences and those of their families. This of course is a more liberal permissive style of education in psychology with an emphasis on ideas and understanding and with a willingness to negotiate topics rather than formally deliver them. This would truly be an education that would 'bring out from within'.

In addition the recognition of artistic approaches in psychology would lead to a greater respect and encouragement of divergent thinking. Students could also be encouraged to read great writers and to respect fiction as psychologically revealing. Single case study work could be more enthusiastically promoted and the value of the study of the individual endorsed. My own belief is that all of these suggestions would lead to more ecologically valid and sensitive research in a general sense and make psychology as a subject a better grounding for life.

Enthusiasm

Education is not merely based on reason, nor is it just the training of reason. Creativity takes place in a context of *wanting* to create, *valuing* creativity, experiencing the joy of creativity. Vitality must precede knowledge and passion and enthusiasm is the first thing students look for, and need, in their teacher. Strangely there is little to no point in bringing this up at staff meetings. Scientists prefer nuts and bolts suggestions and procedures that can guarantee an outcome. Basing a course on enthusiasm is to a positivist (if not to a Kierkegaardian) basing it on air. Of course there is a historical precedent. Antagonism to enthusiasm has its own tradition as scientists and philosophers of old saw it as the attribute of religious fanatics or evangelical powerhouses like the Wesleys (Talbot, 1968, p.15). But really the scientism of behaviourism has also played its part in evacuating passion from reductionist institutions. Perhaps the emotional volatility of the enthusiast is also seen as neurotic (?) at least in psychology but either way the focus on fact has its effects in the draining away of colour from the didactic situation. The advantage of placing the subjective at the heart of psychology and the advantage also of the licence to feel is a potential return of greater warmth, passion and vibrancy to psychology departments and to the student population.

Can two cultures become one?

Psychology is riddled with dichotomies to such a degree that it consists of two very ill-defined cultures. Various terms have been used to describe them: hard and soft; process and person; essentialist and constructionist; experimental and clinical; quantitative and qualitative. The process culture is massively more powerful in the research arena, as a browse through almost any academic publisher's list of latest titles can demonstrate. The person culture is more popular in the teaching situation and with the general public. Advances in psychology, however, often occur when two cultures are synthesised. In the nineteenth-century the two intellectual domains of the sensory and the conceptual were fused by Ebbinghaus's work on memory. In the 1880s Wundt believed that social psychology could only be apprehended rhetorically but then in the 1930s it was fused with experimental psychology. Today cognitivists seek the scientific foundations of cognitive therapy, a therapy which actually grew from psychoanalysis; Hans Eysenck was a pioneer of experimental clinical psychology and work in personality seeks a rapprochement of constructivism and trait approaches (Hampson, 1988). Alas, like all scientists (and artists), psychologists of all persuasions are exceedingly territorial and view encroachments from outside with great suspicion. It is, however, fruitless to create one subdiscipline by destroying another — a common strategy in our subject. Let us hope that the current vitality for mixed-method approaches in psychology breeds tolerance and acceptance of rival perspectives and an attempt towards synthesis that would be a relief for student and professional alike.

17
Conclusions:
the mixed-method future of
psychology

Colour and line

It has not been the purpose of this book to present demonstrated facts about mind or personality to the reader. Artistic psychology is concerned more with eduction of process than instruction in content. The text therefore is written in the Kierkegaard tradition of using one's own struggle to enrich one's creative work; it is not written in the Positivist tradition of being a dispassionate observer of what is the case. The *reading* of people therefore has taken precedence over the observation of them; indwelling and empathising has been seen as more central than measurement and contextualising more essential than analysis. What we have here then are essays, stories and patterns rather than facts, and insights and impressions rather than theories.

This particular tome, however, has not shunned the use of objective standardised methods. As in the detailed single case study of the solo circumnavigator Dodge Morgan in *The Journal of Personality* (Nasby and Read, 1997) it certainly is possible and fruitful to direct these methods in great detail at the individual level. Personnel and occupational psychologists of course rely on this, but in my view the artistic depictions using music, photography and poetry etc. give an added realness, colour and sense of uniqueness. One could hardly prefer to see an EPQ quadrant analysis of Extraversion and Neuroticism with, say, Desmond and Ivo represented simply by dots in EN space.

The experiment in the artistic context

Experimentation is highly, and I think rightly, valued by Western academic psychologists. For fact-finding variables have to be controlled, and of course Piaget (1972) is right, one must check, but it is strangulating, deadening and obsessional to be checking all the time! Experimentation is no panacea. A man will not be able to work out why his marriage failed by doing an experiment; a woman cannot do an experiment to prove why her son has become an habitual car thief at 15 and one cannot do an experiment to demonstrate why self-realisation is a good thing in education. Experiments cannot answer every query.

Scientists are particularly concerned, however, in experimental and outcome research, with 'main effects' — the general finding, and with two, three and higher order interactions of variables. Does a therapeutic technique work better for example for young men or for middle-class people? But as we grade from this into the thousand-way interaction that is the individual person we are into the realm of the organisation of the individual personality, a central issue of artistic psychology. Experimentally science grades into art and we have to move from an elemental to an holistic perspective to capture the phenomena adequately. This blending of the objective and subjective, of the particular and the general will I hope create a psychology that is genuinely commensurate with the complexity and colour that is a living human being. It is tragic that experts on components often 'hold professional views which actively prevent them from grasping the overall picture' (Collins, 1994, p.11); real bridges need to be built then to activate a blended mixed-method psychology.

Pre-emptive science as villainy

The alternative, a total reframing of psychology into pre-emptive science, however, bodes ill. I would go so far as to say (see Chapter 3) that it is the evil depicted in Dickens's *Hard Times* (Dickens, 1907/1961). The denial of feeling; the cunning of the political manoeuvring; the externalising of problems; the obsession with control; the worship of fact; the aggressiveness of dismissals of alternatives; the thirst for 'science power'; the inhibition of self-expression; the trading-in of person for mechanism and the subordinating of person to method — all of this is the product of the quashing of poetry by prose; score by libretto; spirit by reason; intuition by fact and love by logic. Were a building scientist to say to an architect, 'Your designs are not wanted any more, *we* will build buildings now according to scientific laws', one would have the same feeling: the presence of evil. The sacking of (state assisted) Irish poets and their replacement by a computer would eventuate a similar base ambience.

The moral issue

Yet strangely the self-abrogation of neo-classical science is probably seen as 'cleaner' and more virtuous in Christian communities than the Gothic narcissism of artistic psychology. In our culture there is something spiritually lofty about dispassionate objectivity over romantic egocentricity; something high-principled about Apollonian suffering over Dionysiac ecstacy. Irrationality and passion are seen as somehow nefarious and 'lower' than reason and thought, this is so in the writings of psychologists as disparate as Stuart Sutherland and Sigmund Freud. This moral issue in my view is a major hurdle for the acceptability of artistic approaches in Western psychology. Positivism and Structuralism are chosen by people whose temperaments they suit. But to be emotive doesn't mean one lacks emotional coherence and to write of the Impossible in a psychologically revealing way — as does Wilde — doesn't mean that one does not keep a tangential hold on reality. For Pythagoras science, as much as art, *needs* passion. This book has tried therefore to cover fully and broadly the landscape of the mind using both empirical and artistic approaches to do this. It has ranged in places from the burlesque to the ascetic. Some of the images and emotion-laden themes may have shocked the spectator's sensibilities. At its extremes, photographs of painted, powdered and perfumed men might seem to some to be visual violence depicting cobalt-blue mental states and strange sins. If so, then so be it. I make no apologies for them. This is life and this is mind. It is my view that a Rationalism, Structuralism and Positivism dominated psychology is only the power of padded shoulders. Knowledge from passion and understanding from being have their own strength, usefulness and validity and are vital additions to our ideology.

The schizophrenia of schizophrenia research

My own fields within psychology are personality and abnormal psychology and my research over the past 20 years has focussed mainly on paranoia, schizotypy and schizophrenia. Is there any sense of unification in these fields? I think not. Would unification of the empirical and the intuitive be advantageous? That I certainly think is so.

There certainly are two cultures in schizophrenia research and generally in the field of clinical psychology. One is represented by such journals as *The Journal of Critical Psychology, Counselling and Psychotherapy* (formerly *Changes*); *Clinical Psychology Forum*; *Mental Health Care* and *Open Mind* and features the day-to-day, indeed second-by-second battles to cope with mental disorder. The messiness of this whole business is there frankly and starkly on the page and authors adopt a 'real life' tone and manner. Papers are intuitive, rhetorical, often emotive, often funny, generally colourful and basically present clinical psychology, psychotherapy and psychiatry more or less 'as it really is '. One might refer to these journals as representing the 'sharp end' culture.

There is, however, another, quite different culture represented by *The Journal of Abnormal Psychology*; *The British Journal of Clinical Psychology*; *Schizophrenia Bulletin* and *The British Journal of Psychiatry*. Papers in these journals are empirical, objective in tone, contain not a trace of emotion and make next to no reference to sufferers' experiences. There is a 'first person account' section in *Schizophrenia Bulletin* but it is rarely referred to in the body of the journal. This could be called the 'cutting edge' culture which seeks the causes of clinical conditions in a scientific way so as to found treatment and clinical practice on 'sound scientific principles' and 'evidence-based medicine'.

The two cultures exist somewhat uneasily. While the cutting edge culture presents a glossy scientific front to the general field of psychopathology and while publication within it is vital for career advancement the personnel in the sharp end culture often complain that 'in reality' the pronouncements of scientists are contextually insensitive, often damaging (as for example with neuroleptic drugs), not workable, or are of marginal help in the clutter and clammer of day-to-day clinical work — where decisions usually have to be based on educated guesswork, hunches of the moment and sheer psychological common sense. Finding that a technique works for 60 per cent of sufferers in a controlled trial still leaves the overworked therapist, dealing all the time with individuals in their own unique situation, in a chancy spot. The difficulties of applying techniques to harrassed working-class clients in run-down estates is also a common theme.

Fortunately, in clinical psychology there are journals such as *The Journal of Mental Health*, *The Therapist* and *Mental Health Care* where overlap of the sharp end and the cutting edge cultures does take place at least to some degree and papers both of scientific finesse and raunchy realism can sit side-by-side in the same issue. (*Open Mind* also features scientific material as news items.) These journals and publications like them represent to me the way forward for psychology as a discipline. Publications which fuse lab' and life, which present empirical research and also show how it can be taken to the street or the ward are the life's blood of any subject. But the issue of seeking main effects from large samples as compared to the intense study of the singular personality is not one merely of procedural preference or personal taste. It has serious practical consequences.

Psychosis research can become so busy trying to find 'general features of processing' in people with a diagnosis of delusional disorder or schizophrenia, or whatever, that the personnel become in danger of missing the unique personal function of psychosis for the sufferer. For example, in my case, atonement was the central theme to which cognitive and biochemical mechanisms were basically pawns.

When we come to this, psychosis, the most serious problem of them all with a reduced fertility and a disturbingly high suicide rate it becomes clear that the issues faced by this book are far from marginal, anachronistic or a function merely of some intellectual aesthetic. Pre-emptive positivism and the neglect of understanding can kill. Patients can feel alienated, categorised, neglected, treated only as cognitrons or bundles of chemicals. Person-healing obviously can benefit from science but once it becomes slaved to science, to classification, to standardised treatment, people die.

A total psychology

Therapy is very much about facilitating possibilities for the person rather than being a scientific explanatory exercise to find out 'what he or she is really like'. Process research, though it has been attacked by some 'Person' psychologists, is to my mind a valuable ally to the therapist. To know that people with very few friends are very low on self-disclosure for example (Argyle, 1992) is tangible, valuable information. It is a pity that psychotherapists don't become more mindful of it in their relationships with their clients. Research on abnormalities and limitations in body language in neurotic clients with social difficulties has also proved useful in therapy where non-verbal communication has been focussed on specifically (Argyle et al., 1974). Clearly overlap research between social and clinical psychology has promise. Empirical process research on delusion has produced similarly specific suggestions for the therapist (Garety and Freeman, 1999, p.149) and empirical findings on hallucinations have been put to use in the consulting room (P.D.J. Chadwick et al., 1996).

It is my own personal feeling that the artist-experimenter identity is an identity that enables the practitioner to capture both the complexities and subtleties of the individual case and embark on the search for generalities and explanatory mechanisms.

Solely analytical investigators, however, have serious limitations in the more intuitive domains of psychology. As we have seen Carkhuff (1969) found that academic grades in behavioural psychology correlated negatively with success as a therapist and Estes (1938) found that when asking people to match films of people's body language to case study narratives, behavioural psychologists (and other scientists and philosophers) were less and artistic and literary people more successful at the task. Somehow we need personnel who can function both at the level of explanation and that of understanding, who can analyse as well as intuit, who are capable of catching and holding that which easily escapes from our thoughts as well as being at ease with a statistical manual. In other words: we need total psychologists, psychologists who are as much poetical as analytical, as much intuitive as mechanistic. After all if one provided a geologist with a batch of chemical analyses of rocks and some hand specimens of same one would expect him or her to be able to match them up a lot more accurately than would a lay person. If not then we would be entitled to half echo Chapter 3 and ask 'what on earth is going on here?! Who are these people?!'

Final thoughts

In terms of past intellectual and philosophical traditions it is clear that artistic psychology has closer links with Constructivism, Expressionism and Phenomenology than with Structuralism, Rationalism and Positivism. To see psychology partly as the facilitation of possibility (Stevens, 1996) is an Expressionistic theme (Britt, 1999, Chapter 3) rather than a Naturalistic one. It takes us beyond 'what is the case' to new horizons and vistas. This is dream-making and dream-realising rather than 'observation'.

A person, however, has genetic, biochemical, physiological, cognitive, emotional and motivational, social and spiritual aspects. As we go about our daily lives we sense stimuli, categorise situations, call up scripts to deal with them and then enact dramas. We are both scientists and artists, mechanisms, and players in the theatre of existence. To a degree we suffer our temperaments and personalities in a causal sense yet to a degree we also create and mould them and seek meaning in our lives within the constraints of the situations in which we find ourselves. We live out our own dreams and even the dreams of other people for us. We have to negotiate what we are with what we should be; negotiate what we want and what others desire us to want. We have to negotiate our deepest needs with the necessity to manage our impressions on others merely to smooth the path of social life. When we become mentally disordered it is not simply our behaviour that becomes 'un-normal' but our self-integrity that also suffers. The beauty of the personality is damaged such that our criteria of health and illness have and need to have an aesthetic dimension to them yet a dimension of great practical import. It is my hope that the future will bring greater integration of the more artistic with the more scientific (for example developments in Self-theory (Blatt and Zuroff, 1992) with research in paranoia (P.D.J. Chadwick et al., 1996)) to create a person-centred psychopathology such that the focus of old on syndromes and symptoms will pass into history and even the concept of psychopathology itself will yield to a greater acceptance of the natural diversity of persons. This will take us back to the *real* focus of psychology, the study of the individual and their experiences not that of some intangible abstraction of 'Mr and Mrs Average' and their latent structures. When this happens psychology can truly be said to have rediscovered its soul.

Bibliography

American Psychiatric Association (1994) *Diagnostic and Statistical Manual of Mental Disorders* (4th edition), Washington, D.C.: American Psychiatric Association.

Andrews, R. (1992) *Collins Thematic Dictionary of Quotations*, Glasgow: Harper Collins.

Argyle, M. (1992) *The Social Psychology of Everyday Life*, London and New York: Routledge.

Argyle, M. (1996) The experimental study of relationships, in D. Miell and R. Dallos (eds) *Social Interaction and Personal Relationships*, London: Sage, Reading C, pp. 344–56.

Argyle, M., Bryant, B. and Trower, P. (1974) Social skills training and psychotherapy: A comparative study, *Psychological Medicine*, 4 (4; Nov): 435–43.

Assagioli, R. (1975) *Psychosynthesis: A manual of principles and techniques*, London: Turnstone Press.

Bandura, A. (1986) *Social Foundations of Thought and Action: A social cognitive theory*, Englewood Cliffs, N.J.: Prentice Hall.

Banister, P., Burman, E., Parker, I., Taylor, M. and Tindall, C. (1994) *Qualitative Methods in Psychology: A Research Guide*, Buckingham and Philadelphia: Open University Press.

Banville, J. (1994) Oscar's mother, to the life, *The Observer Review*, Sunday 12th June, p.18.

Bartlett, N. (1993) *Who Was That Man? A present for Mr Oscar Wilde.* Harmondsworth: Penguin.

Baumrind, D. (1980) New Directions in Socialisation Research, *American Psychologist*, 35: 639–52.

Baumrind, D. (1989) Rearing Competent Children, in W. Damon (ed) *Child Development Today and Tomorrow*, San Francisco: Jossey-Bass, pp. 349–79.

Beatrice, J. (1985) A psychological comparison of heterosexuals, transvestites, preoperative transsexuals and postoperative transsexuals, *Journal of Nervous and Mental Disease*, 173(6): 358–65.

Beck, A.T. (1976) *Cognitive Therapy and the Emotional Disorders*, New York: International Universities Press.

Beck, A.T. (1987) Cognitive models of depression, *Journal of Cognitive Psychotherapy*, 1: 2–27.

Benedict, R.H.B., Harris, A.E., Markow, T., McCormick, J.A., Nuechterlein, K.H. and Asarnow, R.F. (1994) Effects of Attention Training on Information Processing in Schizophrenia, *Schizophrenia Bulletin*, 20, 3: 537–46.

Benor, D.J. (1990) Survey of Spiritual Healing Research, *Complementary Medicine Research,* 4(3): 9–33.

Bentall, R.P., Jackson, H.F. and Pilgrim, D. (1988) Abandoning the concept of 'schizophrenia': some implications of validity arguments for psychological research into psychotic phenomena, *British Journal of Clinical Psychology,* 27: 303–24.

Berger, J. (1980) *The Success and Failure of Picasso,* London: Writers and Readers Publishing Cooperative.

Bergman, A.J., Harvey, P.D., Mitropoulov, V., Aronson, A., Marder, D., Silverman, J., Trestman, R. and Siever, L.J. (1996) The factor structure of schizotypal symptoms in a clinical population, *Schizophrenia Bulletin,* 22(3): 501–9.

Billig, M., Condor, S., Edwards, D., Gare, M., Middleton, D. and Radley, A. (1988) *Ideological Dilemmas: A social psychology of everyday thinking,* London: Sage.

Birnbaum, M. (1920) *Oscar Wilde: Fragments and Memories,* London: Elkin Mathews, pp. 28–9.

Blake, W. (1989) *A Poison Tree,* in B. Lloyd-Evans (ed) *The Batsford Book of English Poetry,* London: Batsford.

Blatt, S. and Zuroff (1992) Interpersonal relatedness and self-definition: Two prototypes for depression, *Clinical Psychology Review,* 12: 527–62.

Boden, M. (1979) *Piaget,* London: Fontana.

Boyle, M. (1990) *Schizophrenia: A scientific delusion?* London and New York: Routledge.

Brewin, C.R. (1998) Intrusive memories, depression and PTSD, *The Psychologist,* 11, (6; June): 281–3.

Brewin, C.R. and Power, M.J. (1999) Integrating psychological therapies: processes of meaning transformation, *British Journal of Medical Psychology,* 72, (2; June): 143–57.

Britt, D. (ed) (1999) *Modern Art: Impressionism to Post-Modernism,* London: Thames and Hudson.

Brown, G.W. and Harris, T.O. (1978) *Social Origins of Depression: A study of Psychiatric Disorder in Women,* London: Tavistock Publications.

Bruner, J. (1990) *Acts of Meaning,* London: Harvard University Press.

Burch, G. St.J., Steel, C. and Hemsley, D.R. (1998) Oxford-Liverpool Inventory of Feelings and Experiences: Reliability in an experimental population, *British Journal of Clinical Psychology,* 37 (1, February): 107–8.

Burr, V. (1995) *An Introduction to Social Constructionism,* London: Routledge.

Burt, K. and Oaksford, M. (1999) Qualitative Methods: Beyond beliefs and desires. *The Psychologist,* 12, (7; July): 332–5.

Camus, A. (1942/1983) *The Outsider,* Harmondsworth: Penguin.

Camus, A. (1942/1988) *The Myth of Sisyphus,* Harmondsworth: Penguin.

Cardinal, R. and Short, R. (1970) *Surrealism: Permanent Revolution,* London: Studio Vista.

Carkhuff, R.R. (1969) *Helping and Human Relations* (2 vols), New York: Holt, Rinehart and Winston.

Cattell, R.B. (1990) Advances in Cattellian personality theory, in L.A. Pervin (ed) *Handbook of Personality: Theory and Research,* New York: Guildford Press, pp.101–110.

Chadwick, P.D.J., Birchwood, M. and Trower, P. (1996) *Cognitive Therapy for Delusions, Voices and Paranoia,* Chichester: Wiley.

Chadwick, P.K. (1992) *Borderline: A Psychological Study of paranoia and delusional thinking*, London and New York: Routledge.

Chadwick, P.K. (1993) The stepladder to The Impossible: a first hand phenomenological account of a schizoaffective psychotic crisis, *Journal of Mental Health*, 2: 239–50.

Chadwick, P.K. (1995) *Understanding Paranoia: What causes it, how it feels and what to do about it,* London: Thorsons.

Chadwick, P.K. (1996a) In search of 'deep music': artistic approaches to the study of mind, *Clinical Psychology Forum*, 89 (March): 8–11.

Chadwick, P.K. (1996b) A meeting place for science, art and spirituality: the perception of reality in insane and 'supersane' states, *Network: The scientific and medical network review*, 60 (April): 3–8.

Chadwick, P.K. (1997) *Schizophrenia, the positive perspective: In search of dignity for schizophrenic people*, London and New York: Routledge.

Chadwick, P.K. (1998) Is there an 'X factor' in Schizophrenic Illness? *Network: The Scientific and Medical Network Review*, 68, December: 12–14.

Claridge, G.S. (1967) *Personality and Arousal*, Oxford: Pergamon.

Claridge, G.S. (1988) Schizotypy and Schizophrenia in P. McGuffin and P. Bebbington (eds) *Schizophrenia: The Major Issues*, London: Heinemann, Chapter 14, pp. 187–200.

Claridge, G.S. (1990) Can a disease model of schizophrenia survive? in R.P. Bentall (ed) *Reconstructing Schizophrenia,* London and New York: Routledge, Chapter 6, pp. 157–83.

Claridge, G.S. (1997) *Schizotypy: Implications for Illness and Health,* Oxford: Oxford University Press.

Claridge, G.S. and Beech, T. (1995) Fully and quasi-dimensional constructions of schizotypy in A. Raine, T. Lencz and S.A. Mednick (eds) *Schizotypal Personality*, Cambridge: Cambridge University Press, Chapter 9, pp. 192–216.

Claridge, G.S. and Broks, P. (1984) Schizotypy and hemisphere function, 1. Theoretical considerations and the measurement of schizotyp', *Personality and Individual Differences*, 5: 633–48.

Coakley, D. (1994) *Oscar Wilde: The Importance of Being Irish*, Dublin: Town House.

Collins, W. (1994) Not with a bang but a bleep, *The Spectator*, 8th October, pp. 9–12.

Conradi, P. (1988) *Fyodor Dostoyevsky*, Basingstoke: Macmillan.

Csikszentmihalyi, M. (1992) *Flow: The Psychology of Happiness*, London: Rider Press.

Davis, D.R. (1995) *Scenes of Madness: A psychiatrist at the theatre*, London and New York: Routledge.

Deary, I.J. and Matthews, G. (1993) Personality Traits are alive and well, *The Psychologist*, July: 299–311.

Dickens, C. (1907/1961) *Hard Times*, London: Dent.

Digman, J.M. (1990) Personality Structure: Emergence of the Five-Factor Model, *Annual Review of Psychology*, 41: 417–40.

Dimsdale, J.E., Pierce, C., Schoenfeld, D., Brown, A., Zusman, R. and Graham, R. (1986) Suppressed Anger and Blood Pressure: The effects of Race, Sex, Social Class, Obesity and Age, *Psychosomatic Medicine*, 48: 430–6.

Dion, K.K. (1972) Physical attractiveness and evaluation of children's transgressions, *Journal of Personality and Social Psychology*, 24: 207–13.

Dion, K.K., Berscheid, E. and Walster, E. (1972) What is beautiful is good, *Journal of Personality and Social Psychology*, 24: 285–90.

Dixon, N.F. (1981) *Preconscious Processing,* Chichester: Wiley.

Dostoyevsky, F. (1864/1972) *Notes from Underground/The Double (1846)*, Harmondsworth: Penguin.

DSM IV (1994) (see American Psychiatric Association).

Edwards, D. and Potter, J. (1992) *Discursive Psychology*, London: Sage.

Ellis, A. (1962) *Reason and Emotion in Psychotherapy*, New York: Lyle Stuart.

Ellis, L. (1997) *Sexual Orientation – Toward Biological Understanding*. New York: Praeger.

Ellis, L. (ed) (1998) *Males, Females and Behaviour – Toward Biological Understanding*. New York: Praeger.

Ellmann, R. (1959/1982) *James Joyce*, Oxford: Oxford University Press.

Ellmann, R. (1988) *Oscar Wilde*, New York: AlfredA. Knopf.

Emler, N. (1990) A social psychology of reputation, in W. Stroebe and M. Hewstone (eds) *European Review of Social Psychology*, 1: 171–94, Chichester: Wiley.

Ericsson, K.A. and Simon, H.A. (1980) Verbal reports as data, *Psychological Review*, 87: 215–51.

Ericsson, K.A. and Simon, H.A. (1984) *Protocol Analysis,* Cambridge, MA: MIT Press.

Erikson, E.H. (1968) *Identity, Youth and Crisis*, New York: W.W. Norton.

Ernst, B. (1986) *Adventures with Impossible Figures,* Diss, Norfolk: Tarquin Publications.

Estes, S.G. (1938) Judging personality from expressive behaviour, *Journal of Abnormal and Social Psychology*, 33: 217–36.

Eustace, J. (1993) *Studying Family and Community History* (Course DA301). Milton Keynes, Open University Press.

Evans, J.L. (1997) Semantic activation and preconscious processing in schizophrenia and schizotypy, in G.S. Claridge (ed) *Schizotypy: Implications for Illness and Health*, Oxford: Oxford University Press, Chapter 5, pp. 80–97.

Evans, J. (1998) in Doing the academic groove: Why can't social scientists dance? Editorial, *Society Matters*, (Open University) No 6, Autumn/Winter, p.7.

Evison, R. and Horobin, R. (1990) Co-counselling, in J. Rowan and W. Dryden (eds) *Innovative Therapy in Britain*, Milton Keynes: Open University Press.

Eysenck, H.J. (1967) *The Biological Basis of Personality*, Illinois, NJ: Springfield.

Eysenck, H.J. (ed) (1981) *A Model for Personality*, Berlin, Heidelberg: Springer Verlag.

Eysenck, H.J. and Eysenck, S.B.G. (1975) *Manual of the Eysenck Personality Questionnaire* (Junior and Adult) Sevenoaks, Kent: Hodder and Stoughton.

Eysenck, H.J. and Eysenck, M.W. (1985) *Personality and Individual Differences: A natural science approach*, New York: Plenum.

Fenigstein, A. (1984) Self-consciousness and the over-perception of Self as a target, *Journal of Personality and Social Psychology*, 47(4): 860–70.

Flavell, J.H. (1977) *Cognitive Development*, Englewood Cliffs, NJ: Prentice Hall.

Fowler, D., Garety, P. and Kuipers, E. (1995) *Cognitive Behaviour Therapy for Psychosis*, Chichester: Wiley.

Frank, J. (1961) Nihilism and notes from Underground, *The Sewanee Review*, 69, (1; Jan–March), reprinted in H. Bloom (ed) *Fyodor Dostoyevsky*, New York, Philadelphia: Chelsea House Publishers, Chapter 4, pp. 35–58.

Freud, S. (1911) Psychoanalytic notes on an autobiographical account of a case of paranoia (dementia paranoides), Standard Edition, vol 12, London: Hogarth Press, 3–82.

Freud, S. (1915) *A Case of Paranoia Running Counter to the Psychoanalytic Theory of the Disease*, London: Hogarth Press.

Fromm, E. (1947) *Man for Himself*, New York: Rinehart.

Fromm, E. (1957) *The Art of Loving*, London: Allen and Unwin.

Frosh, S. (1994) *Sexual Difference: Masculinity and Psychoanalysis*, London and New York: Routledge.

Frosh, S. (1997) *For and Against Psychoanalysis*, London and New York: Routledge.

Frye, N. (1957) *The Anatomy of Criticism*, Princeton, N.J.: Princeton University Press.

Gagnier, R. (1987) *Idylls of the Market Place: Oscar Wilde and the Victorian public*, Aldershot: Scholar Press.

Garety, P.A. and Freeman, D. (1999) Cognitive approaches to delusions: a critical review of theories and evidence, *British Journal of Clinical Psychology*, 38, 2: 113–54.

Gergen, K.J. (1985) The social constructionist movement in modern psychology, *American Psychologist*, 40: 266–75.

Gergen, K.J. and Gergen, M.M. (1983) Narratives of the Self, in T.R. Sarbin and K.E. Scheibe (eds), *Studies in Social Identity*, New York: Praeger.

Gergen, K.J. and Gergen, M.M. (1983) The social construction of helping relationships, in J.D. Fisher, A. Nadler and B. De Paulo (eds) *New Directions in Helping*, 1: 144–63, New York: Academic Press.

Gillett, G. (1995) The philosophical foundations of qualitative psychology, *The Psychologist,*, 8: 111–14.

Gittings, R., (1978) *Selected Poems and Letters of Keats*, London: Heinemann Educational Books Ltd.

Gleick, J. (1994) *Chaos: Making a New Science*, London: Abacus.

Godden, D.R. and Baddeley, A.D. (1975) Context-dependent memory in two natural environments: on land and underwater, *British Journal of Psychology*, 66: 325–32.

Goffman, E. (1959) *The Presentation of Self in Everyday Life*, Harmondsworth: Penguin.

Goldberg, L.R. (1990) An alternative 'description of personality': the big five factor structure, *Journal of Personality and Social Psychology*, 59: 1216–29.

Goldberg, L.R. (1993) The structure of phenotypic personality traits, *American Psychologist*, 48: 26–34.

Goldberg, L.R. and Rosolack, T.K. (1994) The Big Five factor structure as an integrative framework: An empirical comparison with Eysenck's P-E-N model, in C.F. Halverson Jr., G.A. Kohnstamm and R.P. Martin (eds) *The Developing Structure of Temperament and Personality from Infancy to Adulthood*, New York: Lawrence Erlbaum.

Goodwin, D.W., Powell, B., Bremer, D., Haine, H. and Stern, J. (1969) Alcohol and recall: state dependent effects in man, *Science*, 163: 1358.

Gosselin, C.C. and Eysenck, S.B.G. (1980) The Transvestite Double Image: a preliminary report, *Personality and Individual Differences*, v1, pt.2: 172–3.

Gosselin, C.C. and Wilson, G. (1980) *Sexual Variations,* London: Faber.

Gould, S.J. (1981) *The Mismeasure of Man,* Harmondsworth: Penguin.

Green, B.A. (1979) The effects of distortions of the self: a study of *The Picture of Dorian Gray, Annual of Psychoanalysis,* 7: 391–410.

Gregory, R.L. (1970) *The Intelligent Eye,* London: Weidenfeld and Nicolson.

Grunbaum, A. (1984) *The Foundations of Psychoanalysis: A philosophical critique,* Berkeley CA: University of California Press.

Guilford, J.P. (1959) *Personality,* New York: McGraw Hill.

Haddock, G. and Slade, P.D. (1996) *Cognitive-Behavioural Interventions with Psychotic Disorders,* London and New York: Routledge.

Haley, B. (1985) Wilde's 'Decadence' and the Positivist tradition, *Victorian Studies,* 28(2): 215–29.

Hampson, S.E. (1988) *The Construction of Personality: An Introduction* (2nd edition), London and New York: Routledge.

Harper, D.J. (1994) The professional construction of 'paranoia' and the discursive use of diagnostic criteria, *British Journal of Medical Psychology,* 67: 131–43 and 151–3.

Harré, R. (1983) *Personal Being: A theory for individual psychology,* Oxford: Blackwell.

Harré, R. and Gillett, G. (1994) *The Discursive Mind,* London: Sage.

Harwell, C.W. (ed) (1980) *Disordered Personalities in Literature,* New York: Longman.

Hart-Davis, R. (1962/1989) *Selected Letters of Oscar Wilde,* Oxford: Oxford University Press.

Hart-Davis, R. (1988) *More Letters of Oscar Wilde,* Oxford: Oxford University Press.

Hebdige, D. (1987/1992) A report on the Western Front: Postmodernism and the 'Politics' of style, *Block,* 12, 4–26, reprinted in F. Franscina and J. Harris (eds) *Art in Modern Culture: An anthology of critical texts,* Phaidon, 1992, pp. 331–41.

Henry, J., Pickering, J., Stevens, R., Valentine, E. and Velmans, M. (1997) Towards a psychology of experience, *The Psychologist,* March: 117–20.

Henwood, K.L. and Nicolson, P. (1995) Qualitative Research, *The Psychologist,* 8, (3; March): 109–110.

Henwood, K.L. and Pidgeon, N.F. (1992) Qualitative research and psychological theorising, *British Journal of Psychology,* 83: 97–111.

Henwood, K.L. and Pidgeon, N.F. (1994) Beyond the qualitative paradigm: A framework for introducing diversity in qualitative psychology, *Journal of Community and Applied Social Psychology,* 4; 225–38.

Hillman, J. (1975) *Loose Ends: Primary Papers in Archetypal Psychology,* Zurich: Spring Publications.

Hodges, A. (1983) *Alan Turing: The Enigma,* London: Burnett.

Hodges, R.D. and Scofield, A.M. (1995) Is spiritual healing a valid and effective therapy? *Journal of the Royal Society of Medicine,* 88 (April): 203–7.

Hokanson, J.E. (1961) The effects of Frustration and Anxiety on Aggression, *Journal of Abnormal and Social Psychology,* 62: 346.

Horgan, J. (1992) Quantum philosophy, *Scientific American,* 267, (1; July): 72–80.

Horney, K. (1942) *Self-Analysis,* New York: W.W. Norton.

Hudson, L. (1966) *Contrary Imaginations: A psychological study of the English Schoolboy,* Harmondsworth: Penguin.

Hudson, L. (1966) *Frames of Mind,* Harmondsworth: Penguin.

Hudson, L. (1968) *Frames of Mind: Ability, Perception and Self-Perception in the Arts and Sciences*, London: Methuen.

Hudson, L. (1972) *The Cult of the Fact*, London: Jonathan Cape.

Hunter-Blair, D. (1938) Oscar Wilde as I knew him, *Dublin Review*, (July); p.94.

Jackson, J.W. (ed) (1995) *The Uncollected Oscar Wilde*, London, Fourth Estate.

Jackson, M. (1997) Benign Schizotypy? The case of spiritual experience, in G.S. Claridge (ed) *Schizotypy: Implications for Illness and Health*, Oxford: Oxford University Press, chapter 11, pp. 227–50.

Jackson, M. and Claridge, G.S. (1991) Reliability and Validity of a psychotic traits questionnaire (STQ), *British Journal of Clinical Psychology*, 30(4; November): 311–24.

Jaeger, A. (1983) *Feminist Politics and Human Nature*, New York: Rowman and Allanheld.

James, W. (1890) *Principles of Psychology*, New York: Holt, Rinehart and Winston.

Jamison, K.R. (1993) *Touched with Fire: Manic-Depressive Illness and the Artistic Temperament*, New York: The Free Press.

Johnson, R.A. (1987) *The Psychology of Romantic Love*, London: Arkana.

Joyce, J. (1922) *Ulysses*, Paris: Shakespeare and Company.

Jullian, P. (1969/1994) *Oscar Wilde*, London: Constable.

Jung, C.G. (1955/1985) *Synchronicity: An Acausal Connecting Principle*, London: Ark.

Kaufman, W. (1956) *Existentialism from Dostoyevsky to Sartre*, Cleveland, Ohio: Meridian.

Kaye, C. and Blee, T. (1997) *The Arts in Health Care: A Palette of Possibilities*, London and Bristol: Jessica Kingsley.

Kelly, G. (1955) *The Psychology of Personal Constructs*, New York: W.W. Norton.

Kermode, F. (1966) Mr E.M. Forster as a Symbolist, in M. Bradbury (ed) *Forster: A Collection of Critical Essays*, Englewood Cliffs, N.J.: Prentice Hall Inc., pp. 90–5.

Kessen, W. (1979) The American child and other cultural inventions, *American Psychologist*, 34: 815–20.

Kinderman, P. and Bentall, R.P. (1996) Self-discrepancies and persecutory delusions: Evidence for a defensive model of paranoid ideation, *Journal of Abnormal Psychology*, 105: 106–14.

Kinderman, P. and Bentall, R.P. (1997) Causal attributions in paranoia and depression: internal, personal and situational attributions for negative events, *Journal of Abnormal Psychology*, 106, 2: 341–5.

Kinderman, P., Dunbar, R. and Bentall, R.P. (1998) Theory of Mind deficits and causal attributions, *British Journal of Psychology*, 89, (2; May): 191–204.

Kingdon, D.G. and Turkington, D. (1994) *Cognitive-Behavioural Therapy of Schizophrenia*, Hove: Lawrence Erlbaum Associates.

Kinsey, A.C., Pomeroy, W.B., Martin, C.E. and Gebhard, P.H. (1953/1966) *Sexual Behaviour in the Human Female*, New York: Pocket Books; first published 1953 by W.B. Saunders.

Kline, P. (1981) *Fact and Fantasy in Freudian Theory*, London and New York: Methuen.

Kline, P. (1988) *Psychology Exposed or The Emperor's New Clothes*, London and New York: Routledge.

Knox, M. (1994) *Oscar Wilde: A long and lovely suicide*, New Haven: Yale University Press.

Koestler, A. (1964/1989) *The Act of Creation*, London: Arkana.

Kubler-Ross, E. (1970) *On Death and Dying*, London and New York: Macmillan.

Larkin, P. (1988) *Collected Poems*, London: Faber and Faber.

Lee, D. (1959) *Freedom and Culture*, New York: Prentice Hall.

Lindsay, S.J.E. and Powell, G.E. (1994) *The Handbook of Clinical Adult Psychology*, London and New York: Routledge.

MacKay, C., Cox, T., Burrows, G. and Lazzerini, T. (1978) An inventory for the measurement of self-reported stress and arousal, *British Journal of Social and Clinical Psychology*, 17:283–4.

Magaro, P. (1981) The paranoid and the schizophrenic: The case for Distinct Cognitive Styles, *Schizophrenia Bulletin*, 7: 632–61.

Marzillier, J. (1990) *The Picture of Dorian Gray*: the narcissistic quest for immortality, *Changes* 8, 3: 162–72.

Mason, O., Claridge, G. and Jackson, M. (1995) New scales for the assessment of schizotypy, *Personality and Individual Differences*, 18: 7–13.

McAdams, D.P. (1988) *Power, Intimacy and the Life Story*, London and New York: Guilford Press.

McAdams, D.P. (1993) *Stories We Live By*, New York: Guilford Press.

McCrae, R.R. and Costa, P.T. (1990) *Personality in Adulthood*, New York: Guilford Press.

McCreery, C. and Claridge, G.S. (1995) Out-of-the body experiences a.1 Personality, *Journal of the Society for Psychical Research*, 60: 129–48.

McKay, M. and Fanning, P. (1987) *Self-Esteem*, Oakland CA: New Harbinger Publications.

Medawar, P.B. (1969) *Induction and Intuition in Scientific Thought*, London: Methuen.

Melville, J. (1994) *Mother of Oscar: The life of Jane Francesca Wilde*, London: John Murray.

Mental Health Foundation (1997) *Knowing our Own Minds*, London: Mental Health Foundation.

Mental Health Foundation (2000) *Strategies for Living*, London: Mental Health Foundation.

Miller, G.A., Galanter, E. and Pribram, K.H. (1960) *Plans and the Structure of Behaviour*, London and New York: Holt, Rinehart and Winston.

Milne, D.L. (1999) *Social Therapy: A guide to social supportive interventions for mental health practitioners*, Chichester: Wiley.

Mischel, W. (1973) Toward a cognitive social-learning reconceptualisation of personality, *Psychological Review*, 80: 252–83.

Mischel, W. (1990) Personality dispositions revisited and revised: A view after three decades in L.A. Pervin (ed) *Handbook of Personality: Theory and Research*, New York: Guilford Press, pp. 111–34.

Mochulsky, K. (1971) *Dostoyevsky: His life and work*, translated by M. Minihan, Princeton, N.J.: Princeton University Press.

Mollon, P. (1984) Shame in relation to narcissistic disturbance, *British Journal of Medical Psychology*, 57: 207–14.

Morgan, M. (1990) *File on Wilde*, London: Methuen Drama.

Morgan, M. (1996) Qualitative research: a package deal? *The Psychologist*, 9: 31–2.

Morgan, M. (1998) Qualitative research: science or pseudo-science? *The Psychologist*, 11: 481–3.

Murdoch, I. (1953/1976) *Sartre: Romantic Rationalist*, Glasgow: Fontana/Collins.

Murray, L. (1971) Oscar Wilde's absorption of 'influences': the case history of Chuang Tsu, *Durham University Journal*, 33,1: 1–13.

Mussen, P.H., Conger, J.J., Kagan, J. and Huston, A.C. (1990) *Child Development and Personality*, New York: Harper and Row.

Nasby, W. and Read, N.W. (1997) The inner and outer voyages of a solo circumnavigator: An integrative case study, *Journal of Personality*, 65: 757–1116.

Nowlis, V. (1965) Research with the mood adjective check list in S.S. Tomkins and C.E. Izard (eds) *Affect, Cognition and Personality*, New York: Springer.

Ohayon, M.M., Priest, R.G., Caulet, M. and Guilleminault, C. (1996) Hypnogogic and Hypnopompic hallucinations: pathological phenomena? *The British Journal of Psychiatry*, 169, (October): 459–67.

Orford, J. (1987) *Coping with Disorder in the Family*, London: Croom Helm.

Pater, W. (1873/1990) *Essays on Literature and Art*, J. Uglow (ed), London: Dent.

Pater, W. (1885/1985) *Marius The Epicurean*, Harmondsworth: Penguin.

Pater, W. (1889/1990) Oscar Wilde, in J.W. Jackson (ed) (1995) *The Uncollected Oscar Wilde*, London: Fourth Estate.

Paulhus, D.L. (1986) Self-deception and impression management in test responses, in A. Angleitner and J.S. Wiggins (eds) *Personality Assessment by Questionnaire*, New York: Springer, pp. 142–65.

Pearson, H. (1946/1988) *The Life of Oscar Wilde*, Harmondsworth: Penguin.

Philipp, R. and Roberston, I. (1996) Poetry helps healing, *Lancet*, 347: 332–3.

Piaget, J. (1959) *The Language and Thought of the Child*, London: Routledge and Kegan Paul.

Piaget, J. (1972) *The Insights and Illusions of Philosophy*, London: Routledge and Kegan Paul.

Popper, K.R. (1959) *The Logic of Scientific Discovery*, London: Hutchinson.

Post, F. (1994) Creativity and Psychopathology: a study of 291 world-famous men, *British Journal of Psychiatry*, 165: 22–34.

Post, F. (1996) Verbal creativity, depression and alcoholism: an investigation of one hundred American and British writers, *British Journal of Psychiatry*, 168 (May): 545–55.

Power, M.J. and Brewin, C.R. (eds) (1997) *The Transformation of Meaning in Psychological Therapies: Integrating theory and practice*, Chichester: Wiley.

Quinton, A. (1977) Hermeneutics, in A. Bullock, O. Stallybrass and S. Trumbley, *The Fontana Dictionary of Modern Thought*, London: Fontana.

Raine, A., Lencz, T. and Mednick, S.A. (1995) *Schizotypal Personality*, Cambridge: Cambridge University Press.

Rauschenberg, R. (1990) Robert Rauschenberg interviewed by L. Wijers and M. Kremer, in *Art and Design* No 21: *Art meets Science and Spirituality*, pp. 14–25.

Rhodes, N., Dowker, A. and Claridge, G. (1995) Subject matter and poetic devices in psychotical poetry, *British Journal of Medical Psychology*, 68: 311–22.

Roberts, G. (1991) Delusional belief systems and meaning in life: a preferred reality?, *British Journal of Psychiatry*, 159 (suppl. 14): 19–28.

Robinson, W.P. (ed) (1996) *Social Groups and Identities: Developing the legacy of Henri Tajfel*, Oxford: Butterworth-Heineman.

Rogers, C.R. (1959) A Theory of Therapy, Personality and Interpersonal Relationships, in S. Koch (ed) *Psychology, A Study of a Science*, Vol 3. New York: McGraw Hill, pp. 184–256.

Rogers, C.R. (1969) *Freedom to Learn: A view of what education might become*, Columbus, OH: Charles W. Merrill.

Rogo, D.S. (1990) *Beyond Reality: The role unseen dimensions play in our lives*, Wellingborough, Northants: The Acquarian Press.

Romme, M. and Escher, S. (1993) *Accepting Voices*, London: Mind Publications.

Rowan, J. (1990) *Subpersonalities: The people inside us*, London and New York: Routledge.

Rump, E.E. (1982) Relationships between creativity, arts-orientation and aesthetic preference variables, *Journal of Psychology*, 110: 11–20.

Russell, R. (1994) Do you have a Spiritual Disorder? *The Psychologist*, 7 (8; August): 384.

Sarbin, T.R. and Mancuso, J.C. (1980) *Schizophrenia: Medical diagnosis or verdict?* Elmsford, NY: Pergamon.

Schafer, R. (1976) *A New Language for Psychoanalysis*, London and New Haven: Yale University Press.

Schmidgall, G. (1994) *The Stranger Wilde: Interpreting Oscar*, London: Abacus.

Shapiro, D. (1989) A process of discovery, *The Psychologist*, 2, 4: 153–4.

Shotter, J. (1993) *Cultural Politics of Everyday Life*, Buckingham: Open University Press.

Sidgewick, H.A. (1894) Report of the census of hallucinations, *Proceedings of the Society for Psychical Research*, 26: 259–394.

Skinner, B.F. (1953) *Science and Human Behaviour*, New York: Macmillan.

Smith, J. (1981) Self as experience in Maori culture, in P. Heelas and A. Lock (eds) *Indigenous Psychologies*, London: Academic Press, pp. 145–60.

Spence, D.P. (1987) *The Freudian Metaphor: Toward Paradigm Change in Psychoanalysis*, London and New York: W.W. Norton.

Stein, N.L. and Policastro, M. (1984) The Concept of a Story: A Comparison between Children's and Teachers' Viewpoints, in H. Mandl, N.L. Stein and T. Trabasso (eds) *Learning and Comprehension of Text*, Hillsdale, N.J.: Lawrence Erlbaum.

Stevens, R. (ed) (1996) *Understanding the Self*, London: Sage, in association with The Open University.

Storr, A. (1964) *Sexual Deviation*, London: Penguin.

Storr, A. (1987) Why psychoanalysis is not a science in C. Blakemore (ed) *Mindwaves*, Oxford: Basil Blackwell.

Storr, A. (1996) *Feet of Clay: A study of gurus*, London: Harper Collins.

Sutherland, N.S. (1992) *Irrationality: The enemy within*, London: Constable.

Sweetman, D. (1995) *Paul Gaugin: A complete life*, London: Hodder and Stoughton.

Symons, A. (1891) Review of *Intentions* by O. Wilde, *The Speaker*, 4 (4th July) p.27.

Tajfel, H. (1982) *Social Identity and Intergroup Relations*, Cambridge: Cambridge University Press.

Talbot, N. (1968) *The Major Poems of John Keats*, Sydney: Sydney University Press.

Thomas, D. (1974) *Selected Poems*, London and Melbourne: J.M. Dent.

Thomson, M. (1989) *On Art and Therapy*, London: Virago Press.

Thorne, B. (1993) Person-centred therapy, in W. Dryden (ed) *Individual Therapy: A handbook*, Buckingham: Open University Press.

Tripp, C.A. (1977) *The Homosexual Matrix*, London and New York: Quartet Books.

Tyler, A. (1992) *Saint Maybe*, London: Vintage.

Tyson, P. and Tyson, R.L. (1990) *Psychoanalytic theories of Development: An Integration*, New Haven and London: Yale University Press.

Venables, P.H. and Bailes, K. (1994) The structure of schizotypy, its relation to subdiagnoses of schizophrenia and to sex and age, *British Journal of Clinical Psychology,* 33, (3; September): 277–94.

Vetere, A. (1996) A gender sensitive perspective on personal relationships, in D. Miell and R. Dallos (eds) *Social Interaction and Personal Relationships,* London: Sage, pp. 335–43.

Vollema, M.J. and van den Bosch, R.J. (1995) The multidimensionality of schizotypy, *Schizophrenia Bulletin,* 21(1): 19–31.

Waggoner, H.H. (1966) Notes on the uses of coincidence in the novels of E.M. Forster, in M. Bradbury (ed) *Forster: A collection of critical essays,* Englewood Cliffs, N.J.: Prentice Hall Inc., pp. 81–9.

Walker, K. (1994) Men, women and Friendship: what they say, what they do, *Gender and Society,* 8, (2; June): 246–65.

Warner, R. (1994) *Recovery from Schizophrenia: Psychiatry and Political Economy.* London and New York: Routledge.

Watson, L. and Beaumont, D. (1989) Transvestism: Towards the twenty-first-century, *TV Scene,* No.7 (February): 28–31.

Watts, F. (1996) Are science and religion in conflict? *The Psychologist,* 9 (1; January): 15–18.

West, D.J. (1948) A mass observation questionnaire on hallucinations, *Journal of the Society for Psychical Research,* 34: 187–96.

Wetherell, M. (1996) Life histories/Social histories, in M. Wetherell (ed) *Identities, Groups and Social Issues,* London: Sage, Chapter 6, pp. 299–342.

Wilde, O. (1882/1890a/1995) in J.W. Jackson (ed) *The Uncollected Oscar Wilde,* London: Fourth Estate.

Wilde, O. (1890b/1985) *The Picture of Dorian Gray,* Harmondsworth: Penguin.

Wilde, O. (1891a) Preface to *The Picture of Dorian Gray,* London: Ward Lock.

Wilde, O. (1891b) *Intentions,* London: Osgood, McIlvaine.

Wilde, O. (1994) *Complete Works of Oscar Wilde,* Glasgow: Harper Collins.

Wilde, S. (1987) *Affirmations,* Taos, NM: White Dove International.

Williams, L.M. (1995) Further evidence for a multi-dimensional personality disposition to schizophrenia in terms of cognitive inhibition, *British Journal of Clinical Psychology,* 34 (2; May): 193–213.

Williams, L.M. (1996) Cognitive inhibition and schizophrenic symptom subgroups, *Schizophrenia Bulletin,* 22(1): 139–51.

Winnicott, D.W. (1965) *The Maturational Processes and the Facilitating Environment: Studies in the Theory of Emotional Development,* Madison, Conn.:International University Press.

Zika, S. and Chamberlain, K. (1992) On the relation between meaning in life and psychological well-being, *British Journal of Psychology,* 83: 133–45.

Name Index

Subject Index